AF906205

The Cultural Life of Machine Learning

Jonathan Roberge · Michael Castelle
Editors

The Cultural Life of Machine Learning

An Incursion into Critical AI Studies

palgrave
macmillan

Editors
Jonathan Roberge
Centre Urbanisation Culture Société
Institut national de la recherche scientifique
Quebec City, QC, Canada

Michael Castelle
Centre for Interdisciplinary Methodologies
University of Warwick
Coventry, UK

ISBN 978-3-030-56285-4 ISBN 978-3-030-56286-1 (eBook)
https://doi.org/10.1007/978-3-030-56286-1

© The Editor(s) (if applicable) and The Author(s), under exclusive license to Springer Nature Switzerland AG 2021
Chapter 2 is licensed under the terms of the Creative Commons Attribution 4.0 International License (http://creativecommons.org/licenses/by/4.0/). For further details see license information in the chapter.
This work is subject to copyright. All rights are solely and exclusively licensed by the Publisher, whether the whole or part of the material is concerned, specifically the rights of translation, reprinting, reuse of illustrations, recitation, broadcasting, reproduction on microfilms or in any other physical way, and transmission or information storage and retrieval, electronic adaptation, computer software, or by similar or dissimilar methodology now known or hereafter developed.
The use of general descriptive names, registered names, trademarks, service marks, etc. in this publication does not imply, even in the absence of a specific statement, that such names are exempt from the relevant protective laws and regulations and therefore free for general use.
The publisher, the authors and the editors are safe to assume that the advice and information in this book are believed to be true and accurate at the date of publication. Neither the publisher nor the authors or the editors give a warranty, expressed or implied, with respect to the material contained herein or for any errors or omissions that may have been made. The publisher remains neutral with regard to jurisdictional claims in published maps and institutional affiliations.

Cover illustration: Original artwork by Mario Klingemann

This Palgrave Macmillan imprint is published by the registered company Springer Nature Switzerland AG
The registered company address is: Gewerbestrasse 11, 6330 Cham, Switzerland

Contents

Notes on Contributors

Werner Binder is an amateur Go player and an assistant professor for sociology at the Masaryk University, Brno (Czech Republic). After studies in Mannheim, Potsdam, and Berlin, he earned his Ph.D. at the University of Konstanz with a thesis on the Abu Ghraib Scandal. He is author of *Abu Ghraib und die Folgen* (2013, Transcript), coauthor of *Ungefähres* (2014, Velbrück), and coeditor of *Kippfiguren* (2013, Velbrück). He currently works on the history and methodology of cultural sociology, on populist discourses in Europe and the United States as well as on social imaginaries in the field of digital technologies. Among his recent journal publications are "Biography and Form of Life. Toward a Cultural Analysis of Narrative Interviews" (2019, with Dmitry Kurakin, *Sociológia—Slovak Sociological Review*) and "Social Imaginaries and the Limits of Differential Meaning. A Cultural Sociological Critique of Symbolic Meaning Structures" (2019, *Österreichische Zeitschrift für Soziologie*).

Michael Castelle is an Assistant Professor at the University of Warwick's Centre for Interdisciplinary Methodologies and a Turing Fellow at the Alan Turing Institute. He holds a Ph.D. in Sociology from the University of Chicago and a Sc.B. in Computer Science from Brown University. His current research focuses on the social and historical epistemology of deep learning, with an emphasis on its relationship to sociological and anthropological theory. His previous dissertation work involved the history of transaction processing and messaging middleware in the context of financial exchanges, including implications for a contemporary understanding of marketplace platforms and their regulation.

Daniel Greene is an Assistant Professor of Information Studies at the University of Maryland. His research focuses on the future of work and the fight to define that future in policy, culture, and code. His forthcoming book from the MIT Press, *The Promise of Access*, draws on years of ethnographic research to investigate how the problem of poverty became a problem of technology, exploring the schools and libraries teaching people to code, why they embrace that mission, and how it changes them. Other research explores the design of surveillance systems such as military drones, police body cameras, and human resources software. His work has been published in venues such as *New Media and Society*, the *International Journal of Communication*, and *Research in the Sociology of Work*.

Orit Halpern is an Associate Professor at Concordia University in Montréal. Her work bridges the histories of science, computing, and cybernetics with design and art practice. Her recent monograph, *Beautiful Data* (Duke Press, 2015), is a history of interactivity, data visualization, and ubiquitous computing. She also directs *the Speculative Life Research Cluster*; a research lab working on media, infrastructure, and the Anthropocene at the Milieux Institute for the Arts, Culture, and Technology. Her next book is on extreme infrastructures, computation, ecology, and the future of habitat. She has also published and created works for a variety of venues including *e-flux*, *Rhizome*, *The Journal of Visual Culture*, *Public Culture*, and ZKM in Karlsruhe, Germany.

Anna Lauren Hoffmann is an Assistant Professor with The Information School at the University of Washington. Her research is situated at the intersections of data, technology, culture, and ethics, with particular attention to the ways in which the design and use of information technology can promote or hinder the pursuit of important human values like respect and justice. Her work has appeared in various scholarly journals like *New Media & Society*, *The Library Quarterly*, and *Information, Communication, & Society*. Her writing has also appeared in popular outlets, including *The Guardian*, *The Seattle Times*, and the *Los Angeles Review of Books*.

Théo Lepage-Richer is a Ph.D. Candidate and SSHRC/FRQ-SC Doctoral Fellow in the Department of Modern Culture and Media at

Brown University. His research is broadly concerned with the history and epistemology of machine learning, with a specific focus on the transformation of neural networks from a model of the mind to a functional framework for pattern extraction. Working at the intersection of media studies and science & technology studies, he has published pieces on the commodification of facial recognition as well as on issues of quantification as they pertain to the projection of risk within individuals. Previously, Théo has been a visiting scholar at Charles University and at the Digital Democracies Group at Simon Fraser University.

Fenwick McKelvey is an Associate Professor in Information and Communication Technology Policy in the Department of Communication Studies at Concordia University. He studies the digital politics and policy, appearing frequently as an expert commentator in the media and intervening in media regulatory hearings. He is the author of *Internet Daemons: Digital Communications Possessed* (University of Minnesota Press, 2018), winner of the 2019 Gertrude J. Robinson Book Award. He is coauthor of *The Permanent Campaign: New Media, New Politics* (Peter Lang, 2012) with Greg Elmer and Ganaele Langlois. His research has been published in journals including *New Media and Society*, the *International Journal of Communication*, public outlets such as The Conversation and Policy Options, and been reported by The Globe and Mail, CBC The Weekly and CBC The National. He is also a member of the Educational Review Committee of the Walrus Magazine.

Aaron Mendon-Plasek is a historian of science and technology, scholar, and writer. A Ph.D. Candidate in History at Columbia University, Aaron has a M.A. in History from Columbia, a M.A. in Humanities and Social Thought from NYU, an MFA in Writing from the School of the Art Institute of Chicago, and a B.S. in Physics and Astronomy and a B.A. in Writing from Drake University. He lives in New York with his partner, Sapna Mendon.

Tyler Reigeluth has a Ph.D. in Philosophy from the Université libre de Bruxelles where he worked with the Algorithmic Governmentality FNRS-funded research project. His dissertation problematized the notion of behavior within contemporary machine learning by developing a genealogy of its normative implications. After having carried out post-doctoral positions at the Université du Québec à Montréal and at the

University of Chicago, he is currently a postdoctoral fellow at the Université de Grenoble-Alpes' Institute of Philosophy, within the framework of the Ethics&AI Chair in the Multidisciplinary Institute of Artificial Intelligence (MIAI). His research lies at the intersection of political theory and philosophy of technology and has focused most recently on the normative and epistemological relationships between learning, education, and technics. He co-edited the book *De la ville intelligent à la ville intelligible* (2019).

Jonathan Roberge is an Associate Professor at the Institut National de la Recherche Scientifique (INRS) cross appointed to Urban Studies, Cultural Studies, and Knowledge Mobilization. He funded the Nenic Lab as part of his Canada Research Chair in 2012. He is a member of the Chaire Fernand-Dumont sur la culture at INRS, the Centre interuniversitaire sur la science et la technologie and the Laboratoire de Communication mediatisée par les ordinateurs at UQAM. He is among the first scholars in Canada to have critically focused on algorithms and cultural production. In 2014, he organized the first sociological conference on this topic which culminated into a foundational text in this domain entitled *Algorithmic Cultures* (Routledge, 2016, translated into German at Transcript Verlag, 2017).

Luke Stark is an Assistant Professor in the Faculty of Information and Media Studies at the University of Western Ontario. His work interrogates the historical, social, and ethical impacts of computing and artificial intelligence technologies, particularly those mediating social and emotional expression. His work has appeared in scholarly journals including *The Information Society*, *Social Studies of Science*, and *New Media & Society*, and in popular venues like *Slate*, *The Globe and Mail*, and *The Boston Globe*. He holds a Ph.D. from the Department of Media, Culture, and Communication at New York University.

Ceyda Yolgörmez is a Ph.D. candidate in Social and Cultural Analysis Program at Concordia University. Her research looks at the socialization of AI agents through situated interactions in game contexts. She studies game-playing AIs and focuses on the material-discursive conditions through which specific articulations of their agencies emerge. She is particularly interested in the histories of technologies and techniques of AI that underline the attributions of agency. Alongside this, she thinks about how AI and sociology could come together, how they would benefit each other; and how new forms of intelligences could inform social theory in a deep and meaningful way. A big part of this thinking deals with uncertainty and error, and glitch, and their function in maintaining social order, or bringing social change. She is coordinator of Machine Agencies Research Group, and is member of Speculative Life Research Cluster, and Technoculture, Arts and Games at Milieux Institute.

List of Figures

List of Tables

CHAPTER 1

Toward an End-to-End Sociology of 21st-Century Machine Learning

Jonathan Roberge and Michael Castelle

The world of contemporary machine learning (ML)—specifically in the domain of the multilayered "deep" neural networks, generative adversarial networks, differentiable programming, and related novelties in what is known as artificial intelligence (AI)—poses difficulties for those in the social sciences, like us, who wish to take its rich and varied phenomena as objects of study. We want, ideally, to be able to offer timely contributions to present-day, pressing debates regarding these technologies and their impacts; but at the same time, we would like to make claims that persist beyond the specific features of today's (or yesterday's) innovations. The rapid pace of technical and institutional change in ML today—in which researchers, practitioners, think tanks, and policymakers

J. Roberge
Centre Urbanisation Culture Société, Institut National de La Recherche Scientifique, Quebec City, QC, Canada
e-mail: Jonathan.Roberge@UCS.INRS.Ca

M. Castelle (✉)
Centre for Interdisciplinary Methodologies,
University of Warwick, Coventry, UK
e-mail: M.Castelle.1@warwick.ac.uk

© The Author(s) 2021

J. Roberge and M. Castelle (eds.), *The Cultural Life of Machine Learning*, https://doi.org/10.1007/978-3-030-56286-1_1

are breathlessly playing a game of catch-up with each other—only exacerbates this tension. While the topic of AI has attracted interest from social scientists and humanists in the past, the recent conjunction of ML hype, massive allocations of technological and financial resources, internal scientific controversies about the validity of connectionist approaches, and discourses about hopes and fears all mark the rise to prominence of twenty-first-century machine learning and deep learning (DL) as a paradigmatically novel sociotechnical phenomenon. In a nutshell, what we are witnessing is nothing less than an *epistemic shock* or what Pasquinelli (2015) has referred to as an epistemic "trauma." For scholars of *cultural life*—such as sociologists, media scholars, and those affiliated with science and technology studies—this situation forces us to ask by what methods we can possibly stay up to date with these radical transformations, while also being able to provide commentary of some significance. How, especially, would it be possible to *make sense of* the present challenges posed by ML, but in a way that allows for a more complex (and indeed "deeper") understanding currently unavailable to ML's practitioners? In this introduction, we want to wager that it may be more productive to embrace these tensions than to attempt to fully resolve them. For instance, it is certainly possible to be technically precise while proposing perspectives quite distant from the computing sciences—the different chapters assembled here are a testimony to this—and it is certainly possible to engage with these technologies and their many subtleties while remaining focused (or, indeed, "trained") on the more historical and cultural if not mythical aspects of their deployment. The list of dualities does not stop there, of course. ML and modern AI models are simultaneously agents for epistemology and, increasingly, ontology; that is to say, they are a way of *knowing* as well as of *being* in the world. They are part of a discourse as much as they are a mode of action, and they are a description of the world and its social composition as much as a prescription of what it ought to be. In turn, the study of machine learning must be aware of this epistemological/ontological tension and be willing to carefully navigate it.

It should perhaps not be surprising that this is not the first time that critical reflections on artificial intelligence emerging from the social sciences have had to fight for their legitimacy. In the mid-1980s, Bloomfield's "The Culture of Artificial Intelligence" (1987)—a work today almost entirely forgotten—forcefully argued against the "exclusion of sociological questions from any serious examination of AI" and the "foreclosure of sociology to questions of social impact" (pp. 63–67). Around the same time, a better-remembered piece by Woolgar (1985) raised the question: "why not a sociology of machines?"—primarily to indicate that such an endeavor must go beyond simply examining the impacts of technology and attend to its *genesis* and *social construction*. What these kinds of positions had in common was a commitment to develop a more holistic approach, in which no aspect of these so-called intelligent technologies would be left out of consideration; so we see in Schwartz (1989) the idea that a proper sociology of AI could ask "under what conditions and in what settings is a model deemed adequate?," and in Forsythe's (1993) work the argument that "engineers' assumptions have some unintended negative consequences for their practice, for the systems they build, and (potentially at least) the broader society" (p. 448). Fast forward some 30-plus years, and the need to make social-scientific discourse on what one might call "21st-century" AI both socially pertinent and accurate has returned with a vengeance. If we consider the sociotechnical genesis of these techniques as "upstream" and their eventual social impact as "downstream," then we can see critics like Powles and Nissenbaum (2018), who write of the "seductive diversion of 'solving' bias in artificial intelligence," as warning against an overemphasis on upstream engineering dilemmas without considering how "scientific fairness" comes to be deployed in practice; and we can see Roberge, Senneville, and Morin (2020) discussion of regulatory bodies such as Quebec's Observatory on the Social Impact of AI (OBVIA) as warning of a corresponding overemphasis on "downstream" social impact, which does not see that said social impact is explicitly entangled with the development of the commercial AI research power center known as the Montréal hub.

As a corrective, we want to propose the need for what could be called—with a wink and a nod to deep learning methodology—an *end-to-end* sociology of contemporary ML/AI, which understands this explicit entanglement of "upstream" and "downstream" and instead trains itself on the entire sociotechnical and political process of modern machine learning from genesis to impact and back again. In this, we find ourselves in line with scholars like Sloane and Moss (2019) who have recently argued, for an audience of AI practitioners, that it is necessary to overcome "AI's social science deficit" by "leveraging qualitative ways of knowing the sociotechnical world." Such a stance justifies the value of historical, theoretical, and political research at both an epistemological level of how AI/ML comes to produce and justify knowledge, and at an ontological level of understanding the essence of these technologies and how we can come to coexist with them in everyday practice. But to do so requires an epistemic step that ML practitioners have not fully accepted themselves, namely, to insist on a definition of ML/AI as a "co-production requiring the interaction of social and technical processes" (Holton & Boyd, 2019, p. 2). Radford and Joseph (2020), for their part, have proposed a comparable framework that they call "theory in, theory out," in which "social theory helps us solve problems arising at *every step* in the machine learning for social data pipeline" (p. 2; emphasis added). These perspectives represent threads that weave in and out of the chapters in this book as they address machine learning and artificial intelligence from differing historical, theoretical, and political perspectives from their epistemic genesis to sociotechnical implementations to social impact. These chapters can be seen to represent a different attempt to bring these proposals into reality with empirically motivated thinking and research.

To engage with machine learning requires, to some extent, understanding better what these techniques and technologies are about in the first place for its practitioners. What are the baseline assumptions and technical-historical roots of ML? What ways of knowing do these assumptions promote? While it is not uncommon to read that ML represents a "black boxed" technology by both insiders and outsiders, it is nonetheless important to stress how counterproductive such a claim can be, in part because of its bland ubiquity. Yes, ML can be difficult to grasp due to its apparent (if not always actual) complexity of large numbers of model parameters, the rapid pace of its development in computer science, and the array of sub-techniques it encompasses (whether they be the genres of learning, such as supervised, unsupervised, self-supervised, or the specific algorithmic models such as decision trees, support vector machines, or neural networks). As of late, different scholars have tried to warn that the "widespread notion of algorithms as black boxes may prevent research more than encouraging it" (Bucher, 2016, p. 84; see also Burrell, 2016; Geiger, 2017; Sudmann, 2018). Hence, the contrary dictum—"do not fear the black box" (Bucher, 2016, p. 85)—encourages us to *deconstruct* ML's fundamental claims about itself, while simultaneously paying special attention to its internal logics and characteristics and, to some degree, *aligning* social scientists with AI researchers who are also genuinely curious about the apparent successes and potentially serious limitations of today's ML models (even if their tactics are limited to the quantitative).

While the difficulty of knowing what's going on inside a neural network should not be seen as a conspiracy, it *is* the case that certain ideological underpinnings can be exposed by determining what aspects of the "black box" are in fact known and unknown to practitioners.

One fundamental characteristic of contemporary machine learning, which one can best observe in the "connectionist machine" (Cardon, Cointet, & Mazières, 2018) of deep learning, is precisely this *pragmatic* and *model-centric* culture. It is with deep learning that we can most easily recognize as social scientists that we have moved from an analytical world of the *algorithm* to the world of the *model*, a relatively inert, sequential, and/or recurrent structure of matrices and vectors (which nevertheless is, of course, trained in a processual manner). For DL practitioners, the only truly important "algorithm" dates from the mid-nineteenth century: namely, Cauchy's (1847) method of *gradient descent*. Much of the rest of deep learning's logic often seems more art than science: a grab-bag of techniques that researchers must confront and overcome with practice and for which there can be no formal guidance. These are the notable "Tricks of the Trade" (Orr & Müller, 1998) that the previous marginalized wave of neural network research came to circulate among themselves; today they refer, for example, to the "hyperparameters" that exist outside both the model and the algorithm and yet crucially determine its success (in often unpredictable ways). This relates to a second fundamental characteristic: the flexibility and dynamic, cybernetic quality of contemporary machine learning. Training a model on millions of training examples is a *genetic* process, during which the model *develops over time*. But it is not just the model that develops, but the social world of which the model is but a part; every deep learning researcher is, more so than in other sciences, attuned to *each other* and *each other's models*, because an innovation in one field (such as machine translation) might be profitably transduced to new domains (such as computer vision).

As we can see, it is not just the training processes of contemporary machine learning that randomly explores to find a good local minimum (e.g., using backpropagation and stochastic gradient descent): the entire sociotechnical and cultural endeavor of ML mirrors that mechanism. "Machine learning is not a one-shot process of building a dataset and running a learner," Domingos notes, "but rather an iterative process of running the learner, analyzing the result, modifying the data and/or the learner and repeating" (Domingos, 2012, as cited by Mackenzie,

2015). That the same can be said of both the field's model architectures and the field in general reflects the *self-referentiality* that is a third fundamental characteristic of contemporary machine learning, in which machine learning practitioners, implicitly or explicitly, see their own behavior in terms of the epistemology of their techniques. This inward quality was also found among the researchers of an earlier generation of AI, who saw the height of intelligence as the chess-playing manipulator of symbolic mathematical equations (Cohen-Cole, 2005); today we should be unsurprised that a reinforcement-learning agent with superhuman skill at various Atari video games (Mnih et al., 2013) was considered by some practitioners as a harbinger of machine superintelligence. This represents the logic of a closed community in which the only known social theory is game theory (Castelle, 2020).

Machines using supervised learning to recognize images, speech, and text are not only connectionist, but "inductive machines" by nature (Cardon et al., 2018). ML (and especially DL) methodologies hold firm in this grounded approach where reality emerges from data and knowledge emerges from observation, and the assumptions are often (if not always) straightforward: i.e., that there must be self-evident, objective ties between what is "out there" and what is to be modeled and monitored. These inductivist views, in other words, offer a kind of realism and pragmatism that is only reinforced by the migration of architectures for image recognition—such as the famous ImageNet-based models, which try to identify 1000 different types of objects in bitmap photos (Krizhevsky, Sutskever, & Hinton 2012)—to the more agentive world of real-time surveillance systems (Stark, 2019) or autonomous vehicles (Stilgoe, 2018). These embodied, real-world systems retain the ideology of simpler models, where to "recognize" is to decipher differences in pixels, to "see" is to detect edges, textures, and shapes and to ultimately pair an object with a preexisting label: this is a leopard, this is a container ship, and so on. Instead, these core principles of image recognition have remained unchallenged—namely that the task at hand is one of projecting the realm of the visual onto a flat taxonomy of concepts. And this is where signs of vulnerability inevitably appear: isn't it all too easy to be adequate in this domain? Crawford and Paglen (2019) have notably raised this issue of the fundamental ambiguity of the visual world by noting that "the automated interpretation of images is an inherently social and political project, rather than a purely technical one."

Such an argument nicely sums up what we meant earlier for the necessity of the social sciences to engage with machine learning on its own epistemological grounds. The idea is not to deny the possibility of reflexivity within ML cultures, but to instead relentlessly question the robustness of said reflexivity, especially outside of narrow technical contexts. The debate is thus on, and at present finds itself to be an interesting echo of the argument that the rise of big data should be associated with an "end of theory" (Anderson, 2008). Then, the term "theory" referred to traditional statistical models and scientific hypotheses, which would be hypothetically rendered irrelevant in the face of massive data sets and millions of fine-grained correlations (boyd & Crawford, 2012). But instead of big data's crisis of empiricism, in the case of machine learning we have—as we have suggested above—a crisis of epistemology and ontology, as ML models become more present and take on ever more agency in our everyday lives. At present, machine learning culture is held together by what Elish and boyd (2018) call "epistemological duct tape," and the different chapters in this book are, in part, a testimony to this marked instability.

How to Categorize Meanings

It has become increasingly difficult to ignore the level of hype associated with ML and AI in the past decade, whether it be claims about how the latest developments represent a "tsunami" (Manning, 2015), a "revolution" (Sejnowski, 2018), or—to be more critical—something of a myth (Natale & Ballatore, 2020; Roberge et al., 2020) or a magical tale (Elish & boyd, 2018). This is what we intend to capture in saying that ML has developed a *cultural life* of its own. The question, of course, is to understand how this is possible; and on closer inspection, it seems apparent that what has allowed ML to become such a meaningful endeavor is *its claim to meaning itself*. Once one looks, one begins to see it everywhere: from Mark Zuckerberg noting that "most of [Facebook's] AI research is focused on *understanding the meaning* of what people share" (Zuckerberg, 2015; emphasis added) to Yoshua Bengio for whom the conversation is "about computers *gradually making sense of the world* around us by observation" (Bengio, 2016). Similar quotes can be found regarding specific tasks like object recognition, in which the goal is "to translate the *meaning* of an image" (LeCun, Bengio, & Hinton,

2015) and/or to develop a "*fuller understanding* of the 3D as well as the *semantic* visual world" (Li quoted in Knight, 2016).

This latent desire to "solve" the question of meaning within the formerly deeply symbol-centric world of artificial intelligence here manifests itself as claims of an unfolding conquest, but not everyone is convinced; Mitchell (2018), for example, shows how contemporary AI time and again crashes into the "barrier of meaning." Mitchell argues that this is because AI's associationist training methodologies (a) do not have "commonsense knowledge" of the world and how other actors in the world behave, and (b) are unable to *generalize* to develop more abstract concepts and to "flexibly adapt … concepts to new situations." We would argue that a better distinction might be between *decontextualized* meaning, i.e., the sense-relations that seem to be carried by signs independent of context, and pragmatic *reference*, which is largely dependent on context (Wertsch, 1983). It is with the former that machine learning excels—for example in the "sorting things out" of classification models (Bowker & Star, 1999), and in the sense-relations seemingly captured by word embeddings (Mikolov, Sutskever, Chen, Corrado, & Dean, 2013)—but with the latter, models can only struggle to accommodate pragmatic reference by decontextualizing as much input as possible (one will notice that so-called natural language processing has far more to do with decontextualized sentences of written text than with real-world utterances between two or more humans). ML practitioners, in general, tend to have a limited sense of what "context" is, in contrast to the term's use by anthropologists to indicate how the sociocultural situations in which communicative utterances occur affect and transform their meaning. For ML, this insatiable effort to calculate meaning by relentlessly making so-called context out of *co-text* (Lyons, 1995, p. 271), however, tends to opens the door to existing processes of commensuration (Espeland & Stevens, 1998), and does *not* tend to any increased reflexivity on behalf of its researchers and developers about the nature of communication, meaning, and even learning. Social scientists and philosophers—especially those concerned with hermeneutics, as we will describe below—will recognize the epistemological and ontological issues in the predominance of such a myopic worldview.

What is left after these processes of decontextualization and *entextualization* (Bauman & Briggs, 1990) are the materials for the numerous classification tasks at which modern machine learning excels. In the social-scientific literature it is Mackenzie (2017) who has discussed these models at the greatest length; for him, ML is a "diagramming machine" spanning processes of "vectorization, optimization, probabilization, pattern recognition, regularization, and propagation" (p. 18); and by "diagram" he indicates, via Peirce (1931), a semiotic form that produces meaning *iconically* and *indexically*, or through some kind of similarity and physical contiguity; this, again, differs from the sign-systems dominant in the history of computing, namely those that are largely *symbolic*. So, for example, Mackenzie can see deep learning's fundamental practice of vectorization—which projects all data (whether input, intermediate data, or output) into some high-dimensional vector space—as a historical development of the process of power/knowledge begun with the grids and tables described by Foucault (1970). While this classical episteme was associated primarily with unidimensional and symbolic practices of ordering, ranking, sorting, and joining, such as those of the relational database (Castelle, 2013), the vectorized world is one in which the similarity of data points is literally a geometrical transformation (e.g., the "cosine distance") or sequence of such transformations.

While one might associate the thousand categories of ImageNet-based object recognition models with the regime of hierarchical order, the operationalization of deep learning's object recognition—and its predecessor, pattern recognition—ignores any taxonomy of its object categories (i.e., it ignores the "Net" in the original "ImageNet" database). Instead, ML/DL's conquest of iconicity—its ability to calculate the likeness between a picture of a tiger and an arbitrary value or category denoted as "tiger"—is performed through a layered, directional (and thus indexical) flow of linear and nonlinear transformations. In a well-trained model, this sequence of transformations produces the appropriate category as its output without reference to any "common sense" or semantic knowledge base. But by producing categorical outputs, ML/DL necessary morphs into something prescriptive. To return to Bowker and Star (1999), "each standard and each category valorizes some point of view and silences another" (p. 5). And because the data used today in ML, and especially DL, is *all too human*—from musical taste to surveillance camera footage, from commuting routes to interpersonal conversations—the significance of this becomes enormous.

In his contribution to this volume, Aaron Mendon-Plasek offers an historical account of how precisely machine learning came to categorize meanings. As today's practitioners tend to understand it, machine learning was invented in the late 1950s with Samuel's (1959) checkers-playing program and then goes mysteriously silent for much of the 1960s and 1970s during a period of dominance by "good old fashioned" symbolic AI (in part incurred by Minsky and Papert's attack on neural networks), only for inductive methods to emerge again in the 1980s. Mendon-Plasek detonates this standard just-so narrative by showing how the field of *pattern recognition* in fact emerged in 1955 (with work on character recognition by Oliver Selfridge and Gerald Paul Dinneen), remaining relevant throughout the 1960s and 1970s, and from the outset had a *modus operandi* identical to that of today's machine learning: that of "mechanizing contextually contingent significance." His central argument is that with this framing, the stakes became nothing less than the elaboration of a different *episteme*, in the Foucauldian sense. This epistemic worldview valorized the percentage of correct classifications as the measure of meaning, resulting in a very efficient if mundane "legitimation through performance" (Lash, 2007, p. 67), to which we will come back later in this introduction. However, the notion of a "legitimate" methodology might be something of an oxymoron, as the credit and confidence that produce legitimacy must be mobilized by broader social and cultural forces.

To develop an historical and (socio)-theoretical account of ML is also of interest to Tyler Reigeluth and Michael Castelle in their contribution. The question they raise is of the highest stakes: if machine learning is a kind of "learning," then how should we think of the system of "education" it implicitly proposes? This question forces one to think about the condition of possibilities for, and potential distinction between, human and mechanical/computational/technological ways of acquiring and nurturing knowledge. The authors revisit the work of psychologists Vygotsky, Luria, and Leont'ev, originating in the 1920s and 1930s in the Soviet Union, and their emphasis on the social and cultural dimensions of pedagogy. To learn implies a *genetic* process, i.e., an engagement in a developmental and transformational activity; but it also implies a *dialectical* process occurring between individuals and society: the self, others, and groups of others, i.e., teachers, communities of peers, etc. This is made possible through what Vygotsky calls "*mediation*"—which, usefully for the comparison between human learning and machine learning, can take place as either linguistic/semiotic communications or in the form of technical interventions—which in turn is how learners make sense of culture and the production of meaning. Reigeluth and Castelle go on to (re)frame the issue by arguing, with Vygotsky, that "a concept's meaning actually develops through learning as a social relation … [t]he meaning of a signifier is not presupposed nor is it intrinsically attached to a word. Rather, it is the result of a dialectical process through which meaning develops socially." Here we see a stark distance between what counts as learning in Soviet psychology and what counts as learning for proponents and users of machine learning; for the former, learning is always *fundamentally social*, and for the latter, there is rarely even a concept of a "teacher" (even the "supervision" of supervised learning is merely an inert list of labels). That is to say, learning—as the acquisition and constant transformation of knowledge—goes beyond the finite capabilities of individuals, and it is through sociocultural mediation that it becomes possible and meaningful; and so there must be something fundamentally misguided with most forms of machine learning. This insight mandates the opening of a dialogue between ML, the social sciences, phenomenology, and hermeneutics, rather than foreclosing it.

To be fair, it is not the case that discussions of interpretation, explanation, and understanding are left out of current discussions around ML. They are, in fact, quite prevalent, in the form of the burgeoning literature on "interpretable AI," "explainable AI" (or "xAI"), and "human-understandable AI" (Biran & Cotton, 2017; Gilpin et al., 2018), categories that overlap in various ways but all of which signal a sudden discovery of hermeneutics among computer scientists—without, of course, discovering the word "hermeneutics" itself. These concepts of interpretation, explanation, and understanding indeed have a very long history in philosophical and biblical exegesis, and their respective definitions were at the core of the *Methodenstreit* in the late eighteenth and early nineteenth century that came to define what we now know as the social sciences. But as of yet, there are few in computer science who have dared to make this connection with centuries of existing thought (building up to the philosophical hermeneutics of the late twentieth century), although some interventions have been made on behalf of social and cognitive psychology (Miller, 2019). Instead, the growing autoreferential repurposing and rebranding of these terms into historically detached subfields of, e.g., "xAI" do less to mitigate the black-box qualities and inductive ambiguities of machine learning and instead add yet another layer to the problem by providing approximate, "local surrogate," or linear models instead of addressing the intrinsically interactive, or dialogical, nature of interpretation and understanding (Gadamer, 1977; Mittelstadt, Russell, & Wachter, 2019). Instead, "explainable AI" is largely (if often unconsciously) a positivist project designed to, on the one hand, encourage acceptance of increasingly agentive machine learning models and, on the other, to convince computer scientists that interpretation is an agreed-upon concept which practitioners can "wield ... in a quasi-mathematical way" (Lipton, 2016). Other commentators argue that explainable AI represents a catch-22 in that if it were possible to explain a decision, we would not need to be using ML in the first place (Robbins, 2019). Is it possible to continue along this path in the absence of reflexivity? Can interpretability escape questions about *self-understanding*? Can interrogations about *how* go without interrogations about *why*? These are certainly crucial matters related to meaning-making and situatedness, values and change, and therefore refer to more than simply a question of *method* (Gadamer, 1975).

Fenwick McKelvey's contribution to this volume focuses on the missteps and missed opportunities that have punctuated the relation between machine learning and the social sciences or, in the case of his study, the specific relationship of predictive computational analysis to the rise of the "New Political Science" during the Cold War era. What he offers is a "genealogy of artificial intelligence as a political epistemology" whose goal is to explain "how we came to believe that humans—especially their political behavior—could be modelled by computers in the first place." Certain conditions were necessary to achieve just that, including an emphasis on *how* rather than *why*, a straightforward view of social determinism, and the associated belief that social categories were more important than individual agency or even specific geographical location. Through an integration of the political-scientific ideology known as behavioralism with a nascent mathematical modeling, the Simulmatics Corporation, for instance, was referred to as the "A-bomb of social-science" for its experimental attempts to model the US electorate in terms of "issue clusters" based on surveys and demographic information. These were informed by the assumption of what was called a human "subjective consistency" that would permit not only observing but estimating, and not only simulating and modelling but forecasting and predicting how people would react to different political propositions. Politics was thus to become the object of a kind of cybernetics. One could say that the New Political Science of that time developed as "an engine, not a camera" (MacKenzie, 2006), in which "the opinion poll is an instrument of political action" (Bourdieu, 1979) with substantial implications that, more than ever, we are witnessing today. Specifically, these developments also paved the way for a computational brand of social science to be more and more involved in decision making and, with different degrees of legitimacy, in political steering—e.g., the now-infamous Cambridge Analytica as the predictive core of a propaganda machine. In short, McKelvey describes the origins of a "thin citizenship"—a situation in which "data functions as a proxy for the voter"—which has become utterly dominant today.

ML's Quest for Agency

From what we have seen so far it is clear that machine learning both *represents* and *intervenes*. Yet, it remains to be seen exactly why these two dimensions of meaning making and action are so fundamentally inseparable. ML's "algorithmic modeling" (Breiman, 2001) differs somewhat from traditional statistical modeling, in that the goal of the former is primarily attaining high "prediction" accuracy on a held-out dataset and not necessarily a parsimonious parameterized model as in the latter; i.e., sometimes a neural network with large numbers of uninterpretable parameter weights will do. As such, machine learning culture is more directly involved with the possibility of taking *action*. (For example, in the example of email spam classification, it is not really enough to *assess* an email as being spam or to know why an email has been assessed as spam, but it is very useful to actively *label* it as such and automatically *move* it to the spam folder.) It is likely the case that this agentive use of ML is in part responsible for the increased attention given to machine learning by social scientists in recent years after decades of quiet existence within computer science. While traditional statistical models often remain inside the ivory tower and only induce action through the work of strategic policymakers, machine learning models are readymade as (semi-) autonomous; the act of classification, whose accuracy is optimized during training, can become an act of decision-making during deployment. It is one and the same operation. And just as the model itself is internally a process of small optimizations, so is the *operationalization* of the problem it is trying to solve. The inherent pragmatism of ML compels practitioners to tweak their models (and their surrounding sociotechnical environment) to find, as practical guidebooks recommend, "the level of detection that is useful to you" (Dunning & Friedman quoted in Amoore, 2019, p. 7). The resultant models are thus both flexible and capable of operationalization; their proposed solutions take the form of actions thrown into a greater course-of-life or world action in an attempt to alter that course and produce a desired outcome.

As machine learning's meaning-making and decision-making capabilities become more and more intertwined, so does the relationship between such machines and their practical environment. What counts as agency in these rapidly changing conditions can be described with the help of Latour's (1986) concept of a *cascade*, namely, that ML deployments become part of messy unfoldings and heterogeneous entrenchments. ML models in their deployment come to be mundane; increasingly, they glean, collect, and massage real, in situ datapoints in what is *eo ipso* an effort to channel and triage them—indeed to "sort things out" as mentioned above. While the seemingly inherent commercial value of data is often expressed in catchphrases like "data is the new oil" (Strasser & Edwards, 2017), it is more important to make sense of how the current and broader "datafication" (van Dijck, 2014) and "platformization" of the world (Helmond, 2015) ignite the deployment of ML and vice versa, as if each were the condition of possibility for the other. The clear reality is that as platforms (whether social media, marketplaces, or others) grow they demand the further use of predictive modeling, which conversely becomes more powerful and more intensely developed by training on the massive scale of data aggregated by platforms. At the scale of platforms like Facebook, it is a necessity to leverage machine learning not just to moderate problematic content but also to generate dynamic recommendations, perform facial recognition and other classification on photos, and more (Mackenzie & Munster, 2019). Similarly strong interdependencies between platforms and their ML models are found in the speech recognition of Alexa (Pridmore et al., 2019) or the way Tesla's autonomous vehicles act together as a platform to entrain each other's models (Stilgoe, 2018). In the next section, we will discuss in greater detail the political economy associated with for-profit ML development/deployment; for now, it is important to understand what is at stake in these cases just mentioned, specifically how *actionable* knowledge is in and of itself a form of *interested* knowledge. This is to say, models take action that is not merely "accurate" but in the interest of their employer above all else, as in YouTube's optimization of engagement for its recommendation models (Ribeiro, Ottoni, West, Almeida, & Meira, 2020). As stated by Rieder (2017),

> On the level of signification, data mining techniques attribute meaning to every variable in relation to a purpose; on the level of performativity, the move to increasingly integrated digital infrastructures means that *every classificatory decision can be pushed back into the world instantly*, showing a specific ad, hiding a specific post, refusing a loan to a specific applicant, setting the price of a product to a specific level, and so forth. *No data point remains innocent.* (pp. 110–111)

Another, related way to look at ML's complicated and very much entrenched agency is with its constant attempt at anticipating the near future. ML models exist because they are "predictive" engines, which does not mean that they *will* precisely see the future but that prediction is what they "want" (Mackenzie, 2015). Reigeluth (2018) points to how this is an essentially cybernetic quality; "action," he notes, "is always *ahead of itself*, it is already prediction *in* action, which makes it possible to say that prediction is internal to action" (p. 57; emphasis added). This captures the sense of *anticipation* that is central to both the training process and the execution of ML models. Mackenzie (2015) offers a compact interpretation based on the current *modus operandi* of real-world digital platforms: ML is set in motion by a "desire to predict desire" (p. 431). This desire is captured by various *metrics* that either measure performance of a model directly (e.g., the root-mean-squared error metric) or by indirect *captivation metrics* that measure the amount of user time spent on the platform (Seaver, 2019). For a company like Netflix, success is measured by its ability to choose for its own customers and vice versa, i.e., "the production of sophisticated recommendations produces greater customer satisfaction which produces more customer data which in turn produces more sophisticated recommendations, and so on" (Hallinan & Striphas, 2016, p. 122). Anticipation, expectation, the manufacturing of choice, and informed trading on outcomes all become part of a spiral in which the future's indeterminacy is generated, managed, and potentially conquered. Throughout this process, prediction is inevitably not only just a form of prescription and normalization but of popular legitimacy; consider the $1 million Netflix Prize, which drew attention to big data–based recommendation systems and to Netflix's expertise in said techniques. The more ML prediction is applied, the more it becomes accepted; the more it spreads, the more it gets entrenched in the fabric of everyday life. Following scholars like Benbouzid and Cardon (2018), it would then be possible to assert that prediction has now become a key form of intervention into society in such a fashion that it becomes within ML's agency to be able to fundamentally change that broader reality.

In her contribution to this volume, Ceyda Yolgörmez proposes to take the sociology of AI seriously, both by incorporating STS scholars such as Woolgar and the classical social theorist G. H. Mead alongside Alan Turing, and by moving beyond existing technological-deterministic approaches. Her goal is to reassess the condition of possibility that would make it feasible to think about "AI as an integral part of a social interaction." One such condition is dynamism; something that, as we describe above, is now a fundamental internal aspect of predictive models but also something that is external in those models' capacity to operate in the real world. For Yolgörmez, dynamism is thus synonymous with openness and indeterminacy, which in turn is what makes possible the dialogue between humans and machines. It is as if both human and machine were similarly imperfect in their inability to fully control the space of potential and actual interactions between them. The chapter's main point thus relates to the creation of a "distributed understanding of agency" inspired by Mead, one that would nonetheless allow for a non-negligible dose of autonomy and reflexivity for the actors of such a "new" sociability. For example, Mead (1934) explains the interacting individual as being composed of a *me* which is "the organized set of attitudes of others which one himself assumes," and an *I* in which "we surprise ourselves by our own action." Such a distinction between cognition and action points to a way out of the "barriers of meaning" mentioned in the previous section, a distinction which is currently realized to some extent in the technical innovation of generative adversarial networks (GANs) at the core of the "creative AI" movement; such architectures are composed of two neural networks, a discriminator that learns directly from examples and a generator that attempts to fool the discriminator (Goodfellow et al., 2014). Machine intelligence, in such a case, is capable not only of deviation, spurious correlation, and error, but all these at once, considered as a novel, unique act. As it turns out, if a program in the sociology of AI is to emerge, it would need a theory of novelty to occupy the central stage so that the encounter between humans and machines would become a significant experience seen through a meaningful lens.

Werner Binder's contribution to this volume takes the form of a historical narrative of how games have been instrumental in the development of ML not only as an abstraction, but in the form of specific culturally rich and centuries-old games such as chess and Go. The apparently insurmountable complexity of the latter makes it the perfect challenge for machine learning; one might assume that whoever conquered it would conquer the world. This is indeed what happened in the mid-2010s, when DeepMind's AlphaGo model attempted and ultimately prevailed at beating human professional masters. Match after match, event after event, the rising success of the machine amounted to a "cognitive breach" in that the reports of its technical breakthroughs were in and of itself a demonstration of a deeper, more symbolic debate regarding the nature of intelligence and creativity. As "deep play" or "social drama," *à la* the cultural anthropologists Clifford Geertz and Victor Turner respectively, the stakes could not have been higher for the new wave of "deep learning." AlphaGo embodied what it means for an automated model to combine meaning making and decision making almost seamlessly, and in doing so become an *agent* both epistemologically and ontologically. The strength of the argument is that it is able to detour around the philosophical debates about machine consciousness that have surrounded artificial intelligence for decades. Here, as Binder puts it, the "attribution of agency and intelligence on the basis of an entity's performance has [the] advantage [that] it remains agnostic regarding the question of what intelligence really is." So what kind of a genius player is AlphaGo? What are its "divine" moves and how were they described by the Go community in chat rooms and blogs? Many enthusiastic comments mention the creative and even aggressive style of the machine, with arguments in favor of an "intentional stance" showing "genuine strategic insight" that in turn "defies conventional wisdom," etc. AlphaGo and subsequent iterations learned from self-play; they valued guessing and experience over mathematical prowess, and this is how it became not only successful but respected. The game of Go, all along, has been a reality test, one that DeepMind's brand of machine learning has passed if judged by its "symbolic inclusion" into the broader social imaginary. In the end, that is what was at stake for ML at this crucial historical moment, i.e., the capacity to mingle within the lifeworld and cultural context—in a way, to make sense of its own situatedness.

Context Matters

Earlier in this introduction, we argued that machine learning is never truly devoid of meanings. To interpret and perform, to categorize and implement, is how ML technology finds a place in this world, its situations, and its contexts. As Seaver (2015) notes, "the nice thing about context is that everyone has it." More interesting, however, would be to follow his lead further and consider that the "controversy lies in determining what context is." This is what is finally at stake for ML, namely, the (in)capability to make sense of the fact that context always matters. The question is thus about reflexivity, and the problem is thus about problematization. In a series of recent high-profile interactions and debates between AI researchers Yoshua Bengio and Gary Marcus, the latter criticized ML for its inherent difficulty in engaging with the causal aspects of reality. Marcus' complaint that deep learning has no way of handling compositional thought processes and no way to incorporate and depend on background knowledge is effectively a cognitivist's way of saying that these models do not handle *context*. Tacit understanding, collective representation, and symbolic interaction remain of the utmost importance in social reality despite being ignored for most of the history of ML development. So what is it then that the social sciences can do? What position could they occupy that would not necessarily come to help or save ML, but that would reaffirm the social sciences' own contextual status, i.e., the field's always complicated self-positioning in terms of scientificity and reflexivity? This is also a problem about problematization, one that a social theory of machine learning would have to grasp epistemologically as well as ontologically. A possibility here—albeit by no means the only one—could be to be more sensitive to *hermeneutical* tenets, such as the importance of experience, the active role of interpretation, and the historicity of knowledge. If digital hermeneutics has seen a resurgence of interest of late (e.g., Capurro, 2010; Hongladarom, 2020), it is in part because machines increasingly come to perform acts of interpretation by transforming and transducing signs into other signs, which may then be taken up for interpretations by others. One can then try to apply simple, yet powerful principles such as, for example, the concept of the hermeneutic circle between the whole and the parts; as Gadamer (1975/2004) famously puts it, "The anticipation of meaning in which the whole is envisaged becomes actual understanding when the parts that are determined by the whole themselves also determine this whole." But this is not the type of interpretation that machine learning is attempting at present. Facial or emotion recognition, to give two examples, fundamentally lack an understanding of why faces are historically and axiologically so important in social interaction; what is more, they lack the capacity to reflect on the discriminatory traditions that come with "calculating" facial features as well as awareness of the fact that they reproduce such biases and prejudices (Buolamwini & Gebru, 2018; Introna, 2005; Stark, 2019). Putting the machine learning encoding of "bias" and "prejudice" in perspective is to problematize them; it is to question their broader meaning as a way to gain some distance and, ultimately, some reflexivity.

Issues dealing with "prejudice" are sure to be central in any discussion about context. A fairly common mistake made by those who have studied the polemics between Gadamer's hermeneutics and Habermas' critical theory during the 1960s and 1970s, for instance, is to think that Gadamer was in favor of "prejudice"—what he calls the *Vorstruktur des Verstehens,* the prestructure of understanding—and the authority of tradition, while Habermas was diametrically opposed (see Apel, 1971; Habermas, 1967/1988). In this debate, however, Gadamer never stated that prejudices should be "accepted," but rather that they should be recognized for their entrenchment within a historical condition. And it is these historically entrenched biases that even the social sciences cannot completely free themselves from; Habermas agreed with this, but also insisted that it is possible to see that these historical conditions are rooted in power and coercion. Numerous such convergences exist between hermeneutics and critical theory, the most important of which is that a comprehension of history introduces some sort of critical distance and, at the same time, critique can be supported by a reinterpretation of cultural history (see Bubner, 1975; Hekman, 1986; Roberge, 2011). This, in turn, sheds new light on ML's deficient handling of bias and prejudice. The problem in the current state of affairs is that racist and sexist preconceptions, for example, are treated as if they were a glitch to be fixed technically, one which is before and thus separate from the computational core of ML. In contrast, a critical hermeneutics-based approach would focus on the entire social construction of ML as an *end-to-end problem*, addressing not just how bias and prejudice are molded within ML models but how they are molded in those who seek ML as a solution to social problems. Self-interpretation and critical understanding go hand in hand here, which is also to say that a coherent and reflexive account of ML in general, and ML's relation to bias and prejudice in particular, is by its very essence a political one. As we have said, ML is a vastly interested form of knowledge. Its situatedness is bound with a unique historical moment of political economy, and this book is a testimony to how it could be possible to make sense of this idea. The purpose is not necessarily to align with one specific thesis—for instance, the rise of surveillance capitalism *à la* Zuboff (2019)—as much as to ask tough questions regarding the kinds of value extraction that are now developing, the dynamics of ML's rampant development in contemporary life, and the legitimacy that is given to its deployment in a tripartite and very much intertwined cultural, economic, and political sense.

Théo Lepage-Richer's contribution to this volume explores the limits inherent to ML's knowledge from a historical as well as epistemological perspective. He locates key moments in which the idea of neural networks gained momentum, and examines how researchers came to conceive of the analogy between the brain and the computer as a way to attempt to overcome their respective limitations. A first such moment is the development of the McCulloch-Pitts model in the mid-1940s, in which its two authors posited that a new experimental science could quantitatively determine the operation and thus self-regulation of a mind, be it embodied in the human brain or formed of mechanical wiring. Epistemologically, the model instituted a "shared conceptualization of the unknown as something that can be contained and operationalized by networks of interconnected units." For Lepage-Richer, the model's logic was then picked up in a second, yet closely-related moment corresponding to the emergence of cybernetics in the late 1940s and 1950s. In the work of cyberneticist Norbert Wiener, for instance, a very similar endeavor against uncertainty led him to conflate knowledge and order; when he talks about "the great torrent of disorganization," for instance, he displays a sort of philosophy of nature. Yet more striking is the fact that cybernetics is historically inseparable from the context of the Cold War. Control and communication, for example, were reformulated "in light of new needs and imperatives [where] the laboratory and the battlefield quickly emerged as interchangeable settings in terms of how knowledge was redefined as an adversarial endeavor." From there, the genealogy toward a third, more contemporary moment is quite ambiguous; while today's AI continues to "work" on adversaries, such adversaries have been, as mentioned above, incorporated into the very architectures of neural nets. Targeted perturbations are willingly introduced to expose and then overcome blind spots, as in the case of cybersecurity or the "adversarial examples" that disrupt contemporary neural networks (Goodfellow,

Shlens, & Szegedy, 2015). "Failures are [now] framed," the chapter notes, "as constitutive of neural networks by providing the opportunity to improve future iterations of these systems." And this is where the entire epistemology of connectionist machine learning becomes so problematic, namely, the notion that nothing can truly lie beyond neural networks, not even social and political issues; ML's own failures in terms of biases are effectively recycled and washed away. Instead of being collectively addressed, their consequences are becoming not only understood but accepted as simple engineering problems.

Orit Halpern's contribution to this volume also looks at how the management of uncertainty is the new "core business" of ML. She is especially interested in understanding how today's massive infrastructural endeavors present themselves as a sort of doubling-down, in which an increased penetration of computing allows for an expansion of both science and capital. The Event Horizon Telescope array is her initial case in point; in 2019, its tremendous sensory capabilities allowed it to capture the first image of a black hole using the Earth itself as a sensory recording medium. How is this instrument of extraterritorial political economy able to change what it means to govern life on Earth? For Halpern, the answer to this important question lies in a very practical setting, namely, the Atacama Desert in Chile, which is the location of both the "sublime" infrastructure of radio telescopes and one of the largest lithium mines in existence. The metal is highly strategic as it is one of the lightest and of increasingly high demand in a world of battery-powered devices and vehicles. In Chile, these lithium mines have been privatized along with their water sources, and it is now up to corporate actors to privately handle the environmental footprint of this exploitation. "This new infrastructure of corporate actors," Halpern notes, "[merges] high tech with salt and water in order to support our fantasies of eternal growth." The rise in extraction comes with a rise in an interest in optimizing; applied mathematics and machine learning are deployed in reinforcement. Endless data organized in endless loops, in other words, are there to make the best out of a finitude of resources. Yet, this is not the sum of the Atacama Desert story. During the Pinochet dictatorship, it was used as a site for the summary execution of dissidents. Human memories—those of mothers searching for their children's bodies—thus mesh with the more abstract form of spatial and practical exploration and exploitation of the land. For Halpern, these convergences and their reformulation of time and space create the conditions under which a truly reflexive critique of both modern imperialism and artificial intelligence could (re-)emerge and forge a new meaning for what counts as our human horizon.

In the final contribution to this volume, Luke Stark, Daniel Greene, and Anna Lauren Hoffman propose to contextualize today's primary discourses about the ethics and governance of ML and AI systems. A critical perspective would have to see these discourses as belonging to a broader frame of culture, economy, and politics, especially as these, by their very definition, imply legitimacy and power. A first and rather common proposed solution is to develop more tools and technical fixes, as discussed above; but "fairness," the control of bias, and the like often leave aside important dimensions of the problems they address, so that, for the authors and others in the STS and critical legal studies literature, they turn out to be "entirely insufficient to address the full spectrum of sociotechnical problems created by AI systems." Another fairly common type of governance posits itself through axiological principles, as is the case, for instance, in the Vatican's recent "Call for AI Ethics." The problem then is that in declaration after declaration, the same abstract principles get promoted alongside what is also often a self-promotional attempt by political actors to justify themselves. States and their regulatory bodies face similar issues when it comes to regulating and offering standards. They too are reluctant to propose drastic changes to a field they only partly understand and which they more often than not see as a site of economic growth and/or global competition, including in military terms, and also fail to "address the wide range of AI-equipped analytic technologies designed to surveil elements of human bodies and behavior." Approaches based on human rights tend to have stricter boundaries, but they nonetheless have difficulties grappling with the structural logics that would need to be addressed such as the incompatibility between human rights covenants and corporate systems manufacturers; approaches based on cybersecurity entail similar conflicts. For the authors, what all of these approaches to AI/ML governance have in common is to "seek to restrict debates around the societal impact of AI to a coterie of technical experts whose positions are posited, chiefly by themselves, as technocratic and thus apolitical," and this means it is necessary to develop alternatives, emphasizing communities of practice, which might be inspired by recent labor action by tech workers or by the call for mass mobilization in the abolitionist policies of the Movement for Black Lives. What role can social justice take in ML/AI cultures? How can affected communities come to have a voice in matters of governance? These questions are difficult but essential in the present context.

To understand the cultural life of machine learning is certainly an open endeavor. What the eight chapters assembled here have in common is to problematize the internal logic of these techniques and technologies, but also to offer unexpected possibilities to think anew our relationship with them. For instance, the chapters all point toward the question of *who*, in the end, is the receiver and thus the destination of the varied outputs of deployed machine learning systems. Keeping in line with hermeneutics, it is not unrealistic to say that questions about meanings and significance are questions about appropriation and self-understanding. Individuals can *actively make sense* of these technologies as they are not only the users and consumers of their various enhanced platform settings—"sharing" their ML-massaged data—but are also their real-time interpreters, social actors, and citizens. And this is where issues at an individual level connect with issues of the collective and where questions related to processes of appropriation connect with questions about processes of reflexivity. To be reflexive in the brave new world of ML is to constantly interrogate its purposes, probe its actions, and reassess its broader consequences with the hope that the knowledge being produced might somehow alter its course. Reflexivity is agentic in that regard; and it offers a different kind of "quest for agency" than that of the machine learning models discussed above, one that would have a deeper sense of the politics at play. To (re)politicize the context, to say it *matters*, is thus to recognize that collectivities are being shaped by ML deployment as much as these collectivities have the *capability* to shape ML, most notably in the direction of social justice. This, in turn, implies the necessity for increased dialogue and public debate. It also implies that social science scholars currently vested in the exploration of ML will need to constantly reassess their own (social) role. On the one hand, doing so may very much be about finding better ways to deeply engage with these technologies, i.e., to be hands-on and perform closer and more interested examinations of its contingencies. On the other hand, the critical study of ML/AI deployment might have to find its own stance with the appropriate distance to shed its own specific light on the phenomenon. Are calls for both proximity and distance then antithetical? Does this tension force a double bind that would be problematic to the future of the critical study of machine learning and artificial intelligence? Earlier in this introduction we proposed that it might be better to embrace such tension, and the following chapters reflect their authors' willingness to be daring in this regard.

References

Amoore, L. (2019). Doubt and the agorithm: On the partial accounts of machine learning. *Theory, Culture & Society, 36*(6), 147–169.

Anderson, C. (2008). The end of theory: The data deluge makes the scientific method obsolete. *Wired Magazine, 16*(7).

Apel, K.-O. (1971). *Hermeneutik und Ideologiekritik*. Suhrkamp.

Bauman, R., & Briggs, C. L. (1990). Poetics and performance as critical perspectives on language and social life. *Annual Review of Anthropology, 19*, 59–88.

Benbouzid, B., & Cardon, D. (2018). Machines à prédire. *Reseaux, 211*(5), 9–33.

Bengio, Y. (2016, February 17). *Yoshua Bengio on intelligent machines*. http://www.themindoftheuniverse.org/play?id=Yoshua_Bengio.

Biran, O., & Cotton, C. V. (2017). *Explanation and justification in machine learning: A survey*. IJCAI-17 Workshop on Explainable AI (XAI).

Bloomfield, B. P. (1987). *The question of artificial intelligence*. Routledge.

Bourdieu, P. (1979). Public opinion does not exist. In A. Mattelart & S. Siegelaub (Eds.), *Communication and class struggle* (Vol. 1, pp. 124–130). International General/IMMRC.

Bowker, G., & Star, S. L. (1999). *Sorting things out: Classification and its consequences*. MIT Press.

boyd, d., & Crawford, K. (2012). Critical questions for big data: Provocations for a cultural, technological, and scholarly phenomenon. *Information, Communication & Society, 15*(5), 662–679.

Breiman, L. (2001). Statistical modeling: The two cultures (with comments and a rejoinder by the author). *Statistical Science, 16*(3), 199–231. https://doi.org/10.1214/ss/1009213726.

Bubner, R. (1975). Theory and practice in the light of the hermeneutic-criticist controversy. *Cultural Hermeneutics, 2*, 337–352. https://doi.org/10.1177/019145377500200408.

Bucher, T. (2016). Neither black nor box: Ways of knowing algorithms. In S. Kubitschko & A. Kaun (Eds.), *Innovative methods in media and communication research* (pp. 81–98). Palgrave Macmillan. https://doi.org/10.1007/978-3-319-40700-5_5.

Buolamwini, J., & Gebru, T. (2018). Gender shades: Intersectional accuracy disparities in commercial gender classification. *Conference on Fairness, Accountability and Transparency* (pp. 77–91). http://proceedings.mlr.press/v81/buolamwini18a.html.

Burrell, J. (2016). How the machine 'thinks': Understanding opacity in machine learning algorithms. *Big Data & Society, 3*(1), 1–12. https://doi.org/10.1177/2053951715622512.

Capurro, R. (2010). Digital hermeneutics: An outline. *AI & Society, 25*(1), 35–42. https://doi.org/10.1007/s00146-009-0255-9.

Cardon, D., Cointet, J.-P., & Mazières, A. (2018). Neurons spike back: The invention of inductive machines and the artificial intelligence controversy. *Reśeaux, 5*(211), 173–220.

Castelle, M. (2013). Relational and non-relational models in the entextualization of bureaucracy. *Computational Culture*, 3.

Castelle, M. (2020). The social lives of generative adversarial networks. *Proceedings of the 2020 Conference on Fairness, Accountability, and Transparency* (p. 413). https://doi.org/10.1145/3351095.3373156.

Cauchy, A. (1847). Méthode générale pour la résolution des systemes d'équations simultanées. *Comptes Rendus de l'Académie des Sciences de Paris, 25*(1847), 536–538.

Cohen-Cole, J. (2005). The reflexivity of cognitive science: The scientist as model of human nature. *History of the Human Sciences, 18*(4), 107–139. https://doi.org/10.1177/0952695105058473.

Crawford, K., & Paglen, T. (2019). *Excavating AI: The politics of images in machine learning training sets*. https://www.excavating.ai.

Domingos, P. (2012). A few useful things to know about machine learning. *Communications of the ACM, 55*(10), 78–87. https://doi.org/10.1145/2347736.2347755.

Elish, M. C., & boyd, d. (2018). Situating methods in the magic of Big Data and AI. *Communication Monographs, 85*(1), 57–80. https://doi.org/10.1080/03637751.2017.1375130.

Espeland, W. N., & Stevens, M. L. (1998). Commensuration as a social process. *Annual Review of Sociology, 24*(1), 313–343. https://doi.org/10.1146/annurev.soc.24.1.313.

Forsythe, D. E. (1993). Engineering knowledge: The construction of knowledge in artificial intelligence. *Social Studies of Science, 23*(3), 445–477.

Foucault, M. (1970). *The order of things: An archaeology of the human sciences*. Vintage.

Gadamer, H.-G. (1975/2004). *Truth and method*. Continuum Books.

Gadamer, H.-G. (1977). *Philosophical hermeneutics*. University of California Press.

Geiger, R. S. (2017). Beyond opening up the black box: Investigating the role of algorithmic systems in Wikipedian organizational culture. *Big Data & Society, 4*(2). https://doi.org/10.1177/2053951717730735.

Gilpin, L. H., Bau, D., Yuan, B. Z., Bajwa, A., Specter, M., & Kagal, L. (2018). Explaining explanations: An overview of interpretability of machine learning.

2018 IEEE 5th International Conference on Data Science and Advanced Analytics (DSAA), 80–89. https://doi.org/10.1109/DSAA.2018.00018.

Goodfellow, I., Pouget-Abadie, J., Mirza, M., Xu, B., Warde-Farley, D., Ozair, S., Courville, A., & Bengio, Y. (2014). *Generative adversarial networks* [Cs, Stat]. http://arxiv.org/abs/1406.2661.

Goodfellow, I. J., Shlens, J., & Szegedy, C. (2015). *Explaining and harnessing adversarial examples* [Cs, Stat]. http://arxiv.org/abs/1412.6572.

Habermas, J. (1967/1988). *On the logic of the social sciences*. MIT Press.

Hallinan, B., & Striphas, T. (2016). Recommended for you: The Netflix Prize and the production of algorithmic culture. *New Media & Society, 18*(1), 117–137. https://doi.org/10.1177/1461444814538646.

Hekman, S. J. (1986). *Hermeneutics and the sociology of knowledge*. Polity.

Helmond, A. (2015). The platformization of the web: Making web data platform ready. *Social Media + Society, 1*(2). https://doi.org/10.1177/2056305115603080.

Holton, R., & Boyd, R. (2019). 'Where are the people? What are they doing? Why are they doing it?'(Mindell) Situating artificial intelligence within a socio-technical framework. *Journal of Sociology*. https://doi.org/10.1177/1440783319873046.

Hongladarom, S. (2020). Machine hermeneutics, postphenomenology, and facial recognition technology. *AI & Society*. https://doi.org/10.1007/s00146-020-00951-x.

Introna, L. D. (2005). Disclosive ethics and information technology: Disclosing facial recognition systems. *Ethics and Information Technology, 7*(2), 75–86.

Knight, W. (2016, January 26). *Next big test for AI: Making sense of the world*. MIT Technology Review. https://www.technologyreview.com/2016/01/26/163630/next-big-test-for-ai-making-sense-of-the-world/.

Krizhevsky, A., Sutskever, I., & Hinton, G. E. (2012). ImageNet classification with deep convolutional neural networks. In P. L. Bartlett, F. C. N. Pereira, C. J. C. Burges, L. Bottou, & K. Q. Weinberger (Eds.), *Advances in neural information processing systems 25: 26th Annual Conference on Neural Information Processing Systems 2012. Proceedings of a meeting held December 3–6, 2012, Lake Tahoe, Nevada, United States* (pp. 1106–1114). http://papers.nips.cc/paper/4824-imagenet-classification-with-deep-convolutional-neural-networks.

Lash, S. (2007). Power after hegemony: Cultural studies in mutation? *Theory, Culture & Society, 24*(3), 55–78. https://doi.org/10.1177/0263276407075956.

Latour, B. (1986). Visualisation and cognition: Drawing things together. In H. Kuklick (Ed.), *Knowledge and society studies in the sociology of culture past and present* (pp. 1–40). Jai Press.

LeCun, Y., Bengio, Y., & Hinton, G. (2015). Deep learning. *Nature, 521*(7553), 436–444. https://doi.org/10.1038/nature14539.

Lipton, Z. C. (2016). *The mythos of model interpretability* [Cs, Stat]. http://arxiv.org/abs/1606.03490.

Lyons, J. (1995). *Linguistic semantics: An introduction*. Cambridge University Press.

Mackenzie, A. (2015). The production of prediction: What does machine learning want? *European Journal of Cultural Studies, 18*(4–5), 429–445. https://doi.org/10.1177/1367549415577384.

Mackenzie, A. (2017). *Machine learners: Archaeology of a data practice*. MIT Press.

Mackenzie, A., & Munster, A. (2019). Platform seeing: Image ensembles and their invisualities. *Theory, Culture & Society, 36*(5), 3–22. https://doi.org/10.1177/0263276419847508.

MacKenzie, D. (2006). *An engine, not a camera: How financial models shape markets*. MIT Press.

Manning, C. D. (2015). Computational linguistics and deep learning. *Computational Linguistics, 41*(4), 701–707.

Mead, G. H. (1934). *Mind, self & society from the standpoint of a social behaviorist*. University of Chicago Press.

Mikolov, T., Sutskever, I., Chen, K., Corrado, G., & Dean, J. (2013). Distributed representations of words and phrases and their compositionality. *Proceedings of the 26th International Conference on Neural Information Processing Systems* (Vol. 2, pp. 3111–3119). http://dl.acm.org/citation.cfm?id=2999792.2999959.

Miller, T. (2019). Explanation in artificial intelligence: Insights from the social sciences. *Artificial Intelligence, 267*, 1–38. https://doi.org/10.1016/j.artint.2018.07.007.

Mitchell, M. (2018, November 5). Artificial intelligence hits the barrier of meaning. *The New York Times*. Opinion sec. https://www.nytimes.com/2018/11/05/opinion/artificial-intelligence-machine-learning.html.

Mittelstadt, B., Russell, C., & Wachter, S. (2019). Explaining explanations in AI. *Proceedings of the Conference on Fairness, Accountability, and Transparency* (pp. 279–288). https://doi.org/10.1145/3287560.3287574.

Mnih, V., Kavukcuoglu, K., Silver, D., Graves, A., Antonoglou, I., Wierstra, D., & Riedmiller, M. (2013). *Playing Atari with deep reinforcement learning* [Cs]. http://arxiv.org/abs/1312.5602.

Natale, S., & Ballatore, A. (2020). Imagining the thinking machine: Technological myths and the rise of artificial intelligence. *Convergence, 26*(1), 3–18. https://doi.org/10.1177/1354856517715164.

Orr, G. B., & Müller, K.-R. (Eds.). (1998). *Neural networks: Tricks of the trade*. Springer-Verlag.

Pasquinelli, M. (Ed.). (2015). *Alleys of your mind: Augmented intelligence and its traumas*. Meson Press.

Peirce, C. S. (1931). *Collected papers of Charles Sanders Peirce* (Vol. 2). Harvard University Press.

Powles, J., & Nissenbaum, H. (2018, December 7). *The seductive diversion of "solving" bias in artificial intelligence*. Medium. https://onezero.medium.com/the-seductive-diversion-of-solving-bias-in-artificial-intelligence-890df5e5ef53.

Pridmore, J., Zimmer, M., Vitak, J., Mols, A., Trottier, D., Kumar, P. C., & Liao, Y. (2019). Intelligent personal assistants and the intercultural negotiations of dataveillance in platformed households. *Surveillance & Society, 17*(1/2), 125–131. https://doi.org/10.24908/ss.v17i1/2.12936.

Radford, J., & Joseph, K. (2020). Theory in, theory out: The uses of social theory in machine learning for social science. *Frontiers in Big Data, 3*. https://doi.org/10.3389/fdata.2020.00018.

Reigeluth, T. (2018). Algorithmic prediction as a social activity. *Réseaux*, No 211(5), 35–67.

Ribeiro, M. H., Ottoni, R., West, R., Almeida, V. A. F., & Meira, W. (2020). Auditing radicalization pathways on YouTube. *Proceedings of the 2020 Conference on Fairness, Accountability, and Transparency* (pp. 131–141). https://doi.org/10.1145/3351095.3372879.

Rieder, B. (2017). Scrutinizing an algorithmic technique: The Bayes classifier as interested reading of reality. *Information, Communication & Society, 20*(1), 100–117. https://doi.org/10.1080/1369118X.2016.1181195.

Robbins, S. (2019). A misdirected principle with a catch: Explicability for AI. *Minds and Machines, 29*(4), 495–514. https://doi.org/10.1007/s11023-019-09509-3.

Roberge, J. (2011). What is critical hermeneutics? *Thesis Eleven*. https://doi.org/10.1177/0725513611411682.

Roberge, J., Senneville, M., & Morin, K. (2020). How to translate artificial intelligence? Myths and justifications in public discourse. *Big Data & Society, 7*(1). https://doi.org/10.1177/2053951720919968.

Samuel, A. L. (1959). Some studies in machine learning using the game of checkers. *IBM Journal of Research and Development, 3*(3), 210–229. https://doi.org/10.1147/rd.33.0210.

Schwartz, R. D. (1989). Artificial intelligence as a sociological phenomenon. *The Canadian Journal of Sociology / Cahiers Canadiens de Sociologie, 14*(2), 179–202. https://doi.org/10.2307/3341290.

Seaver, N. (2015). The nice thing about context is that everyone has it. *Media, Culture & Society, 37*(7), 1101–1109. https://doi.org/10.1177/0163443715594102.

Seaver, N. (2019). Captivating algorithms: Recommender systems as traps. *Journal of Material Culture, 24*(4), 421–436. https://doi.org/10.1177/1359183518820366.

Sejnowski, T. J. (2018). *The deep learning revolution*. MIT Press.

Sloane, M., & Moss, E. (2019). AI's social sciences deficit. *Nature Machine Intelligence, 1*(8), 330–331. https://doi.org/10.1038/s42256-019-0084-6.

Stark, L. (2019). Facial recognition is the plutonium of AI. *XRDS: Crossroads, the ACM Magazine for Students, 25*(3), 50–55. https://doi.org/10.1145/3313129.

Stilgoe, J. (2018). Machine learning, social learning and the governance of self-driving cars. *Social Studies of Science, 48*(1), 25–56. https://doi.org/10.1177/0306312717741687.

Strasser, B. J., & Edwards, P. N. (2017). Big Data is the answer ... but what is the question? *Osiris, 32*(1), 328–345. https://doi.org/10.1086/694223.

Sudmann, A. (2018). On the media-political dimension of artificial intelligence: Deep learning as a black box and OpenAI. *Digital Culture & Society, 4*(1), 181–200. https://doi.org/10.14361/dcs-2018-0111.

van Dijck, J. (2014). Datafication, dataism and dataveillance: Big Data between scientific paradigm and ideology. *Surveillance & Society, 12*(2), 197–208. https://doi.org/10.24908/ss.v12i2.4776.

Wertsch, J. V. (1983). The role of semiosis in L. S. Vygotsky's theory of human cognition. In B. Bain (Ed.), *The sociogenesis of language and human conduct*. Plenum Press.

Woolgar, S. (1985). Why not a sociology of machines? The case of sociology and artificial intelligence. *Sociology, 19*, 557–572.

Zuboff, P. S. (2019). *The age of surveillance capitalism: The fight for a human future at the new frontier of power*. Profile Books.

Zuckerberg, M. (2015, June 30). *For the next hour I'll be here answering your questions on Facebook* [Facebook post]. Facebook. https://www.facebook.com/zuck/posts/10102213601037571?comment_id=10102213705932361&offset=0&total_comments=33321&comment_tracking=%7B%22tn%22%3A%22R9%22%7D.

Seaver, N. (2015). The nice thing about context is that everyone has it. Media, Culture & Society, 37(7), 1101-1109. https://doi.org/10.1177/0163443715594102.

CHAPTER 2

Mechanized Significance and Machine Learning: Why It Became Thinkable and Preferable to Teach Machines to Judge the World

Aaron Mendon-Plasek

> Wherever and whenever groups of people come to agree about what knowledge is, they have practically and provisionally solved the problem of how to array and order themselves. To have knowledge is to belong to some sort of ordered life; to have some sort of ordered life is to have shared knowledge.[1]
>
> —Steven Shapin and Simon Shaffer, *Leviathan and the Air-Pump*

Judging Learning Machines and Making Comments Toxic

Machine learning is often seen as either an early-twenty-first or late-twentieth-century subfield of artificial intelligence drawing on techniques in the fields of operations research, cybernetics, cognitive science, and

A. Mendon-Plasek (✉)
Department of History, Columbia University, New York, NY, United States
e-mail: aaron.plasek@columbia.edu

© The Author(s) 2021

J. Roberge and M. Castelle (eds.), *The Cultural Life of Machine Learning*, https://doi.org/10.1007/978-3-030-56286-1_2

statistics.[2] This chapter, by contrast, shows how the problem-framing strategies and practices of machine learning now in ascendancy were articulated, made durable, and widely circulated by researchers working on pattern recognition problems from the 1950s to the 1970s.[3] Developed through the interactions between different communities, research problems, and computing devices in 1950s and 1960s, pattern recognition researchers sought to mechanize the identification of contextual significance, standardize comparisons of different machine learning systems, and codify a body of training, techniques, and reasoning by inaugurating a new discipline. The slow and uneven forging of a novel constellation of practices, concerns, and values through pattern recognition research changed both what it meant to provide an adequate description of the world even as it caused researchers to reimagine their own scientific self-identities.

Early mid-1950s pattern recognition researchers articulated a conception of *contextual significance* that could be performed by humans or machines, and that emphasized performance *reliability* in parity with human judgment and *robust* performance in the face of never-seen-before new data. This notion of *contextual significance*, as discussed in section "How Identifying Significance Became a Branch of Engineering", was exemplified and circulated in the Cold War research problem of optical character recognition (henceforth *OCR*), and encouraged a form of problem solving that sought to produce useful decisions purely through learning from examples. The multiple meanings of *learning* in pattern recognition, identified in section "Pattern Recognition Eats the World: Learning as a Solution to Technical Problems and to Questions of Social Order", were aspirational in that they were expressions of researcher ambitions for what machines *could* and *should* be taught to do. This polysemous *learning*, instantiated mathematically in late 1950s pattern recognition as a *loss function* borrowed from statistical decision theory, fused day-to-day technical decisions for building pattern recognition systems with attitudes that linked *creativity* to mechanical schemes for generating contextual significance. The theoretical conception of "learning" from examples offered as a solution to the problem of contextual significance was analogically seen as a solution for deciding social questions. This occurred, as sketched out in section "Incomparable Alphabet Learning Machines and a Game with the World", because of two questions of knowledge that pattern recognition researchers faced in the late 1950s and 1960s. The first question was at the level of the individual laboratory: namely, how to evaluate, compare, and judge different OCR systems which used different methods, devices, and data sets? Establishing learning criteria also had a pragmatic benefit of having the pattern recognition systems judge and improve their own performance given new data. The second question was one of professional identity: namely, what made pattern recognition constitute a distinct discipline deserving of its own conferences, jobs, and funding? Both questions tied workaday technical practices to national funding agencies and transnational communities of knowledge production; but, more importantly, both questions were interwoven with each other such that the forms of learning offered as a solution to one question at the level of individual labs constrained disciplinary possibility at the national level, and vice versa. Researchers found a solution to these duel questions of how to judge pattern recognition systems and how to legitimize their discipline via the mid-1960s problem-solving strategies of *supervised* and *unsupervised learning*.

Researchers seeking to make pattern recognition into a reputable field of inquiry saw their object of study as the mechanical identification of significance and the reproduction of human judgment. They emphasized building "learning machines" that reliably performed a specific task within a narrow context despite wide variations in input, and were tied to a way of formulating problems that encompassed disparate activities: spotting missiles in the sky or spotting card catalog subjects in thousands of papers; disambiguating polysemy in machine translation or disambiguating particle tracks in bubble chambers; identifying unstable governments in the Cold War world or identifying individual alphanumeric characters on paper. The contextual flexibility and robustness of pattern recognition was tied, in part, to letting the phenomenon of interest be defined by the statistical properties of the data. "Solutions to the problem of knowledge," Shapin and Shaffer have compellingly argued, "are solutions to the problem of social order."[4] For theoretically-inclined pattern recognition researchers there was little difference between looking for patterns in the natural world and looking for patterns in human society. If humans and machines could make the same classifications in a particular task (e.g., to recognize the letter "A," a tank, a fingerprint, a population), machines could make social judgments.[5] Because *significance* in pattern recognition was tied to a way of problem-framing for which *learning* was seen as the answer, mere narratives of the development of supervised and unsupervised learning miss the point. Textbook definitions of supervised and unsupervised learning as self-evident synchronic ordering principles of machine learning miss the point: for the historian it is precisely *why* these forms of learning became stable, durable ordering principles that *need to be explained*.[6] To trace the shifting notion of *learning* in the larger matrix of tacit problem-framing strategies shared by pattern recognition researchers, we need to look at "substitut[ing actions] for concepts and practices for meanings."[7]

Examples from the history of science are instructive. To historicize scientific objectivity, Daston and Galison (2010) adopt a "bottom-up" historiographic method in which "ideal and ethos are gradually built up and bodied out by thousands of concrete actions, as a mosaic takes shape from thousands of tiny fragments of glass."[8] To follow the changing "collective" knowledge and the various kinds of disciplined "knowing sel[ves]" that such collective knowledge requires, they examine the images of scientific atlases and the practices and values these atlases manifest. I sketch a genealogy of *learning* in the then-nascent field of pattern recognition in the 1950s and 1960s, including how technical and professional contingency informed practices of communal- and self-valuing, by a careful examination of the central research problem of pattern recognition at that time: optical character recognition. OCR research in the 1950s and 1960s did not center on one algorithm or one broad collection of techniques, but articulated a set of specific concerns built into the pattern recognition problem-framing for which messy data was no more or less preferable to high-quality, expensively produced, well-curated data sets. While OCR work did not provide prestige and visibility to the field of pattern recognition, the development and circulation of pattern recognition work in the 1960s across a variety of domains, and its attendant forms of *learning*, provided a blueprint for *how* to solve a problem and, more importantly, what *counted* as a good problem.

Today machine learning reformulates the original sin of incomplete knowledge into an epistemic virtue of greater contextual sensitivity. For example, Google's *Perspective* API uses a machine learning classifier to estimate the likelihood of a comment to be "perceived as 'toxic,'" and was intended to "help increase participation, quality, and empathy in online conversation at scale" by curtailing "abuse and harassment online."[9] The classifier was trained on comments labeled "toxic" or not, but to have enough labeled comments a data set first had to be produced. Crowd-sourced workers rated more than 100,000 Wikipedia talk page comments from "very healthy" to "very toxic" according to how they saw each comment as "a rude, disrespectful, or unreasonable comment that is likely to make you leave a discussion."[10] The ambiguity of the definition was purposeful, in the hopes of facilitating decision-making more responsive to the contextual and positional ambiguities spanning race, gender, nationality, ethnicity, sexuality, and class in disparate "toxic" commenting practices. As Perspective's project manager has said, "We want to build machine-assisted moderation tools to flag things for a human to review, but we don't want some central definition or someone to say what is good and bad."[11] A neural network classifier was then trained using the comments and human classifications to replicate the human ratings for each comment.[12] This classifier, so trained, was used "as a surrogate for crowd workers" to label all *63 million* Wikipedia talk page comments spanning 2004–2015 as "toxic" or not.[13] In effect, to both those being surveyed and Perspective's developers, what constitutes "toxicity" is known by its imagined effect, and only ever probabilistically. While such *ignorance-as-generality* may rightly give us pause when applied to high-stakes decisions, the advantages of this strategy in low-stakes decisions become more apparent when applied to the problem of OCR discussed in the next section.

We can see other problem-framing concerns endemic to machine learning in the case of Perspective, especially in how machine learning systems are fixed when discovered to make improper decisions or classifications. With the *New York Times*, the *Economist*, Wikipedia, and the *Guardian* emblazoned on Perspective's website as "partner experiments," Perspective's public release in 2017 by Google and Jigsaw soon exposed that Perspective's classifier rated comments with words denoting historically marginalized gender, sexual, and racial identities (e.g., "woman," "black," "gay," "asian," "homosexual," etc.) as more probable to be perceived as toxic.[14] The classifier's problem, developers contended, was that in the training corpus these identity words were "over-represented in abusive and toxic comments" because these terms disproportionately appeared in online attacks.[15] The "toxicity" classifier trained on this data "overgeneralized and learned to disproportionately associate those [identity] terms with the toxicity label."[16] The solution, developers continued, was to de-toxify these identity words in the corpus by adding more nontoxic comments containing identity terms and then retraining the classifier on this new corpus. Fixing the classifier by adding more data under the justification of bringing the training data into greater fidelity with social reality *did* achieve the desired technical result, and, for our purposes, illustrated two key epistemic values. First, for Perspective's "toxicity" classifier to work, it needs to be able to identity *contextual significance*: namely, that the same data (e.g., words, n-grams) may produce different effects (e.g., a person leaving a conversation or staying) in different contexts (e.g., different online platforms, different identities). Second, in order to be useful even when encountering new forms of toxic speech, the classifier needs *contextual robustness:* namely, that decisions or categories (e.g., "toxic" speech) developed from past data (e.g., the training corpus) will continue to be correct for future as-yet-unseen data. As we shall see in the following section, *contextual significance*, *contextual robustness*, and *ignorance-as-generality* were carefully constructed epistemic hedges tied together through a conception of *mechanized significance* in mid-century pattern recognition problems.

How Identifying Significance Became a Branch of Engineering

"Pattern recognition," Oliver Selfridge wrote for a 1955 Western Joint Computer Conference session on "Learning Machines," is "the extraction of the significant features ... from a background of irrelevant detail" performed by a machine that "learns" by "build[ing] up sequences [of mathematical operations] 'like'" but not identical to those previously efficacious at a specific task.[17] The chair of the session, Willis Ware, then at RAND, explicitly noted the "'Giant Brain' ballyhoo" surrounding "learning machines" and observed that these programs "may be said to 'think' only to the extent that their users and designers have been able to penetrate sufficiently deeply into a problem so that all possible situations which might arise have been examined[.]"[18] This machine learning was not learning to accommodate new tasks in completely unforeseen situations.[19] Nor was this the learning of Allen Newell's "ultracomplicated problems" that "deal[t] with a complex task by adaptation" in which "relevant information is inexhaustible," "potential solutions [are] neither enumerable nor simply representable," and that took chess as the exemplar problem par excellence.[20] Rather, the open-ended research question, as Selfridge's collaborator Gerald Paul Dinneen put it, was

> to design a machine which will recognize patterns. We shall call any possible visual image, no matter how cluttered or indistinct, a configuration. A pattern is an equivalence class consisting of all those configurations which cause the same output in the machine.[21]

"Good" features were obtained by mathematical "sequences of operations" performed on the digitized images whose values empirically distinguished between equivalence classes for the letters *A* and *O*.[22,23] Such good features were ideally insensitive to "variations [that] ought not affect the valuation" like letter size, position, angle, and letter font.[24]

Rejecting straight lines as "too simple" a task and faces as "too complicated," Selfridge and Dinneen settled on identifying printed black "A"s and "O"s on paper, which were chosen for their respective asymmetry and symmetry.[25] In contrast to AI and its operations research and proof-proving roots, the point was not "to build an efficient reading machine, but rather to study how such a machine might work" to handle the enormous variability of input letters—especially *A*s and *O*s the machine had never encountered and even beyond what the Lincoln Lab researchers could anticipate.[26] This situation was *not* the same as AI's mid-1950s obsessions with heuristic problem solving of mathematical questions, automatic translations facilitated by programming compilers, or logistical operations of bureaucracies. Pattern recognition for Selfridge and Dinneen was about mechanizing a particular notion of contextual significance that valorized the reliability of machine performance (i.e., correct classification) for a task given novel data with deformations that are not known or anticipated at the outset.[27]

Such contextual significance meant that the letter *A* might differ for two different sets of "A"-labeled images in potentially contradictory ways. This might appear to be a wildly idiosyncratic way of identifying anything—whether letters, EKGs, faces, fingerprints, or cats—hopelessly sensitive to the peculiarities of the features selected and the training data used. However, Selfridge reframed this sensitivity to individual examples as a virtue. By identifying a problem in which such a strategy was preferable—namely, that of *optical character recognition*—and noting analogically how this sensitivity to training data was what facilitated humans' comparably superior capacity for finding significance, Selfridge made experience the sole source of contextual significance:

> Now significance is a function of, first, context, and second, experience.... [O]f course, context is a function of experience. But more than that, *experience alone affects the kind of thing we regard as significant.*[28]

If humans could learn significance (and indeed, everything else that they can learn) solely through experiencing the world, Selfridge contended, why couldn't machines learn an image recognition task solely from labeled images? The "recognition of simple shapes in a visual field, such as block capital letters," was a useful test case.[29]

But how did identifying two letters generalize in any way to a method for identifying contextual significance? As seen above, for Selfridge and Dinneen the letters *A* and *O* each constituted an *equivalence class*, which was defined as whatever feature values consistently picked out "A"-labeled images as *A*s and "O"-labeled images as *O*s.[30] These equivalence classes were not an ideal *A* or *O* around which each letter image was an imperfect copy. Rather, an equivalence class defined the values of a feature (or features) that categorized images as the same letter: say, many different "A"s as *the* letter *A*, even if all "A" images have "no one thing in common that makes us use the same [letter name] for all."[31] This is why equivalence classes were so named: pattern recognition was, Selfridge contended, "classifying configurations of data into classes of equivalent significance so that very many different configurations all belong in the same equivalence class."[32]

This method illustrated what researchers would later call the "two subsidiary problems" of pattern recognition: "what to measure and how to process the measurements."[33] Selfridge's answer to the former problem dictated his answer to the latter, forming a hermeneutic circle between observed image *features* (i.e., the series of preprocessing operations performed on each letter), the data *configurations* (i.e., the collection of labeled "A" and "O" images), and *equivalence classes* (i.e., the particular feature attributes that distinguish *A*s and *O*s). Building, evaluating, and improving a learning machine could only be achieved by understanding the relations between individual *features, configurations, and equivalence classes* themselves and the machine's performance as a coherent whole in relation to these individual parts. More or less useful features and equivalence classes could be determined via iterative computational guessing and checking different combinations of *features, configurations,* and *equivalence classes*. Any "sequence of operations" that produced features with values that distinguished *A*s and *O*s could work and could be checked via (potentially laborious) trial and error—whether digital computers or humans were doing the trial and error, for Selfridge, mattered not.[34]

Learning as feature selection improvement in pattern recognition did not foreground expertise, in part, because, as Ware noted, Selfridge's and Dinneen's learning machine papers dealt with "the learning of pattern recognition by a maturing individual" (i.e., a child learning to read) while Newell's problem of chess-playing expertise examined "the action of an entire man as he copes with complicated problems of his life."[35] Ware's pronouncements had the form of normative statements about task complexity, but, in practice, were a statement on the permissible simplifying assumptions for problem inputs precisely because this was one strategy for comparing one problem to another. For Selfridge and Dinneen, input letter images were "well organized in two spatial dimensions and exhibit[ed] a well defined topology"; for Newell, problem inputs were "the highest level of complexity—[that of] the game" and involved "a multitude of input data which must be inspected at many levels."[36] Both Selfridge and Dinneen's OCR problem and Newell's chess-playing program had to learn "criteria for decision[s that] are a priori unstated."[37] Already between the letter-learning and chess-playing problems were all the hallmarks of what Newell would later identify as two distinct dispositions "to construct [scientific] theories" dictating for the researchers "what is important, what problems can be solved, [and] what possibilities exist for theoretical extension," including the ways in which learning criteria were specified.[38] Pattern recognition researchers, like Selfridge and Dinneen and others at the Lincoln Laboratory, employed "sets of continuous variables as the underlying state descriptions," and were trained in the problems and problem-solving strategies of electrical engineering.[39] So informed by training and the task of building an OCR machine, pattern recognition, as exemplified by Selfridge's and Dinneen's 1955 papers, offered a vision of a nascent disciplinary formation that combined different notions of *learning* that reflected these researchers' ambitions for a machine able to distinguish *contextual significance* while maintaining *contextually robust* performance when encountering new data.

Pattern Recognition Eats the World: Learning as a Solution to Technical Problems and to Questions of Social Order

What could people do using pattern recognition that they couldn't do before? What made pattern recognition's problem-framing not merely rhetorically compelling but intellectually preferable for some communities? Which communities celebrated and were empowered by these capacities? Pattern-learning machines offered a way of imperfectly knowing the world via its provisional and piecemeal traces.[40] Mid-century pattern recognition shared with mid-century cybernetics what Andrew Pickering calls a "black box ontology," in which the world is filled with black boxes "that [do] something, that one does something to, and that does something back," and for which its internal workings are opaque to us.[41] Pattern recognition systems, like the cybernetic systems Pickering discusses, attempted to "go on in a constructive and creative fashion in a world of exceedingly complex systems" that might never reasonably be understood or derived from first principles.[42] Given these parallels between cybernetics and pattern recognition, it is no surprise that Selfridge worked as Norbert Wiener's assistant in graduate school, and copy-edited a draft of Wiener's *Cybernetics*.[43] The framing of Selfridge's 1955 pattern recognition paper echoes cybernetics' "ontology of unknowability" in how, for example, the ideal letter *A* is never known or pregiven, but an effective equivalence class can always be learned. For all their similarities, however, pattern recognition distinguished itself from cybernetics in valorizing knowledge as a kind of classification. Representing phenomena as aggregates-of-features was a strategy for reproducing (human) judgment (insofar as these "judgments" could be translated into classification decisions) that also held the possibility of being robust to unexpected new data.

Researchers working on pattern recognition problems were engaged in an intellectually stimulating but professionally fraught endeavor in the 1950s and 1960s since pattern recognition was seen by many as applied engineering and not an intellectual arena able to facilitate professional advancement. Work in pattern recognition was accordingly often conducted as a tertiary research pursuit. Selfridge, Dinneen, and others did pattern recognition research informally, during lunch hours.[44] Their ability to use the Test Memory Computer at Lincoln Laboratory to conduct machine learning experiments was made possible, in part, by the computer's reduced use as a support for the Whirlwind Computer employed in the service of the Department of Defense's Semi-Automatic Ground Environment (SAGE) project.[45] Established disciplines' funding for pattern recognition projects was often in service to a particular military problem to be solved in corporate labs like Bell, Philco, IBM, RAND, and GE, and were in sharp contrast to the few-strings-attached ARPA funding of coeval AI research found in university labs at MIT, Carnegie Mellon, and Stanford often discussed in the history of computing.[46]

Those working on pattern recognition and seeking professional advancement through the pursuit of a disciplinary identity were confronted by pattern recognition's methodological disunity and a vast sea of clever, ad hoc mechanical jury-rigged prototypes. The strategies that developed in response to the problems of recognizing alphanumeric letters in particular, both typed and handwritten, on paper and elsewhere, was a key site in which virtues were formed and justified. Pattern recognition work, especially OCR work in laboratories, in panels at international conferences, government funding agencies, and in individual lives was a critical trading zone that shaped these concerns about how to know the world. What was shared by early pattern recognition research was a set of intellectual ambitions, problem-framing strategies, institutional priorities and norms, and computing practices endemic to OCR work exemplified by Selfridge and Dinneen's 1955 efforts. OCR facilitated the circulation of pattern recognition's methods and values because of its practical application in a variety of disparate domains as well as for the ease with which its methods were generalized and repurposed for non-OCR problems.[47]

A key facet of the "black box ontology" in pattern recognition's framing of good problems was the plurality of meanings of *learning*. In practice, these different meanings of learning were expressed mathematically by the use of the *loss function* that represented the numerically-defined "costs" of a particular decision or action. While pattern recognition learning had not yet become synonymous with minimizing the loss function by the early 1960s, this form of learning was seen as a viable strategy to realizing three ambitions. First, this conception of learning could serve as a decision procedure for *mimicking* (human) judgment for narrow, well-defined cases. Second, this learning *generated* trust through its repeated use when, as researchers described it, "we do not understand our problem well enough to pre-program reasonable sets of characterizers."[48] Third, the idea of learning as "problems of successive estimation of unknown parameters" served as an aid to solving problems when the optimal method was unclear but data was plentiful.[49] All three notions of learning were aspirational, and all three constrained and spurred local day-to-day engineering decisions about how to build, compare, and improve pattern recognition machines, and what forms of professional advancement were available to researchers. More importantly, these conceptions of learning informed what constituted knowledge and the human capacity for identifying significance, and continue to buoy and justify claims of machine learning efficacy today. We treat each of these three in turn.

Mechanical Schemes for Imitating Human Judgment

Pattern recognition provided a strategy for reproducing *any* classification humans could make for a finite collection of images (or any other categorical data) *by definition*. Insofar as classification was a synecdoche for significance, identifying importance became a problem of engineering. Finding the image features correlated to whatever humans employed in the same classification was a problem that could itself be partially automated. Picking out *A*s and *O*s became possible not only for labeled images (where you already had the answer), but also for *A*s and *O*s in unexpected images not anticipated by programmers themselves. This strategy could be applied to a universe of decision problems, as was articulated by pattern recognition researchers by the late 1960s:

> [W]e often speak of the character-recognition problem, the problem of analyzing electrocardiograms, the photointerpretation problem, and so on. Yet each of these is in reality not a single problem but a problem area, an entire ensemble of problems. The problems within an area are generally governed by a number of important parameters. Each proposed application, each choice of parameters, specifies a new problem from the ensemble—there are literally an infinity of problems.[50]

This ambition to produce a methodology able to handle any and all decision problems led to a disciplinary identity crisis for pattern recognition similar to that experienced by statistics in the twentieth century and data science today, and which manifests in the confusion and conflation of the terms artificial intelligence and machine learning.[51] That pattern recognition might be a generalized classification procedure was a self-evident good to be much lauded. But the ambition of universal applicability for many pattern recognition researchers as a completely general form of machine learning also contributed to much hand-wringing in the 1960s and early 1970s about what made pattern recognition a unique field distinct from other engineering or scientific disciplines.

Making Computers a Reliable Interface with the World Through Patterns-for-Agents

Pattern recognition was a hodgepodge of technical and social strategies for inventing and ensuring *reliability* for machines directly interfacing with a messy, inconsistent, and ever-changing real world. What reliability was, or, how it could be measured, often came down to local laboratory decisions about what constituted a "task" and how that task was to be integrated into the sensibilities, infrastructures, and worldview of those needing the task to be done.[52] The decision to restrict pattern recognition tasks to an extremely narrow range of actions and possibilities for purposes of reliability also became a strategy to establish credibility. Pattern recognition, Donald MacKay wrote, "cannot ultimately be separated from that of the organization of action: activity in view of ends."[53] In stark contrast to some applications of machine learning today, the fact that mid-century pattern recognition was *limited* to a specific context of use for a particular agent was considered a *virtue* of the approach. Pattern recognition implicitly had "the notion of pattern-for-an-agent" built in such that "the problem of pattern-recognition is always ill-defined until the class of agents in question, and their repertoire, have been specified in relevant detail."[54] The kind of trust provided by patterns-for-an-agent arose through the machine's repeated use in well-defined situations and not from computing operations per second, the speed and capacity of computer memory, or the availability of ever-larger digitized data sets.

Today we are sensitive to how the repurposing of an existing pattern-for-an-agent can produce fictitious inductive claims, and that when such pattern learning machines are used to arbitrate or assist in the adjudication of social decisions involving historically marginalized groups, such reused "patterns" produce unjust, unfair, and inegalitarian decisions. Selfridge's articulation of pattern recognition and its implementation by Lincoln Lab researchers may strike contemporary readers as woefully unconcerned about the idiosyncrasies of their labeled training data.[55] Such concerns, though justified, erase the intellectual virtues that produced and constrained the possibilities for a particular system to establish credibility.[56] Curation of training data for a particular use case was provisional, as we have seen with Selfridge and Dinneen's 1955 work, in that it relied on how features changed across available but arbitrary examples: as MacKay put it, "our notion of pattern is relative, [but] it is not on that account subjective."[57] What made classifications stick was relative difference: there was no absolute definition of classification to which one would *want* to appeal. Nor, for the problems like OCR or image classification, was there a special set of data to *appeal to* because the techniques were a strategy for machine performance reliability.[58] What they did have to identify were the variability of important differences to the problem. However, picking features, as just one decision of many in building a pattern recognition system, tended to be based "upon intuition, personal feelings, and preferences," a host of pragmatic engineering concerns, and the particular system in which it would be used.[59]

For pattern recognition researchers, a particular learning machine gained its credibility not through mathematical proof but by its consistent uniform performance at a specific task that was responsive to and not incapacitated by unexpected, even contradictory, information. Researchers building learning machines funded by the military and employed in university labs and in commercial corporations didn't need a machine to generate its own goals in a well-defined axiomatic system as was espoused by some prominent mid-century researchers in artificial intelligence.[60] Pattern recognition researchers instead needed a machine to reliably perform a well-defined task in which the enumeration of all potential inputs or the rules governing these inputs was not pragmatically possible.[61] By 1961 OCR systems still required a "consistently high quality of the input patterns, and [had] a limitation of the recognizable alphabet to at most several hundred members *with each allowable size and style variation of each character counting as a separate member*."[62] Reliability was often as much of an aspiration as it was an established fact of practice. This placed concerted attention in pattern recognition on the "prerecognition image processing," to clean up the image, and which, in fact, was inherently "dangerous" since removing the "salt and pepper" imperfections on character images "without first recognizing the character ... will undoubtedly do harm at times, and do some good at other times."[63]

A Decision Procedure When You Don't Know the Problem Solution Space

Insofar as pattern recognition had a methodological theory, it was through an "effective transformation of a perception-recognition problem," such as optical character recognition,"into a classification problem."[64] Such a transformation informed the ways in which data was to be valued, and how the identification of significant information might be *performed and judged*. Which statistical techniques were brought to bear in a particular pattern recognition project varied, in part, on whether the "pattern" in question was for use in (1) textual work (e.g., OCR, information processing, machine translation, hand-printed letters, etc.), (2) social and scientific judgment, data processing, and surveillance (e.g., bacteria colony formation, emission line spectra, tank images, maintenance schedules, fingerprinting, speech processing, etc.), or (3) the studies of "perception," including efforts to build and employ neural networks.[65] Of these three, from the late 1950s to early 1970s, OCR circulated throughout the pattern recognition community as a key exemplar problem from which practitioners learned, remixed, and reified problem-solving strategies, and that brought together practitioners with different skills, training, and goals.[66] OCR work facilitated the introduction and circulation of statistical decision theory as a particular method and form of solution that reshaped the ambitions of pattern recognition, as one pattern recognition researcher wrote in 1968, from a "narrow esoteric field of electronic computer applications" to "one of the most ambitious scientific ventures of this century[.]"[67] The following section investigates how this transformation of pattern recognition from "esoteric" to universal occurred through a sustained inability of researchers to agree upon the appropriate ways to measure machine learning performance in OCR pattern recognition systems. The use of decision theory's loss functions was one strategy that fostered this transformation. The loss function was made durable, in part, by the loss function's ability to satisfy social, political, and disciplinary needs as well as facilitating the intellectual creativity of both statisticians and engineers involved.

Incomparable Alphabet Learning Machines and a Game with the World

The overwhelming predominance of OCR systems as the de facto use case of pattern recognition ensured that the process of accounting for variance in training "features" was often decisive to a system's effectiveness. In practice, as late as 1968, commercial OCR systems compared test characters against ideal character "masks" for typed text, which, while a technique of pattern recognition, was not an example in the machine learning tradition that this chapter has been tracking.[68] Identifying characters via a set of features was sometimes used to identify handwriting, but such strategies tended to produce more errors as a function of the number of possible characters and were usually more computationally intensive than mask approaches.[69]

The practice of learning typed letters and typed letter features empirically from training data as outlined by Selfridge in 1955 remained more of an aspiration in the early 1960s than a physically realized working system, but this may have reflected a belief about the demand for "self-programming reading machines."[70] "No one," writes J. Rabinow in 1968, "has ever asked us to build [a self-programming reading machine]—not even semi-seriously." Rabinow continues:

> Most of the reading machines built today are used in business where the OCR machine reads a prescribed font. In most other situations the number of fonts is quite limited and 5 to 10 specific fonts are usually more than enough. In the case of the Post Office, particularly in the case of zip codes, we can normalize the size and do some feature analysis and guess the numbers. But if one wanted to build a self-programming alphanumeric reader for the Post Office, one would be faced with the fact that there just isn't enough information. This is true both because the number of characters to be read on any envelope is too small, and because one envelope has no relationship to the one before.... As far as I know, there is no self-programming machine, but we all think it would be fun to make one.[71]

Yet there were already considerable efforts underway to identify hand-printed alphanumeric characters in the same conference proceedings containing Rabinow's statement. An ARPA funded project at RAND called GRAIL tracked a user's light pen strokes to correctly recognize character inputs "with about" (Groner's words) 90–95% accuracy largely for the purpose of making programming flowcharts.[72] The System Development Corporation, also supported by ARPA, built a similar light pen system that did the same thing with no recognition accuracy mentioned.[73] Both used dictionaries of pen stroke gestures associated with each symbol.

An OCR problem similar to Selfridge's was pursued by John Munson at Stanford Research Institute (SRI) with funding from the US Army and Navy. Here the task was to take paper "Fortran coding sheets" at the Applied Physics Laboratory at SRI, filled out by hand, and accept them as Fortran programs to be run directly by the machine after being scanned. First, the SRI team used a TV camera to ingest the handwriting characters as 24 by 24 black-and-white grids for "3 alphabets of FORTRAN characters from each of 12 writers" from which character features were calculated with "three 85-weight dot product units per category[.]"[74] Alphabet sets from four additional writers were used to test the system's capacity to recognize Fortran characters, which "achieved a correct classification rate of 80%" but for which Munson estimated could be "raised to 85%, or at best to perhaps 90%."[75] Their future work entailed building an "ad hoc" method using "a decision tree, a huge look up table, a weighted decision, and adaptive process, or a combination" that would provide a list of answers accompanied by confidence probabilities that would achieve "on the order of 90% or better" for individual characters.[76] For the specific task of reading Fortran code as input, they hoped to use Fortran syntax itself to further correct letter recognition so as to "produce text of 99% accuracy or better."[77]

Despite such optimism, Munson was painfully aware that such error rate measures were themselves highly idiosyncratic, depending on the way the data set was created, digitized, and stored, the various learning procedures employed, the kind of classification process attempted, and the criteria for success. This made it dubious to attempt to compare reported error rates between different systems or OCR projects. Munson concluded:

> We view the problem [of handprinted text recognition] in the five stages of data preparation, data input, preprocessing, classification, and context analysis.... We believe that these stages must all be kept in view, however, because a change in performance in one greatly affects the demands put on another. We have tried to establish a framework in which, if the outcome of an experiment is x% correct classification of characters or lines of text, the meaning and value of the result will be clear.[78]

The prevalence of a prototype-and-try attitude toward pattern recognition systems by engineers further exacerbated the difficulty of comparing the efficacy of different OCR programs across different data sets. An OCR program that worked well for one data set would do poorly for a different data set. The issue was not simply what contemporaries might call "overfitting," but rather that the data sets might have antithetical feature values for the same equivalence class.[79] A researcher could always select an ad hoc criteria to compare different machine learning systems, but such comparisons required much labor, money, and institutional infrastructure. Given that most projects were task specific, few resources were usually given for building standards across projects, organizations, or institutions, except when demands were imposed by research funders. Any claims about the "correctness" or "generalizability" of learning programs to "read" the zip codes for the US Post Office,[80] the finance forms for the US Army, student information for the Chicago Board of Education, or driver's license applications for the State of Michigan, or for "automatic newspaper [re]production" for international publishers, were entirely pegged to their institutional contexts and assumptions, and rendered incommensurable when these "tasks" were considered outside of the insitutions in which they were performed.[81] In practice, other concerns could render pattern recognition system accuracy comparisons moot: cost-effectiveness, for instance, was often prioritized even over higher recognition accuracy.[82]

Theoretical studies of pattern recognition were grounded in statistical decision theory as well as signal-to-noise problems in radar, telecommunications, and other applications of information-theoretic measurements. Building on both Fisher's and Pearson and Neyman's hypothesis-testing frameworks, statistical decision theory involved calculating a problem-specific "decision function" to decide how many "stages" of experimental observations were necessary before making a "terminal decision" about which hypothesis to accept given the opportunity cost of incorrect decisions and the possibility of additional experimentation.[83] Much of the initial development of decision theory was done by Abraham Wald, who fled Nazi-occupied Austria to the US in 1938 via the assistance of the Cowles Commission, joined Columbia University's faculty in 1941, and would die in a plane crash in India in December 1950.[84] During this brief time, Wald's work made important contributions to statistics: first, by his singular explication of statistical decision theory in 1939, and, second, via his development of sequential analysis to decision theory in 1943 as part of the Statistics Research Group at Columbia.[85] Both efforts were combined in his definitive Office-of-Naval-Research-sponsored monograph entitled *Statistical Decision Functions* published the year of his death.[86]

Wald's productive insight was to conflate statistical decisions—what Wald, following Neyman, labels "the problem of inductive behavior"—as a generalized zero-sum two-person *game* between an "experimenter" and "Nature."[87] The *game* is the possible choices available to both experimenter and Nature. For the experimenter: a choice of a "decision function" from all possible decisions and the subsequent decision results (i.e., observations). For Nature: a "choice of [the] true distribution."[88] Wald did the difficult mathematical gymnastics of expanding this game to include *infinite* possible choices for both experimenter and Nature, incorporating the use of sequential testing so that after each observation a new decision (e.g., make a classification or take an additional observation) is made in response to the history of previous actions taken by the experimenter.[89]

Here then we can begin to see the analogical and mathematical similarities between Wald's decision theory and pattern recognition's OCR problem. In 1957 C. K. Chow, working "in the Electromechanisms Department of the Burroughs Corporation Research Center at Paoli, PA," suggested decision theory should be used in pattern recognition[90]:

> [The optical character] recognition problem is considered to be that of testing multiple hypotheses in the statistical inference. Consequently, the design and evaluation of a recognition system is comparable to a statistical test. Results of decision theory can be applied.[91]

Mindful of the experimental difficulties of comparing error rates of different OCR systems, Chow noted, "Cases may arise where different misrecognitions have different consequences; e.g., the registering of a four as an asterisk may not be as serious an error as registering it as a nine."[92] Decision theory offered a ready-made toolkit that could compare engineered pattern recognition systems in more meaningful ways using the concept of a "loss" function:

> The criterion of minimum error rate is then no longer appropriate. Instead, the criterion of minimum risk is employed. Proper weights indicate the loss incurred by the system for every possible decision. Proper weights are

> assigned to measure the consequences of errors, rejections, and correct recognitions. These weights indicate the loss incurred by the system for every possible decision. The loss, which should be regarded as negative utility, may actually represent loss in dollars or unit of utility in measuring the consequence of the system decision.[93]

Chow employed nomenclature already matter-of-factly used in Wald's 1939 and 1945 papers, including the use of vectors as features typically found in pattern recognition in the 1960s, and was a very early example of Bayesian decision theory employed to a pattern recognition problem. Given "noise statistics, the signal structure, and preassigned weights," all of which could be determined empirically for a particular OCR system, Chow could not only describe the optimal possible performance for any system according to a particular decision criteria (like the minimization of probability of misclassification), but, more importantly, Chow could describe the ways these different systems would degrade "from characters being corrupted by printing deterioration and/or inherent noise of the [OCR] devices."[94]

Obtaining empirical probability distributions of actual machines was a formidable challenge to making Chow's result usable. However, what did facilitate the circulation of Chow's union of OCR to decision theory was the approach's agnosticism as to (1) how to choose the features to be examined for a particular pattern recognition problem and (2) how patterns of features might be learned by a particular pattern recognition system. Though beyond the temporal scope of this chapter, agnosticism to these two questions in the 1960s structured the possibility for pattern recognition as a field, and set the stage for pattern recognition's conflation with machine learning in the 1970s and then subsequent appropriation by artificial intelligence in the 1980s. Today's machine learning ontology of supervised and unsupervised learning—"learning with a teacher" (using labeled data) and "learning without a teacher" (using unlabeled data), respectively—developed largely in 1960s pattern recognition communities concerned with language and judgement (as already suggested in section "A Decision Procedure When You Don't Know the Problem Solution Space"), and kept Chow's agnosticism tied initially to communities familiar with signal processing in engineering applications.[95]

In 1962, following Chow in examining "how to process a set of measurements once that set has been decided upon" and not "what to measure," N. Abramson, working at Stanford Electronics Laboratory, and

D. Braverman, working at Caltech, presented a strategy for "the optimal use of a sequence of prior observations in order to recognize patterns…of a visual, aural, or electromagnetic origin."[96] Employing the framing of decision theory, they "show[ed] that the use of prior observations for pattern recognition may be described as a process of learning the statistical characteristics of the patterns involved"—in effect, they presented the paradigm, methods, and notation of *supervised learning*, everything but the word "supervised" itself.[97] Using supervised learning one could either assume prior probability distributions of the relevant categories and use estimated statistical parameters as the "true" values (i.e., the "parametric" case), or use empirical observations as the "true" values (i.e., the "nonparametric" case).[98] By 1964, the then-named *supervised* problem was contrasted with the "nonsupervised" case in which the categories are not known beforehand.[99] If these considerations offered a theoretical framework by which different machines might be usefully compared, this framework was largely ignored by many engineers building prototype pattern recognition systems till the early 1970s. Why?

The prominence of OCR as an applied problem produced a builder/theorist divide such that "when builders of pattern recognition devices confronted people working on theoretical aspects of pattern classification, especially statistical classification, there was a tendency to question, in the name of practicality and simplicity, the need for theoretical studies in this area."[100] If my OCR learning machine identifies the right letter 99% of the time for my data, a pattern-recognition builder might say, why resort to the mathematical sophistry of the theorists?—this attitude was only exacerbated for engineers by the theorists' "penchant for presenting their work in the unfortunate 'theorem-proof, theorem-proof' style" that was endemic to Wald's work and statistical decision theory generally.[101] However, ad hoc tinkering and iteration made it difficult for engineers to estimate the challenge of a particular pattern recognition problem except in hindsight. This made it risky—both professionally and financially—to apply pattern recognition to new problems for system builders and their government sponsors; problems anticipated to be solved with ease took years even as other problems thought to be difficult were solved relatively quickly.

Writing in 1968, one researcher summarized the situation: "What is evident is that to a large extent, until very recently, theoretical developments and practical implementation have taken independent paths with little interaction."[102] And elsewhere: "we have a jumble of published and unpublished experimental and theoretical results, engineering successes and failures, comments, criticisms and philosophical arguments out of which, hopefully, will emerge some order and maturing of the field."[103] Theorizing was a potential means of bringing pattern recognition to bear on new problems by finding ways to categorize the complexity of the particular application and so offer some procedure for estimating the resources required to develop new solutions to new problems and to translate existing solutions into new contexts. But it was also a strategy to unify a hodgepodge of researchers into a *discipline* with its own conferences, revenue streams, professional opportunities, training pipelines, and modes of prestige. By the late 1960s, the desire to know when, why, and how such mechanized classifications-as-judgment would fail "require[d] ... a soul-searching methodological examination of the entire enterprise of pattern recognition" that had personal as well as intellectual consequences.[104]

Epilogues, Epistemic Impotence, and Rearguing the Past

The Search for Impotence, Mechanized Intuition, & Disciplinary Coherence

Early pattern recognition in the 1950s and 1960s, as articulated by Selfridge and many others, inhabited two registers of discourse. The first register was pedestrian and born of a perceived need for reliability in the face of variegated social data that *could not be anticipated* (i.e., contextual robustness). The second register, in its extreme form, was the very pinnacle of hubris that sought to reproduce the contextual significance of human perception, and even what humans did or could not know, and that made even hyperbolic coeval claims about producing "intelligence" in artificial intelligence seem levelheaded by comparison.[105] Both were necessary but not sufficient to argue that pattern recognition was "a vast and explicit endeavor at mechanization of the most fundamental human function of perception and concept formation."[106] While the second conference proceedings on the Methodologies of Pattern Recognition in 1969 opened by labeling the field as "one of the most ambitious scientific ventures of this century, requiring collaboration of electronic engineers, physicists, physiologists, psychologists, logicians, mathematicians, and philosophers," the task of changing pattern recognition "from the status of a programming stunt to ... a respectable branch of scientific art" would be achieved, in part, by "explor[ing] the limits beyond which [pattern recognition] will not work."[107] Louis Fein's "Impotence Principles for Machine Intelligence," the closing paper in the proceedings of first IEEE pattern recognition workshop in 1966, claimed that "the most secure part of our present knowledge is knowing what it is that we cannot know or do," and cited Godel's theorems in mathematics, the relativity postulate in relativity, Heisenberg's uncertainty principle in quantum mechanics, the second law of thermodynamics, and others as examples.[108] This "important lesson from the history of science," Fein claimed, had been ignored in "the field of information systems, computers, and automata[.]"[109] Common to all these impotence principles was a concern for generalized applicability of possible solutions.

The search for generalized rules took many forms, including ways of thematically combining pattern recognition work as a discipline and making this knowledge available to researchers in different disciplines. In the second IEEE conference, one researcher observed the tendency in pattern recognition "towards [...] solutions of very limited problems" and "the scarcity of and means for carrying out comparative evaluations of different approaches," hindered the dissemination of pattern recognition research, and the "unif[ication] of the field."[110] Writing half a century ago, this researcher offered a solution to these challenges remarkly similar in substance to those frequently proffered today: namely, developing a "modus operandi of systems study" for use by "non-specialists" spanning from data set creation to final implementation and its subsequent effects.[111]

Even given the mathematical tools of decision theory numerous researchers noted it was not "adequate for the solution of pattern recognition problems."[112] One paper noted decision theory "has had an impact only when it has been supplemented by a substantial amount of heuristic thinking."[113] "For the nonformalizable aspects of design," they concluded, "interactive approaches, namely those in which the human is part of the loop in the design process [...] seem to be most promising."[114] Another paper noted how pattern recognition involved "inductive ambiguity" in the "act of generating hypotheses" as a result of "extra-evidential factors" that "are entirely invisible," and that was contingent such that "two hypotheses which are equally well confirmed by the evidence may have different credibilities depending on how well they harmonize with other hypotheses in a theory."[115] A 1971 conference paper entitled "A 'Crisis' in the Theory of Pattern Recognition," asked, "what is the novelty, then, that the researchers are after in the theory of pattern recognition?"[116] No longer, the Russian scientist Alexander Lerner argued, was "learning [...] a mysterious phenomenon inherent to living beings"; now it was about minimizing the loss function.[117] What distinguished pattern recognition from other disciplines? Noting that "physicists are aware that facts alone are not sufficient to select a true theory," Lerner suggested that picking a "true" theory requires a "selection [that] has been done without any formal rules, by intuition."[118] "Computer intuition," Lerner argued, in pattern recognition was "the introduction of an a priori orderliness [that] enables one to select the best rule from a set of rules that minimize the empirical risk."[119]

These efforts ultimately highlighted two existential threats to pattern recognition: (1) a confusion among individual researchers about what constituted a good pattern recognition question, and (2) an ambiguity about what distinguished pattern recognition as a distinct field of inquiry (from cybernetics, artificial intelligence, statistics, etc.). Both concerns were manifested through the singular inability of pattern recognition researchers to usefully compare different pattern recognition systems and approaches. By the mid-1970s, *supervised* and *unsupervised learning* were established as durable categories that continue to dictate possibility in machine learning to this day, but, as we have seen, were originally developed in the early 1960s. This ontology of learning forged in pattern recognition, and later incorporated into machine learning (the disciplinary formation) *as* machine learning (the set of techniques) did not dispel the practitioners' sense of the diverse activities that were to constitute the discipline. This was demonstrated in part by a 1973 textbook entitled "Pattern Classification and Scene Analysis," with chapters on "Bayes Decision Theory," "Supervised Learning," "Unsupervised Learning," and "Linear Discriminant Functions," that began by noting that "this diversity [of the contributions from many different disciplines] also presents serious problems to anyone writing a book on [pattern recognition]."[120] They continue:

> [Classification theory] provides formal mathematical procedures for classifying patterns once they have been represented abstractly as vectors. Attempts to find domain-independent procedures for constructing these vector representations have not yielded generally useful results. Instead, every problem area has acquired a collection of procedures suited to its special characteristics.[121]

The inability to theorize how to vectorize the world and incorporate these non-necessary "extra-evidential factors," in hindsight, became precisely one of the key concerns that differentiated pattern recognition as a discipline and shaped the manner in which supervised and unsupervised learning was subsequently valorized and circulated in the late 1970s and early 1980s.

Pattern recognition did not attain the kind of disciplinary prominence or prestige implied by Watanabe's claim of "the most ambitious scientific ventures of [the twentieth] century."[122] However, the methodologies and epistemological virtues developed in 1950s and 1960s pattern recognition have today become ubiquitous across a dizzying array of disciplines, subjects, and problem domains as machine learning. By the late 1970s, the previous heterogeneity of forms of learning denoted by "machine learning" in the 1950s and 1960s appears to have collapsed into the categories of unsupervised and supervised learning made durable in the 1960s pattern recognition research literature.

Why the Paucity of Early Machine Learning Histories Has Social and Political Consequences

Histories of machine learning, insofar as they are offered as standalone pieces or as addendums to the history of artificial intelligence, tend to narrate the period from the late mid-1950s to the late 1970s as one in which little progress in machine learning occurred, often using neural network "connectionist" touchstones as a proxy for machine learning progress and foregrounding "AI winters" as a primary driver of machine learning success or failure in both the twentieth and twenty-first centuries. This reflects an instrumental view of the history of science in line with Robert Merton's sociology of science in which the objective is to help scientists do better science.[123] Such views of the purpose of the history of science are even shared by the celebrated author of *The Art of Computer Programming* and ACM Turing Award winner Donald Knuth, who has argued that more recent histories of computer science are "dumbed down" in an ill-advised attempt to make it accessible to a reading public beyond computer scientists.[124] Internalist histories of computer science, Knuth notes, can teach future computer scientists, help them learn from past failures, and develop imagination. For Knuth, the value of these histories should be judged accordingly to how well they succeed at these tasks, but also seems to protect claims of scientific priority and to engage in a certain kind of nostalgia in which prominent scientists become role models. I have no interest in critiquing such uses of history—anymore than I would demand a person read a poem for *only* a particular set of results. Perhaps most readers who have made it this far into the paper will disagree with such a constrained understanding of what history does or should do.[125]

Different histories are written for different purposes, in response to different concerns, and by people with different lived experiences and worldviews. Let Knuth have his technical histories. Let everyone who wants to watch *The Theory of Everything, The Imitation Game,* or *Hidden Figures* as a playbook for a career in cosmology, computing, or aerospace do so. However, historians are painfully aware of how stories we tell about ourselves produce the possibilities for our own action in both subtle and not subtle ways. Our understandings of race, gender, sexuality, and class are profoundly inflected by how we narrate our histories. The U.S. Civil War was about slavery. We shape our world and selves by the stories we tell and the details we choose to make significant. The story of Geoff Hinton unable to find a job because he was working on neural networks isn't just a story about the state of the field; it's a subtle commentary by the story teller about the kinds of values or kind of life a researcher *should* have. Einstein invented relativity while working at a patent office. These stories do work for the people who repeat them even as they are also constrained by them. AI winters are the result of researchers overpromising and under delivering rather than a consequence of a Department of Defense shakeup for which artificial intelligence research was an afterthought—*that* story continues to constrain and suggest possibilities for many machine learning researchers today. The development of supervised and unsupervised learning was a particular answer to the problems of knowledge posed within a defuse, transnational network of individuals and institutions across dozens of countries that comprised the pattern recognition community from the 1950s to the 1970s. I sought to recover the epistemic assumptions of this community by tracing the various instantiations of OCR work in local laboratories and in the international technical literature to understand how machine learning came to be seen by some as a compelling method to make social decisions. This led me to a number of new actors who were largely elided in the histories of artificial intelligence, including women and non-white actors who I have cited in this paper that have made important contributions to machine learning and for which further study is required. The present prominence of machine learning in data science and computer science is often narrated in dramatic fashion as a sudden superiority of neural networks over other AI approaches at the end of the twentieth century and the start of the twenty-first. However, as has been shown here, much of the ontology of machine learning and its attendant epistemic justification was set out by the early 1960s. Contemporary debates about the generalizability of machine learning in social decisions rehearses many of the same debates pattern recognition researchers had with each other in the 1960s about how to compare different learning machines using different data sets.

The early 1950s to mid-1970s was an intellectually capacious and generative period for machine learning in the twentieth century—*not* because of any single technical advance but because the research problem of pattern recognition established virtues, practices, and organizing principles for how a useful question was to be identified. Such problem-framing strategies for technical problems circulated across geography and disciplines, in part, because it was also recognized as valuable knowledge by those not doing pattern recognition work. Rather than taking the machine learning terms of supervised and unsupervised learning as self-evident, I see them as research practices in need of explanation, in part, because they inform what constitutes evidence for questions of race, gender, and socioeconomic class now explicitly debated through the implementation of machine learning systems to make important social decisions. The history presented here reflects my questions on the interweaving of technical solutions as political solutions by many contemporary machine learning systems, including Perspective, that are offered as solutions to questions of social order. Narratives pertaining to machine learning are some of the props by which we envision possibility and feasibility. "Now anyone can deploy Google's troll-fighting AI" said *Wired* when Perspective was publicly released, six months before the discovery of the model's propensity to label identity words as "toxic" discourse.[126] Historical narratives and actors who have been underrepresented in the historiography of AI undoubtedly have shaped current day practices. To ignore these historical contingencies in the implementation of machine learning is a shortcoming. Let us be clear-eyed about the amount of work a history of machine learning entails, to what purposes we would put it to, and the generosity of the communities that make this work possible. Let us also be mindful of the challenging situation of early career scholars who recognize that time is not a panacea for justice, and that the insight and intelligence with which we address machine learning systems today will be the linchpin of future bad laws we must later protest.

Acknowledgements My gratitude to Michael Castelle and Jonathan Roberge for the opportunity to present an early version of this work at the 2018 Cultural Life of Machine Learning AoIR preconference workshop, and for their patience with my incessant revising of this chapter. I have been fortunate to have presented aspects of this research at 4S (2017, 2019), SHOT/SIGCIS (2016, 2018), and SLSA (2017), and the present work has benefitted from these conversations. Research in this paper was generously supported, in part, by a NSF Doctoral Dissertation improvement grant (#1829357). While not directly cited in this paper, this research has been informed by archive collections at the US National Archives in Maryland, the Computer History Museum, University of Chicago, Columbia University, University of Southern California, UCLA, MIT, and Stanford University. Rob Hunt assisted in the conversion of citations to APA style. Finally, the author humbly thanks Matthew Jones, Eamonn Bell, Michael Castelle, Susannah Glickman, and Matthew Wilson Plasek for their valuable attention, advice, encouragement, and kindness. Special thanks to my partner, Sapna Mendon-Plasek, whose unflagging support and love, equanimity during a pandemic, and extraordinary magnanimity, all while defending her own dissertation, made this chapter both possible and much better than it would have been otherwise.

Notes

1. Shapin and Schaffer (1985, p. xlix).
2. Marcus and Davis (2019), Broussard (2018), and Jordan and Mitchell (2015), for instance, situate machine learning as a subfield of artificial intelligence. Valuable historical, sociological, and popular inquiries of artificial intelligence largely distinct from the pattern recognition qua machine learning work discussed in this chapter include Garvey (2019), Dick (2011, 2015), November (2012), Wilson (2010), Nilsson (2010), Boden (1987, 2006), Roland and Shiman (2002), Cordeschi (2002), Forsythe (2001), Crevier (1993), Edwards (1996), Haugeland (1985), Newell (1982), and McCorduck (1979). For operations research, see Thomas (2015), Erikson et al. (2013), and Mirowski (2002). For cybernetics, see Carr (2020), Peters (2016), Kline (2015), Medina (2011), Pickering (2010), and Galison (1994). For cognitive science, see Boden (2006). Valuable historical studies of statistics, risk, and quantification include Dryer (2019), Daston (2018), Igo (2007, 2018), Radin (2017), Bouk (2015), Porter (1986, 1995), Stigler (1986, 1999), Desrosières (1998), Daston (1995), Hacking (1990), and Gigerenzer et al. (1989).

3. Plasek (2016) notes that "the sheer volume and ambit of technical publications produced" indicated a distinct machine learning tradition both simultaneous to and more prolific than early AI research (p. 6). Independently Cardon, Cointet, and Mazières (2018) suggested distinct "connectionist" and "symbolic" approaches using co-citation networks in technical computing literature, noting an excess of connectionist publications over symbolic publications from the 1940s to the mid-1960s. They narrate the second half of the twentieth century and the early twenty-first century as a competition between these two approaches (and their intellectual descendants) and as a series of "AI winters." Jones (2018) offers a high-level overview of loosely the same period, but focuses on the transnational development of machine learning via debates in exploratory data analysis, pattern recognition, and statistics, especially as these fields changed through interactions between computing practices and modes of epistemic valuing. Nilsson (2010), although ostensibly a monograph of AI histories written by a participant-observer, examines a number of machine learning touchstones (e.g., see chapter 29), and remains valuable for its breadth of scope despite historical idiosyncrasies that reflect Nilsson's own career. For a technical, participant-observer examination of the touchstones, practices, and narratives of contemporary machine learning researchers, see Mackenzie (2017). For recent explorations of machine learning systems and the contingency in the construction of data sets, see, for instance, Pasquinelli and Joler (2020), Crawford and Paglen (2019), Radin (2017), and many others investigating fairness, accountability, transparency, and ethics of machine learning systems (see note 5).
4. Shapin and Schaffer (1985, p. 332).
5. Regarding computing infrastructures broadly interpreted and their impact on vulnerable populations, see the ACM Conference on Fairness, Accountability, and Transparency (FAccT*). Important references on the subject include Sweeney (2013), O'Neil (2016), Barocas and Selbst (2016), Noble (2018), Eubanks (2018), Buolamwini and Gebru (2018), Ensign, Friedler, Neville, Scheidegger, and Venkatasubramanian (2018), and Benjamin (2019).
6. For the same reasons the usual list of mid-century neural network touchstones often provided as a stand-in for machine learning histories obscures more than it reveals. For common internalist touchstones of connectionist literature, see McCulloch and Pitts (1943), Hebb (1949), Selfridge (1955, 1959), Rosenblatt (1956, 1957), Samuel (1959), and Minsky and Papert (1969), and, when extended into the 1980s to include backwards-propagation, Rumelhart, Hinton, and Williams (1985, 1986a, 1986b), and Hinton (1989). The scientific priority of

late twentieth century neural network research remains controversial in internalist debates: see, for instance, Schmidhuber (2015).

7. Daston and Galison (2010, p. 52).
8. Daston and Galison (2010, p. 52).
9. Google (2017a, 2017b). Perspective API was not recommended "as a tool for automated moderation" when released in 2017, but as a tool to assist human online content moderators (Google, 2017b). By 2019 Perspective offered a variety of classifiers, including "severe toxicity," "identity attack," "insult," "profanity," "threat," "sexually explicit," "flirtation," and a specific *New York Times* classifier (Conversation AI, 2019).
10. Google (2017a); see also Wulczyn, Thain, and Dixon (2017, pp. 1391, 1392–1393); Dixon et al. (2018, p. 68). Each comment was labeled by at least ten workers to ensure uniformity in responses (Wulczyn et al., 2017). Regarding online content moderation and crowdsourced labor, see Gray and Suri (2019) and Gillespie (2018).
11. Marvin (2019).
12. Wulczyn et al. (2017).
13. Wulczyn et al. (2017, pp. 1391, 1394). As of June 4, 2020, an updated version of Google (2017b), lists the "Wikipedia Machine Annotations of Talk Pages" data set as including *all* English Wikipedia talk page comments from 2001–2015, with "approximately 95 million comments."
14. "I am a gay black woman," for example, was scored by Perspective as 87% likely to be seen as "toxic" while "I am a man" was 20% (West, 2017).
15. Jigsaw (2018).
16. Dixon et al. (2018, p. 67).
17. Selfridge (1955, pp. 91, 93).
18. Ware (1955, p. 85).
19. "Machine learning" denoted a field of inquiry at least two years prior to the 1956 Dartmouth Artificial Intelligence conference proposal frequently cited for the use of the neologism "artificial intelligence." See Booth and Booth (1953, p. 211) for a very early use of the term "machine learning" to connote a field of inquiry; see McCarthy, Minsky, Rochester, and Shannon (1955) for a very early use of the term "artificial intelligence."
20. Newell (1955, pp. 101, 108); see also Ensmenger (2012), and Heath and Allum (1997). Newell identified such "design problems" as computer programming, machine translation, and "abstracting scientific articles" as problems having these characteristics. However, chess became an exemplar for the kind of problem that mid-century logosymbolic AI often studied: research problems in which the logosymbolic rules that

dictate possibility could be enumerated in theory even if they could not be exhaustively computed because of limited computing power, time constraints, etc. (Newell, 1955, p. 104). Such learning in the AI context constituted strategies to "extend the set of [rule] expressions" to arrive at a *well-defined* answer or final "goal state," as exemplified by the Logical Theorist, the General Problem Solver, MYCIN, DENDRIL, and others. Newell writes later that learning is "really concerned with generality—with producing a machine general enough to transcend the vision of its designers," but this vision is specifically one in which "the standard schemes of repetition with the modification of statistical weights is not the most fruitful way to proceed" (Newell, 1963, p. v). In contrast, learning in mid-century pattern recognition emphasized the variability of "correct" answers.

21. Dinneen (1955, p. 94). Regarding the nature of Selfridge and Dinneen's collaboration: "Over the past months in a series of after-hour and luncheon meetings, a group of us at the [Lincoln] laboratory have speculated on problems in this area.... Selfridge and I have begun an investigation of one aspect of pattern recognition, that is, the recognition of simple visual patterns" (Dinneen, 1955, p. 94). Dinneen, then a newly minted PhD in 1955 who had just joined Lincoln Labs at MIT in 1954, would go on to become the director of the Lincoln Laboratory at MIT, and later the assistant secretary of defense during the Carter administration.
22. Selfridge (1955, p. 93). Black and white letter images were mapped onto 90 × 90 grids, with black cells having the value 1 and white cells 0 (Dinneen, 1955, p. 94). Two operations were used to produce features: (1) the "averaging function" "eliminate[d] small pieces of noise, isolated 1's in a field of 0's" (Selfridge, 1955, p. 92); (2) the "edging operation" "tends to bring out edges and corners [...] by evaluating the radial asymmetry around each 1 in the image, and keeping only those 1's which have more than a certain amount" (Dinneen, 1955, p. 98; Selfridge, 1955, p. 92).
23. This paper concerns itself with equivalence classes used by the historical actors discussed. For an introduction to the complex history of mathematical equivalence, see Asghari (2019).
24. Selfridge (1955, p. 92).
25. Dinneen (1955, p. 94).
26. Dinneen (1955, p. 94).
27. See Note 34.
28. Selfridge (1955, p. 92, emphasis mine).
29. Selfridge (1955, p. 92).
30. Dinneen (1955, p. 94). This system used sequences of averaging and edging operations to produce "blobs" that were subsequently counted to

distinguish *A*s and *O*s. Blob-counting, in principle, could not distinguish between *C*s and *U*s (Selfridge, 1955, p. 94), and so serves as an example of a feature that cannot, in principle, distinguish all letter patterns.
31. See "family resemblances" in Wittgenstein (1953, p. 31e).
32. Selfridge (1955, p. 92). Selfridge and Dinneen's notion of equivalence class is very similar to Pitts and McCulloch's "equivalent apparitions" that "share a common figure and define a group of transformations that take the equivalents into one another but preserve the figure invariant" (Pitts & McCulloch, 1947, pp. 127–128). Selfridge and Pitts were roommates in graduate school working under Norbert Wiener. Selfridge reports: "The cognition aspect was first sort of tackled by McCulloch and Pitts in their papers in 1943 and 1947. So I talked with Walter [Pitts] a lot about certain things in cognition and the first paper on my work on pattern recognition systems was at the 1955 … conference" (Husbands & Selfridge, 2008, p. 400).
33. Abramson and Braverman (1962, p. S58). Some argued that the first subsidiary problem was a special case of the second: see, for example, Fu (1968a, pp. 2–3).
34. "[T]he whole process of Pattern Recognition is inevitably tied up with ways of determining significance. I suggest—this is my own fancy—that this is the distinction usually made between machines and men.… I do not, however, believe it is a valid distinction" (Selfridge, 1955, p. 92).
35. Ware (1955, p. 85).
36. Ware (1955, p. 85).
37. Ware (1955, p. 85). Newell articulated this difference in inputs for artificial intelligence and pattern recognition, in part, as "problem-solving versus recognition," respectively: "Those thinking within the framework of continuous systems concentrated on pattern recognition as the key type of task for machines to do—character recognition, speech recognition, and visual-pattern recognition.… Contrariwise, those thinking within the framework of symbolic systems concentrated on problem-solving as the key type of task for machines to do—game playing, theorem proving, and puzzle solving" (Newell, 1982, p. 12).
38. Newell (1982, p. 11).
39. In his post hoc history of the mid-1950s split between pattern recognition and artificial intelligence, Newell (1982) notes, that pattern recognition researchers "follow[ed] the lead of physical science and engineering" and employed "differential equations, excitatory and inhibitory networks, statistical and probabilistic systems" (p. 11). "[T]he major historical effect of this [split between symbolic systems and continuous systems] in the sixties," Newell writes, "was the rather complete separation of those who thought in terms of continuous systems from those who thought in terms of programming systems. The former

were the cybernetics and the engineers concerned with pattern recognition. The latter became the AI community. The separation has been strongly institutionalized. The continuous-system fold ended up in electrical engineering departments; the AI folk ended up in computer science departments" (Newell, 1982, p. 11).

40. A vast literature attests that combinations of mathematical practices, institutional contingencies, labor, cultural values and shared norms, and material computation often inform the ways historical actors understand the world and their relationship to it. For example, Monte Carlo simulations were a way to perform the necessary calculations to build the hydrogen bomb, but came to be seen by some as the correct way of understanding particle physics and so the world (Galison, 1996, 1997). Other examples include proof-proving (Dick, 2011, MacKenzie 2001), precision and the stock market (MacKenzie, 1993, 2008), global climate (Edwards, 2013), computing (Jones, 2016), aerial bombing (Dryer, 2019), scientific atlases (Daston & Galison, 2007), biology (Stevens, 2013), cells (Landecker, 2007), and many, many others.
41. Pickering (2010, p. 20).
42. Pickering (2010, p. 381). Pickering borrows the phrase "exceedingly complex systems" from Stafford Beer. For a study of how cybernetics was employed to make social and political decisions outside of the US context, see, for instance, Medina (2011) and Peters (2016). For cybernetics in the US Cold War context, see Kline (2015).
43. Husbands and Selfridge (2008, p. 398) and Kline (2015, p. 154).
44. See note 21.
45. Lincoln Lab (1955, p. 8). Elided in the historical sources I have located are the Memory Test Computer operators, who were almost certainly women, and whose efforts were likely vital to executing the OCR program. See Dinneen's acknowledgements in note 55. For discussions of SAGE, see Slayton (2013, chapter 1), Edwards (1996, chapter 3), and Light (2003, chapter 2).
46. This account is documented in Edwards' *The Closed World* (1996), McCorduck's *Machines Who Think* (1979), and many others.
47. For explication of trading zones in the history of science, see Galison (2010, 2011); for succinct summary, see Galison (1999).
48. Uhr (1968, p. 159).
49. Fu (1968b, pp. 399–400). The polysemy of learning was not uniformly well-received by pattern recognition researchers: "Through an abuse of the language, the words recognition and learning have been applied to machine systems which implement classification and estimation algorithms" (Kanal, 1968b, p. x).
50. Munson (1969, p. 417).

51. This confusion is due to the appropriation of pattern recognition practices back into the field of artificial intelligence as machine learning in the late 1970s and 1980s. Katz (2017) traces this "malleability of the AI label" today as a "pretext for imposing more metrics upon human endeavors and advancing traditional neoliberal policies" (pp. 1, 2). That may very well be how this confusion has been put to use in the twenty-first century, but the *existence* of this confusion has historical origins that cannot be reduced to claims about discourse, rampant neoliberalism, or corporate takeovers. To do so erases precisely the history I seek to recover.
52. The creation of *precision* in nuclear intercontinental ballistic missiles (MacKenzie, 1993), the application of computer systems to prove proofs and be justified by formal mathematical verification (Dick, 2011, MacKenzie, 2001), and the development of antilock brakes (Johnson, 2009) offer useful parallels for the production of knowledge informed by individual professionalization, local laboratory practices, and transnational knowledge communities.
53. MacKay (1969, p. 409). MacKay was a British physicist, neuroscientist, and early member of the Ratio club.
54. MacKay (1969, p. 409).
55. Dinneen writes in his acknowledgments that "It would have been impossible to obtain the experimental results without the excellent assistance of Miss B. Jensen and Mrs. M. Kannel in programming, coding, and operating the Memory Test Computer. I wish to acknowledge the excellent co-operation of those responsible for the operation of the Memory Test Computer" (Dinneen, 1955, p. 100). The COVID-19 pandemic has made additional archival visits to obtain more information about Jensen and Kannel impossible at the time of writing. For important monographs on gender and labor in the history of mid-twentieth century computing in US and UK contexts, see Ensmenger (2010), Abbate (2012), Hicks (2017), and Rankin (2018).
56. My thinking about the role of disciplinary repertoires in the construction of arguments has benefited and been informed by Slayton (2013).
57. MacKay (1969, p. 410).
58. See, for instance, Brick (1969): "Redundancy, reliability, and uncertainty considerations may make it advantageous to avoid a clear-cut decision, therefore indicating a modus operandi whereby several solutions are encompassed as lower-level processes within a higher-level framework. The ultimate resolution might therefore reside in a meta-structure designed to take advantage of the inherent redundancies" (p. 76).
59. Brick (1969, p. 78).
60. For machine-generated goals in artificial intelligence, see, for instance, Newell (1955, p. 9).

61. Contrast this with Newell's discussion of the meaning of "heuristic": "A 'heuristic program,' to be considered successful, must work well on a variety of problems, *and may often be excused if it fails on some*. We often find it worthwhile to introduce a heuristic method which happens to cause occasional failures, if there is an over-all improvement in performance. But imperfect methods are not necessarily heuristic, nor vice versa. Hence 'heuristic' should not be regarded as opposite to 'foolproof'; this has caused some confusion in the literature" (Newell, 1955, p. 9, footnote 1, emphasis mine).
62. M. E. Stevens (1961a, p. 333).
63. Rabinow (1968, p. 14).
64. Kanal (1968b, p. xi).
65. The tripartite varieties of "pattern" activity I put forth is informed, in part, by the three-part organization of Kanal (1968a, pp. iii–v) and M. E. Stevens (1961a, p. 333). By 1968, the proceedings of the first workshop on pattern recognition sponsored by the IEEE dedicated the first third explicitly to "character recognition," and most papers in that volume used OCR—whether hand printed or typed—as the applied example (Kanal, 1968a). If desire and funding to build reading machines originated from 1950s machine translation research, dedicated, in part, to translating Russian science articles into English (Gordon, 2015), the desire for reading machines was sustained by a belief in the late 1950s and early 1960s in the promise of the information sciences to produce "an understanding of [the researcher] himself, how he thinks, how he comes to understand, how he learns, what he wants his goals to be, and why"—technology would change our science and so change ourselves (Swanson, 1966, p. iii). No doubt this situation was made possible in a very direct way by the Department of Defense and National Science Foundation funding made available for "basic research" at universities and companies during the Cold War. For a history of this transition of research from universities to private companies, see Rhode (2013).
66. OCR was not a problem limited to pattern recognition or machine learning. Writing in 1961 for the National Bureau of Standards, Mary Elizabeth Stevens' extraordinary 1958 survey observes, "'That the blind may read' is the earliest recorded objective for research attempts to develop devices capable of reproducing and transcribing printed, typed, or handwritten characters" (M. E. Stevens, 1961b, pp. 2, 152). Likewise, J. Rabinow's 1968 "State of the Art of Reading Machines" review for the first IEEE Workshop on Pattern Recognition notes, "My own involvement with reading machines came via the route of trying to aid the blind and, particularly, in an attempt to convert an optical image to a tactile one. Even in 1938 this was an old idea and it has been resurrected many times since" (Rabinow, 1968, p. 3, see also pp. 25–26).

For the central role of embodiment and disability regarding conceptions of information in cybernetics and communication engineering, see Mills (2011). For the role of reading, disability, and media affordances, see Mills (2012).

67. Watanabe (1969, p. vii).
68. Rabinow (1968, p. 20). Comparing data to an ideal mask, depending on interpretation of features and weights, could be considered a part of the machine learning tradition. However, for the purposes of our discussion, the commercial OCR systems did not "learn" in the senses described in "How Identifying Significance Became a Branch of Engineering" and "Pattern Recognition Eats the World: Learning as a Solution to Technical Problems and to Questions of Social Order".
69. Rabinow (1968, pp. 20–21).
70. In 1958 Selfridge presented a pattern recognition strategy capable of learning letter features in a system he called "pandemonium," in an explicit reference to Milton's *Paradise Lost* (see Selfridge, 1959), but, despite pandemonium's prominence in some historical accounts, this system was not widely imitated.
71. Rabinow (1968, pp. 23–24).
72. Groner (1968, p. 103).
73. Bernstein (1968).
74. Munson (1968, pp. 126–127).
75. Munson (1968, pp. 129, 130).
76. Munson (1968, p. 136).
77. Munson (1968, p. 137).
78. Munson (1968, p. 139).
79. See the *U*s and *C*s example in note 30.
80. Rabinow (1968, pp. 27–28) and Hessinger (1968).
81. For these last 4 examples, see Sheinberg (1968, pp. 38–39).
82. See, for instance, Chow (1957, p. 252) and Brick (1969, p. 76).
83. Wald (1950, pp. 21–22, 10, 28–29). For a discussion of Wald's statistical "general [decision] problem" in relationship to Neyman-Pearson hypothesis testing, see especially Wald (1939, p. 300). For an internalist historical account of the mathematics of decision theory, see Wald (1950, pp. 28–31). For an example of Wald's work on quality control in US factories, see Columbia Statistical Research Group (1945). For a broader historical account of decision theory as it pertained to operations research, linear programming, and systems design in the US and UK contexts, see Thomas (2015). For the interwoven transnational application of the decision theory in rural Indian reconstruction and US military contexts, especially constructions of certainty in political discourse via "confidence interval logics" and "deconstruction data" sites, see Dryer (2019), especially Chapter 4. For the debates about

Cold War "rationality," of which Wald's decision theory is an important rhetorical and technical tool for debate, see Erikson et al. (2013).

84. Weiss (1992, pp. 335–336).
85. Wald's 1939 paper was cited as his most important contribution by his friend and colleague Jacob Wolfowitz (Wald, 1939; Wolfowitz, 1952). In this paper Wald articulated a very early, very generalized version of statistical decision theory, while also introducing loss functions, Bayes decision solutions, the minimax procedure, and more that comprises elementary textbook machine learning today. Wald's sequential analysis work was classified in 1943, but later published in Wald (1945). See "historical note" in Wald (1945, pp. 119–122).
86. Wald (1950); see also Wald (1949).
87. Wald (1950, pp. 24, 26–27).
88. Wald (1950, p. 27).
89. Weiss (1992) notes: "The Bayesian approach to statistical problems is at least partly a reaction to minimax decision rules.... [M]inimax decision rules are often very conservative. This was inevitable, considering the fact that they come from the theory of zero-sum two-person games, in which players are forced to be antagonistic. If the statistician is playing against Nature, the question is whether nature is that malevolent. A Bayesian feels that he knows what a priori distribution is being used by nature" (p. 340). Wald (1950) notes: "Whereas the experimenter wishes to maximize the risk ... we can hardly say that Nature wishes to maximize [risk]. Nevertheless, since Nature's choice is unknown to the experimenter, it is perhaps not unreasonable for the experimenter to behave as if Nature wanted to maximize the risk" (p. 27).
90. Chow (1957, p. 254).
91. Chow (1957, p. 249, see also p. 248).
92. Chow (1957, p. 249).
93. Chow (1957, p. 249).
94. Chow (1957, p. 247).
95. The phrases and metaphors of *learning with/without a teacher* have a long history. For early examples, see Turing (1948) and Booth and Booth (1953). In the explicit context of supervised and unsupervised learning, see Cooper (1969, p. 99).
96. Abramson and Braverman (1962, p. S58).
97. Abramson and Braverman (1962, p. S58).
98. For the historical source providing this explanation, see Cooper (1969, p. 99).
99. Cooper (1969).
100. Kanal (1968b, p. ix).
101. Kanal, (1968b, p. x). See also Kanal and Chandrasekaran (1969, 324).

102. Kanal (1968b, p. ix). Kanal notes that "most of the commercially available optical character readers have used heuristic techniques almost exclusively. Part of the reason for this is that, often, commercial readers have been developed by hardware oriented engineers not familiar with or convinced about statistical classification theory" (p. ix).
103. Kanal (1968b, p. vii).
104. Watanabe (1969, p. vii).
105. For an elegant articulation of both "registers," see, for instance, Kanal and Chandrasekaran (1969, pp. 317–318).
106. Watanabe (1969, p. vii).
107. Watanabe (1969, p. vii).
108. Fein (1968, p. 443).
109. Fein (1968, p. 445).
110. Brick (1969, pp. 75, 83). For a detailed list of "feature extraction" techniques, "classification and recognition (decision) techniques" and much more, see pp. 89–96.
111. Brick (1969, pp. 78, 80).
112. Kanal and Chandrasekaran (1969, p. 324).
113. Kanal and Chandrasekaran (1969, p. 324).
114. Kanal and Chandrasekaran (1969, p. 331).
115. Watanabe (1969, pp. 521–522, 525).
116. Lerner (1972, p. 368).
117. Lerner (1972, p. 368).
118. Lerner (1972, p. 369).
119. Lerner (1972, p. 371).
120. Duda and Hart (1973, p. vii).
121. Duda and Hart (1973, p. vii).
122. Watanbe (1969, p. vii).
123. See Zuckerman (1988) for a discussion of Merton's sociological project.
124. See Haigh (2015) for discussion and references to Knuth's lecture entitled "Let's Not Dumb Down the History of Computer Science."
125. For an introduction to history of such internalist and externalist debates in the history of science and science and technology studies, see, for instance, Daston (2009).
126. Greenburg (2017).

References

Abbate, J. (2012). *Recoding gender: Women's changing participation in computing*. MIT Press.

Abramson, N., & Braverman, D. (1962). Learning to recognize patterns in a random environment. *IRE Transactions on Information Theory, 8*(5), 58–63.

Asghari, A. (2019). Equivalence: An attempt at a history of an idea. *Synthese, 196,* 4657–4677.

Barocas, S., & Selbst, A. (2016). Big Data's Disparate Impact. *California Law Review, 104,* 671–732.

Benjamin, R. (2019). *Race after technology: Abolitionist tools for the New Jim Code*. Polity.

Bernstein, M. (1968). A method for recognizing handprinted characters in real time. In L. Kanal (Ed.), *Pattern recognition: Proceedings of the IEEE Workshop on Pattern Recognition, held at Dorado, Puerto Rico* (pp. 109–114). Thompson Book Company.

Boden, M. (1987). *Artificial Intelligence and Natural Man* (2nd ed.). Basic Books. (Originally published in 1977.)

Boden, M. (2006). *Mind as machine: A history of cognitive science* (2 Vols.). Oxford University Press.

Booth, A., & Booth, K. (1953). *Automatic digital calculators* (1st ed.). Butterworths Scientific Publications.

Bouk, D. (2015). *How our days became numbered: Risk and the rise of the statistical individual.* University of Chicago Press.

Brick, D. (1969). Pattern Recognition, The Challenge, Are We Meeting It? In S. Watanabe (Ed.), *Methodologies of pattern recognition: Proceedings of the International Conference on Methodologies of Pattern Recognition* (pp. 75–96). Academic Press.

Broussard, M. (2018). *Artificial unintelligence: How computers misunderstand the world.* MIT Press.

Buolamwini, J., & Gebru, T. (2018). Gender shades: Intersectional accuracy disparities in commercial gender classification. *Proceedings of the 1st Conference on Fairness, Accountability and Transparency,* in *Proceedings of Machine Learning Research, 81,* 77–91.

Cardon, D., Cointet, J., & Mazières, A. (2018). La revanche des neurones: L'invention des machines inductives et la controverse de l'intelligence artificielle. *Réseaux, 211*(5), 173–220 (Translated by Elizabeth Libbrecht into English as "Neurons spike back: The invention of inductive machines and the artificial intelligence controversy").

Carr, D. J. Z. (2020). 'Ghastly marionettes' and the political metaphysics of cognitive liberalism: Anti-behaviorism, language, and the origins of totalitarianism. *History of the Human Sciences, 33*(1), 147–174.

Chow, C. K. (1957). An optimum character recognition system using decision functions. *IRE Transactions on Electronic Computers, EC-6*(4), 247–254.

Columbia University Statistical Research Group. (1945). *Sequential analysis when the quality being tested is whether a lot differs from a standard.* Columbia University Press.

Conversation AI. (2019, November 2). *Perspective API reference*. GitHub. https://web.archive.org/web/20191102181003/https://github.com/conversationai/perspectiveapi/blob/master/api_reference.md#alpha.

Cooper, P. (1969). Nonsupervised learning in statistical pattern recognition. In S. Watanabe (Ed.), *Methodologies of pattern recognition: Proceedings of the International Conference on Methodologies of Pattern Recognition* (pp. 409–416). Academic Press.

Cordeschi, R. (2002). *The discovery of the artificial: Behavior, mind, and machines before and beyond cybernetics*. Kluwer Academic Publishers.

Crawford, K., & Paglen, T. (2019, September 19). *Excavating AI: The politics of training sets for machine learning*. https://excavating.ai.

Crevier, D. (1993). *AI: the tumultuous history of the search for artificial intelligence*. Basic Books.

Daston, L. (1995). *Classical probability in the enlightenment*. Princeton University Press.

Daston, L. (2009). Science studies and the history of science. *Critical Inquiry, 35*(4), 798–813.

Daston, L. (2018). Calculation and the division of labor, 1750–1950. *Bulletin of the German Historical Institute, 62*, 9–30.

Daston, L., & Galison, P. (2007). *Objectivity*. Zone Books.

Desrosiéres, A. (1998). *The politics of large numbers: A history of statistical reasoning*. (C. Naish, Trans.). Harvard University Press. (Originally published as *La politique des grands nombres: Histoire de la raison statistique* in 1993.)

Dick, S. (2011). AfterMath: The work of proof in the age of human-machine collaboration. *Isis, 102*(3), 494–505.

Dick, S. (2015). Of models and machines: Implementing bounded rationality. *Isis, 106*(3), 623–634.

Dinneen, G. P. (1955). Programming pattern recognition. In *Proceedings of the March 1–3, 1955, Western Joint Computer Conference* (pp. 94–100). Association of Computing Machinery.

Dixon, L., Li, J., Sorensen, J., Thain, N., & Vasserman, L. (2018). Measuring and mitigating unintended bias in text classification. In *Proceedings of the 2018 AAAI/ACM Conference on AI, Ethics, and Society* (pp. 67–73).

Dryer, T. (2019). *Designing certainty: The rise of algorithmic computing in an age of anxiety, 1920–1970* (Doctoral dissertation, University of California, San Diego).

Duda, R., & Hart, P. (1973). *Pattern classification and scene analysis*. John Wiley & Sons.

Edwards, P. (1996). *The closed world: Computers and the politics of discourse in Cold War America*. MIT Press.

Edwards, P. (2013). *A vast machine: Computer models, climate data, and the politics of global warming*. MIT Press.

Ensign, D., Friedler, S. A., Neville, S., Scheidegger, C., & Venkatasubramanian, S. (2018). Runaway feedback loops in predictive policing. *Proceedings of the 1st Conference on Fairness, Accountability and Transparency*, in *Proceedings of Machine Learning Research, 81,* 160–171.

Ensmenger, N. (2010). *The computer boys take over: Computers, programmers, and the politics of technical expertise*. MIT Press.

Ensmenger, N. (2012). Is chess the drosophila of artificial intelligence? A social history of an algorithm. *Social Studies of Science, 42*(1), 5–30.

Erikson, P., Klein, J., Daston, L., Lemov, R., Sturm, T., & Gordon, M. (2013). *How reason almost lost its mind: The strange career of cold war rationality.* University of Chicago Press.

Eubanks, V. (2018). *Automating inequality: How high-tech tools profile, police, and punish the poor*. St. Martin's Press.

Fein, L. (1968). Impotence principles for machine intelligence. In L. Kanal (Ed.), *Pattern recognition: Proceedings of the IEEE Workshop on Pattern Recognition, held at Dorado, Puerto Rico* (pp. 443–447). Thompson Book Company.

Forsythe, D. (2001). *Studying those who study us: An anthropologist in the world of artificial intelligence*. Stanford University Press.

Fu, K. S. (1968a). *Sequential methods in pattern recognition and machine learning*. Academic Press.

Fu, K. S. (1968b). Learning techniques in pattern recognition systems. In L. Kanal (Ed.), *Pattern recognition: Proceedings of the IEEE Workshop on Pattern Recognition, held at Dorado, Puerto Rico* (pp. 399–407). Thompson Book Company.

Galison, P. (1994). The ontology of the enemy: Norbert Wiener and the cybernetic vision. *Critical Inquiry, 21*(1), 228–266.

Galison, P. (1996). Computer simulations and the trading zone. In P. Galison & D. Stump (Eds.), *The disunity of science: Boundaries, contexts, and power* (pp. 118–157). Stanford University Press.

Galison, P. (1997). *Image and logic: A material culture of microphysics*. University of Chicago Press.

Galison, P. (1999). Trading zone: Coordinating action and belief. In M. Biagioli (Ed.), *The science studies reader* (pp. 137–160). Routledge.

Galison, P. (2010). Trading with the enemy. In M. Gorman (Ed.), *Trading zones and interactional expertise: Creating new kinds of collaboration* (pp. 25–52). MIT Press.

Galison, P. (2011). Computer simulations and the trading zone. In G. Gramelsberger (Ed.), *From science to computational science* (pp. 118–157). Diaphanes.

Garvey, C. (2019). Artificial intelligence and Japan's fifth generation: The information society, neoliberalism, and alternative modernities. *Pacific Historical Review, 88,* 620–659.

Gigerenzer, G., Swijtink, Z., Porter, T., Daston, L., Beatty, J., & Krüger, L. (1989). *The Empire of chance: How probability changed science and everyday Life*. Cambridge University Press.

Gillespie, T. (2018). *Custodians of the internet: Platforms, content moderation, and the hidden decisions that shape social media*. Yale University Press.

Google. (2017a, September 14). *Perspective*. Jigsaw and Google Counter Abuse Technology Team. https://web.archive.org/web/20170914183727/https://www.perspectiveapi.com/#/.

Google. (2017b, September 7). *Conversation AI*. Jigsaw and Google Counter Abuse Technology Team. https://web.archive.org/web/20170907112911mp_/https://conversationai.github.io.

Gordin, M. (2015). *Scientific babel: How science was done before and after global English*. University of Chicago Press.

Gray, M., & Suri, S. (2019). *Ghost work: How to stop Silicon Valley from building a new global underclass*. Houghton Mifflin Harcourt.

Greenburg, A. (2017, February 23). Now anyone can deploy Google's Troll-Fighting AI. *Wired*. https://www.wired.com/2017/02/googles-troll-fighting-ai-now-belongs-world/.

Groner, G. (1968). Real-time recognition of handprinted symbols. In L. Kanal (Ed.), *Pattern recognition: Proceedings of the IEEE Workshop on Pattern Recognition, held at Dorado, Puerto Rico* (pp. 103–108). Thompson Book Company.

Hacking, I. (1990). *The taming of chance*. Cambridge University Press.

Haigh, T. (2015). The tears of Donald Knuth. *Communications of the ACM, 58*(1), 40–44.

Haugeland, J. (1985). *Artificial intelligence: The very idea*. MIT Press.

Heath, D., & Allum, D. (1997). The historical development of computer chess and its impact on artificial intelligence. *AAAI Technical Report WS-97-04*, 63–68.

Hebb, D. O. (1949). *The organization of behavior: A neuropsychological theory*. John Wiley & Sons, Inc./Chapman & Hall, Limited.

Hessinger, R. W. (1968). Optical character recognition in the post office. In L. Kanal (Ed.), *Pattern recognition: Proceedings of the IEEE Workshop on Pattern Recognition, held at Dorado, Puerto Rico* (pp. 41–45). Thompson Book Company.

Hicks, M. (2017). *Programmed inequality*. MIT Press.

Hinton, G. (1989). Connectionist learning procedures. *Artificial Intelligence, 40*, 185–234.

Husbands, P., & Selfridge, O. (2008). An interview with Oliver Selfridge. In P. Husbands, O. Holland, and M. Wheeler (Eds.), *The mechanical mind in history*. MIT Press.

Igo, S. (2007). *The averaged American: Surveys, citizens, and the making of the mass public*. Harvard University Press.

Igo, S. (2018). *The known citizen: A history of privacy in modern America*. Harvard University Press.

Jigsaw. (2018, March 9). Unintended bias and names of frequently targeted groups. *Medium*. https://medium.com/the-false-positive/unintended-bias-and-names-of-frequently-targeted-groups-8e0b81f80a23.

Johnson, A. (2009). *Hitting the Brakes: Engineering Design and the Production of Knowledge*. Duke University Press.

Jones, M. (2016). *Reckoning with matter: Calculating machines, innovation, and thinking about thinking from Pascal to Babbage*. University of Chicago Press.

Jones, M. (2018). How we became instrumentalists (again): Data positivism since World War II. *Historical Studies in the Natural Sciences, 48*(5), 673–684.

Jordan, M., & Mitchell, T. (2015). Machine learning: Trends, perspectives, and prospects. *Science, 349*(6245), 255–260.

Kanal, L. (Ed.). (1968a). *Pattern recognition: Proceedings of the IEEE Workshop on Pattern Recognition, held at Dorado, Puerto Rico*. Thompson Book Company.

Kanal, L. (1968b). Preface. In L. Kanal (Ed.), *Pattern recognition: Proceedings of the IEEE Workshop on Pattern Recognition, held at Dorado, Puerto Rico* (pp. vii–xii). Thompson Book Company.

Kanal, L. & Chandrasekaran, B. (1969). Recognition, Machine 'Recognition' and Statistical Approaches. In S. Watanabe (Ed.), *Methodologies of pattern recognition: Proceedings of the International Conference on Methodologies of Pattern Recognition* (pp. 317–332). Academic Press.

Katz, Y. (2017, November 17). *Manufacturing an artificial intelligence revolution*. https://dx.doi.org/10.2139/ssrn.3078224.

Kline, R. (2015). *The cybernetics moment: Or why we call our age the information age*. Johns Hopkins University Press.

Landecker, H. (2007). *Culturing life: How cells became technologies*. Harvard University Press.

Lerner, A. (1972). A "Crisis" in the Theory of Pattern Recognition. In S. Watanabe (Ed.), *Frontiers of Pattern Recognition: Proceedings of the 1971 International Conference on Frontiers of Pattern Recognition* (pp. 367–372). Academic Press.

Light, J. (2003). *From warfare to welfare: Defense intellectuals and urban problems in Cold War America*. John Hopkins University Press.

Lincoln Laboratory. (1955, May 9). *Memory test computer programming reference manual (Memorandum 6 M-2527-2)*. Division 6, Lincoln Laboratory, Massachusetts Institute of Technology.

MacKay, D. (1969). Recognition and action. In S. Watanabe (Ed.), *Methodologies of pattern recognition: Proceedings of the International Conference on Methodologies of Pattern Recognition* (pp. 409–416). Academic Press.

Mackenzie, A. (2017). *Machine learners: Archaeology of a data practice*. MIT Press.

MacKenzie, D. (1993). *Inventing accuracy: A historical sociology of nuclear missile guidance*. MIT Press.

MacKenzie, D. (2001). *Mechanizing proof: Computing, risk, and trust*. MIT Press.

MacKenzie, D. (2008). *An engine, not a camera: How financial models shape markets*. MIT Press.

Marcus, G., & Davis, E. (2019). *Rebooting AI: Building artificial intelligence we can trust*. Pantheon Books.

Marvin, R. (2019, January 29). How Google's jigsaw is trying to detoxify the internet. *PC magazine*. https://www.pcmag.com/news/how-googles-jigsaw-is-trying-to-detoxify-the-internet.

McCarthy, J., Minsky, M., Rochester, N., & Shannon, C. (1955). A proposal for the Dartmouth Summer research project on artificial intelligence.

McCorduck, P. (2004). *Machines who think: A personal inquiry into the history and prospects of artificial intelligence* (2nd ed.). A. K. Peters, Ltd. (Original work published 1979).

McCulloch, W., & Pitts, W. (1943). A logical calculus of the ideas immanent in nervous activity. *Bulletin of Mathematical Biophysics, 5*, 115–133.

Medina, E. (2011). *Cybernetic revolutionaries: Technology and politics in Allende's Chile*. MIT Press.

Mills, M. (2011). On disability and cybernetics: Helen Keller, Norbert Wiener, and the Hearing Glove. *Differences: A Journal of Feminist Cultural Studies, 22*(2/3), 74–111.

Mills, M. (2012, December). What should we call reading? *Flow 17*. https://www.flowjournal.org/2012/12/what-should-we-call-reading/.

Minsky, M., & Papert, S. A. (2017). *Perceptrons: An introduction to computational geometry*. MIT Press (Original work published 1969).

Mirowski, P. (2002). *Machine dreams: Economics becomes a cyborg science*. Cambridge University Press.

Munson, J. H. (1968). The recognition of hand-printed text. In L. Kanal (Ed.), *Pattern recognition: Proceedings of the IEEE Workshop on Pattern Recognition, held at Dorado, Puerto Rico* (pp. 115–140). Thompson Book Company.

Munson, J. H. (1969). Some views on pattern-recognition methodology. In S. Watanabe (Ed.), *Methodologies of pattern recognition: Proceedings of the International Conference on Methodologies of Pattern Recognition* (pp. 417–436). Academic Press.

Newell, A. (1955). The chess machine: An example of dealing with a complex task by adaptation. In *Proceedings of the March 1–3, 1955, Western Joint Computer Conference* (pp. 101–108). Association of Computing Machinery.

Newell, A. (1963). *Learning, generality, and problem-solving (Memo Rm-3285-1-Pr)*. RAND.

Newell, A. (1982, October 28). *Intellectual issues in the history of artificial intelligence (CMU-CS-82-142)*. Department of Computer Science, Carnegie-Mellon University, DARPA.

Nilsson, N. (2010). *The quest for artificial intelligence: A history of ideas and achievements*. Cambridge University Press.

Noble, S. U. (2018). *Algorithms of oppression: How search engines reinforce racism*. NYU Press.

November, J. (2012). *Biomedical computing: Digitizing life in the United States*. John Hopkins University Press.

O'Neil, C. (2016). *Weapons of math destruction: How big data increases inequality and threatens democracy*. Crown.

Pasquinelli, M., & Joler, V. (2020, May 1). *The nooscope manifested: Artificial intelligence as instrument of knowledge extractivism*. KIM HfG Karlsruhe and Share Lab. http://nooscope.ai.

Peters, B. (2016). *How not to network a nation: The uneasy history of the Soviet internet*. MIT Press.

Pickering, A. (2010). *The cybernetic brain: Sketches of another future*. University of Chicago Press.

Pitts, W., & McCulloch, W. (1947). How we know universals: The perception of auditory and visual forms. *Bulletin of Mathematical Biophysics, 9*, 127–147.

Plasek, A. 2016. On the cruelty of really writing a history of machine learning. *IEEE Annals of the History of Computing*, *38*(4), 6–8.

Porter, T. (1986). *The rise of statistical thinking: 1820–1900*. Princeton University.

Porter, T. (1995). *Trust in numbers: The pursuit of objectivity in science and public Life*. Princeton University.

Rabinow, J. (1968). The present state of the art of reading machines. In L. Kanal (Ed.), *Pattern recognition: Proceedings of the IEEE Workshop on Pattern Recognition, held at Dorado, Puerto Rico* (pp. 3–29). Thompson Book Company.

Radin, J. (2017). "Digital natives": How medical and indigenous histories matter for big data. *Osiris, 32*(1), 43–64.

Rankin, J. L. (2018). *A people's history of computing in the United States*. Harvard University Press.

Rhode, J. (2013). *Armed with expertise: The militarization of American social research during the Cold War*. Cornell University Press.

Roland, A., & Shiman, P. (2002). *Strategic computing: DARPA and the quest for machine intelligence, 1983–1993*. MIT Press.

Rosenblatt, F. (1956). The perceptron: A probabilistic model for information storage and retrieval in the brain. *Psychological Review, 65*, 386–407.

Rosenblatt, F. (1957). *The perceptron: A perceiving and recognizing automaton (85-460-1)*. Cornell Aeronautical Laboratory.

Rumelhart, D., Hinton, G., & Williams, R. (1985). *Learning internal representations by error propagation* (Report 8506). Institute for Cognitive Science, University of California, San Diego. La Jolla, California.

Rumelhart, D., Hinton, G., & Williams, R. (1986a). Learning internal representations by error propagation. In D. Rumelhart, J. McClelland, and the PDP Research Group (Eds.), *Parallel distributed processing: Explorations in the microstructure of cognition* (Vol. 1, pp. 318–362). Bradford Books/MIT Press.

Rumelhart, D., Hinton, G., & Williams, R. (1986b). Learning representations by back-propagating errors. *Nature, 323*(6088), 533–536.

Samuel, A. (1959). Some studies of machine learning using the game of checkers. *IBM Journal of Research and Development, 3*(3), 210–229.

Schmidhuber, J. (2015, June). Critique of paper by 'deep learning conspiracy' *Nature 521*, 436. https://web.archive.org/web/20161218043301/https://plus.google.com/100849856540000067209/posts/9BDtGwCDL7D.

Selfridge, O. (1955). Pattern recognition and modern computers. In *Proceedings of the March 1–3, 1955, Western Joint Computer Conference* (pp. 51–93). Association of Computing Machinery.

Selfridge, O. (1959). Pandemonium: A paradigm for learning. In *The mechanisation of thought processes: Proceedings of a Symposium Held at the National Physics Laboratory on 24th, 25th, 26th, and 27th November 1958* (pp. 1:513–526). Her Majesty's Stationery Office.

Shapin, S., & Schaffer, S. (2011). *Leviathan and the air-pump: Hobbes, Boyle, and the experimental life*. Princeton University Press (Original work published 1985).

Sheinberg, I. (1968). Optical character recognition for information management. In L. Kanal (Ed.), *Pattern recognition: Proceedings of the IEEE Workshop on Pattern Recognition, held at Dorado, Puerto Rico* (pp. 41–45). Thompson Book Company.

Slayton, R. (2013). *Arguments that count: Physics, computing, and missile defense, 1949–2012*. MIT Press.

Stevens, M. E. (1961a). Abstract shape recognition by machine. In *Proceedings of the December 12–14, 1961, Eastern Joint Computer Conference: Computers—Key to total systems control* (pp. 332–351). Association for Computing Machinery.

Stevens, M. E. (1961b). *Automatic character recognition: A state-of-the-art report (technical note#112)*. National Bureau of Standards, US Department of Commerce.

Stevens, H. (2013). *Life out of sequence: A data-driven history of bioinformatics*. University of Chicago Press.

Stigler, S. (1986). *The history of statistics: The measurement of uncertainty before 1900*. Belknap Press, Harvard University Press.

Stigler, S. (1999). *Statistics on the table: The history of statistical concepts and methods*. Harvard University Press.

Swanson, R. (1966). *Information sciences, 1965 (AFOSR 66-0139)*. Air Force Office of Scientific Research, Office of Aerospace Research, United States Air Force.

Sweeney, L. (2013). Discrimination in online ad delivery. *Queue, 11*(3), 10.

Thomas, W. (2015). *Rational action: The sciences of policy in Britain and America, 1940–1960*. MIT Press.

Turing, A. (1948). *Intelligent machinery: A report by A. M. Turing*. National Physical Laboratory.

Uhr, L. (1968). Feature discovery and pattern description. In L. Kanal (Ed.), *Pattern recognition: Proceedings of the IEEE Workshop on Pattern Recognition, held at Dorado, Puerto Rico* (pp. 159–181). Thompson Book Company.

Wald, A. (1939). Contributions to the theory of statistical estimation and testing hypotheses. *The Annals of Mathematical Statistics, 10*(4), 299–326.

Wald, A. (1945). Sequential tests of statistical hypotheses. *The Annals of Mathematical Statistics, 16*(2), 117–186.

Wald, A. (1949). Statistical decision functions. *The Annals of Mathematical Statistics, 20*(2), 165–205.

Wald, A. (1950). *Statistical decision functions*. Wiley.

Ware, W. (1955). Introduction to session on learning machines. In *Proceedings of the March 1–3, 1955, Western Joint Computer Conference* (p. 85). Association of Computing Machinery.

Watanabe, S. (1969). Preface. In S. Watanabe (Ed.), *Methodologies of pattern recognition: Proceedings of the International Conference on Methodologies of Pattern Recognition* (pp. vii–viii). Academic Press.

Weiss, L. (1992). Introduction to Wald (1949) statistical decision function. In N. Johnson & S. Kotz (Eds.), *Breakthroughs in Statistics*. Springer.

West, J. [@jessamyn]. (2017, August 24). *I tested 14 sentences for "perceived toxicity" using perspectives. Least toxic: I am a man. Most toxic: I am a gay black woman. Come on* [Tweet]. Twitter. https://twitter.com/jessamyn/status/900867154412699649.

Wilson, E. (2010). *Affect and artificial intelligence*. University of Washington Press.

Wittgenstein, L. (1999). *Philosophical investigations* (G. E. M. Anscombe, Trans., 2nd ed.). Blackwell Publishers (Original work published 1953).

Wolfowitz, J. (1952). Abraham Wald, 1902–1950. *The Annals of Mathematical Statistics, 23*(1), 1–13.

Wulczyn, E., Thain, N., & Dixon, L. (2017). Ex machina: Personal attacks seen at scale. In *Proceedings of the 26th International Conference on World*

Wide Web, WWW '17 (pp. 1391–1399). International World Wide Web Conferences Steering Committee.
Zuckerman, H. (1988). The sociology of science. In N. Smelser (Ed.), *Handbook of sociology* (pp. 511–574). Sage.

Open Access This chapter is licensed under the terms of the Creative Commons Attribution 4.0 International License (http://creativecommons.org/licenses/by/4.0/), which permits use, sharing, adaptation, distribution and reproduction in any medium or format, as long as you give appropriate credit to the original author(s) and the source, provide a link to the Creative Commons licence and indicate if changes were made.

The images or other third party material in this chapter are included in the chapter's Creative Commons licence, unless indicated otherwise in a credit line to the material. If material is not included in the chapter's Creative Commons licence and your intended use is not permitted by statutory regulation or exceeds the permitted use, you will need to obtain permission directly from the copyright holder.

CHAPTER 3

What Kind of Learning Is Machine Learning?

Tyler Reigeluth and Michael Castelle

Introduction

At the outset of his 1803 lectures on pedagogy, Kant (1803/2007) famously stated that "The human being is the only creature that must be educated." He explains that human nature is indeterminate and needs to be given care, discipline, and instruction; i.e., humans can only achieve their full potential by developing a *second* nature. We have since grown accustomed to framing this indeterminacy of human development in terms of debates around "nurture versus nature," a dichotomous trope which Enlightenment philosophy can be seen as foreshadowing (Keller, 2008). Kant did not, of course, foresee that humans would one day build artificial entities that could *themselves* learn—but if he had, he might have argued that they would also need to be educated in a similar manner to humans. While the idea that learning machines require an "education"

T. Reigeluth (✉)
Ethics & AI Chair, Université Grenoble Alpes, Grenoble, France
e-mail: tyler.reigeluth@ulb.ac.be

M. Castelle
Centre for Interdisciplinary Methodologies,
University of Warwick, Coventry, UK
e-mail: M.Castelle.1@warwick.ac.uk

© The Author(s) 2021

J. Roberge and M. Castelle (eds.), *The Cultural Life of Machine Learning*, https://doi.org/10.1007/978-3-030-56286-1_3

seems strange from the perspective of contemporary machine learning, such a notion is in fact present near artificial intelligence's inception. Specifically, in the 1948 paper "Intelligent Machinery"—which would remain unpublished until the late 1960s—Alan Turing (1948/1969) acknowledges that learning by machines would, just as in the case of learning by humans, necessarily involve the *social* roles of teachers, peers, and the larger community:

> Although we have abandoned the plan to make a 'whole man', we should be wise to sometimes compare the circumstances of our machine with those of a man. It would be quite unfair to expect a machine straight from the factory to compete on equal terms with a university graduate. The graduate has had contact with human beings for twenty years or more. This contact has been modifying his behaviour pattern throughout that period. His teachers have been intentionally trying to modify it. At the end of the period a large number of standard routines will have been superimposed on the original pattern of his brain. These routines will be known to the community as a whole. He is then in a position to try out new combinations of these routines, to make slight variations on them, and to apply them in new ways.

What Turing understood (i.e., the fundamentally social and situated nature of learning), contemporary approaches to machine learning (including the twenty-first-century revival of neural networks known as *deep learning*) have all but forgotten or neglected. Our claim in this essay is that we need a *social theory of machine learning*: i.e., a theory that accounts for the interactive underpinnings and dynamics of artificial "learning" processes, even those thought to be "unsupervised." But in doing so, however, we must be careful not to resort to the term "social" as a self-explanatory term that is simply opposed to the "technical" and does not require further elaboration, for to do so would only reiterate a longstanding—and philosophically problematic, as pointed out by Simondon (1958)—antagonism between the realms of culture and technique. In other words, our attempt to sketch a social theory of machine learning should not be interpreted as simply another demonstration that the models learned by algorithms bear the mark of the humans who design and train them (Diakopoulos, 2014); nor are we simply advancing another claim that opening the algorithm's "black box" will reveal the social norms embedded within its operations (Pasquale, 2015).

What we are interested in instead is how machine learning behaviors unfold and develop meaning and purpose as a socially recognizable form of activity (i.e., as Turing says above with respect to human-based education, "these routines will be known to the community as a whole"). That is, we want to approach machine learning *with reference to, and in comparison with, our understandings of human learning in society*. But to do so we must acknowledge that machine learning algorithms are not merely executors or implementors of prior or external social norms or knowledge; instead, their activity reshapes collective activity as much as it is shaped by it (Grosman & Reigeluth, 2019).

Developing such a social theory of machine learning is necessarily a critical enterprise—not in the sense of attacking claims of machine "learning" from the outside, but of establishing the conditions upon which claims of "machine learning" could be convincingly held. In order to do this, we will compare and contrast contemporary machine learning in practice with one of the most distinctive sociotechnical approaches to pedagogy and learning, namely, what has come to be called *activity theory*. This multidisciplinary perspective builds from the transformational works of the Soviet cultural-historical psychologists Vygotsky, Leont'ev, and Luria. Activity theory differs from American behaviorist and cognitivist theories of learning in that it does not depend on a dualism between behavior and mind, between individual action and sociocultural practice, or between action and interaction.[1] We suggest that activity theory—aspects of which have also been taken up and expanded by other contemporary theories such as situated learning (Lave & Wenger, 1991)—can provide an essential, albeit general, framework for developing a social theory of machine learning.[2]

For the purposes of this essay, however, we will mostly be drawing on Vygotsky's programmatic contributions around the processes of *concept development* and analogizing them to the classification practices of machine learning models. Vygotsky's (1987) central idea is that concepts are not abstract content that is acquired, copied, or directly incorporated by an individual; instead, concepts develop through learning and through a process of *generalization* (p. 47)—a term which, as we will discuss below, is also used extensively in machine learning. For the learner, a concept has value and meaning by representing a solution to a *lived* problem, which may further enable the learner to solve *future* problems. Vygotsky thus offers a dialectical account of conceptualization in which learners and concepts *develop together*. The activity of learning drives the individual's development forward, and both the individual and social meaning of concepts transform through that same learning activity. In other words, concept learning is a *genetic* (i.e., developmental and processual) social activity in which individuals take part in meaning-making and, in doing so, transform both themselves and society.[3]

While concept development and generalization are certainly not the only learning processes addressed by Vygotsky's work, they do offer an ideal problem space to explore machine learning, insofar as the latter—in the form of object recognition models in computer vision, for example—is overwhelmingly presented in terms of being able to *generalize* the detection of higher-level *concepts* such as "giraffe" or "butterfly" in previously unseen images (Chollet, 2018). Vygotsky's approach, as well as those sociocultural approaches to learning that grew out of it, can help renew our understanding of what it means to learn in ways other than the "optimization"-oriented approach that is generally used by machine learning practitioners. Our hope is that by applying socially oriented theories of learning to the field of machine learning, we can help provoke deeper discussions about what exactly we should expect from machine "learning." For example, one central (yet largely implicit) normative premise that polarizes debates around machine learning is the idea that, ideally, machines would ultimately automate the process of learning because, after all, automation is what machines do best. This in turn implies that "full" machine learning will only be achieved when the machine learns "by itself" (in what is called *unsupervised learning*). Where does this fetish for self-sufficiency come from? Why *should* we expect that from machine learning techniques, however "deep" they may prove to be, when such a fundamental asociality is considered a contradiction in the context of human learning?[4]

A Brief History of Human Theories of Learning in Machine Learning and Artificial Intelligence

The recent enthusiasm on the part of researchers and the popular media for artificial intelligence represents the result of the increased relevance in recent decades of the field and methodology of *machine learning* (ML) and, specifically, *deep learning* (DL). While not all contemporary machine learning techniques are "deep" and/or connectionist in nature, it is the case that the particular methodologies of ML/DL—in which a model is trained and progressively evaluated on subsets of a large corpus of data, whether manually labeled or not—induces an experimental approach that diverges from previous AI regimes in the 1970s and early 1980s (Langley, 1988). Specifically, the importance of the term "learning" and its metaphors was at a low point in that previous era of cognitivism and "good old-fashioned AI" (GOFAI), in part due to well-known critiques—such as the attacks by Chomsky (1959) on Skinner and by Minsky and Papert (1969) on the Perceptron, which rejected behaviorist and connectionist approaches, respectively—that set the stage for an intellectual environment in which a framework largely (if not exclusively) devoted to rule-based symbol processing could become "the only game in town" (Sejnowski, 2018, p. 250).

The early-1980s *Handbook of Artificial Intelligence* describes how, after Minsky and Papert's 1969 devastation of (single-layer) connectionism, "those ... who continued to work with adaptive systems ceased to consider themselves AI researchers ... [A]daptive-systems techniques are presently applied to problems in pattern recognition and control theory" (Cohen & Feigenbaum, 1982, p. 326). Instead, by the 1970s, according to the authors, AI researchers mainly "adopted the view that learning is a complex and difficult process and that, consequently, a learning system cannot be expected to learn high-level concepts by starting without any knowledge at all" (p. 326). This period, then, was characterized by a belief that tabula rasa-style systems that learned by example were infeasible; and indeed, the idea that the acquisition of new knowledge required an existing base of knowledge was a good fit with Chomsky's "innate grammar" view of language. This was combined with a specific ideology, highlighted by the historian Cohen-Cole (2005), in which cognitive science and AI came to be unconsciously and reflexively based on a conception of intelligence inspired by the intellectual pursuits of cognitive scientists and AI researchers themselves (e.g., highly trained in the physical and mathematical sciences, good at chess, etc.).[5] It was in part because the goals for AI were so lofty—and specifically constrained to a domain of symbolic-centric rationality—that starting from scratch seemed intuitively implausible (and we see this again today in the demands for "artificial general intelligence").[6]

With cognitive science and AI practitioners in the United States considering themselves part of a revolution against the previous behaviorist tradition in psychology, which was in part characterized by a dependence on experiments on animals, it should not be surprising that there is little reference to theories of animal learning in those fields. There were, of course, some in cognitive science and AI who made explicit references to *human* theories of learning in their work, such as Seymour Papert, who studied under the Swiss psychologist and learning theorist Jean Piaget—best known in the United States as a proponent of a discrete, staged development of child intelligence—before joining MIT's AI Lab (Boden, 1978; Papert, Apostel, Grize, Papert, & Piaget, 1963; Piaget, 1970). However, the cognitive science community remained largely indifferent or hostile to Piaget, a situation illustrated by a fizzled 1975 debate between Piaget and Chomsky in France (Piattelli-Palmarini, 1980).[7] Even Papert (1980), in his work on the programming language Logo, described his main influence from Piaget as "a model of children as builders of their own intellectual structures" and his view of "Piagetian learning" as being equivalent to "learning without being taught" (p. 7)—emphasizing the AI field's intrinsically asocial, individualist, and innatist perspective (Ames, 2018). References to Vygotsky were also, unsurprisingly, rare in the cognitive science and AI literature, in part perhaps because of an early, disparaging misreading of Vygotsky by the cognitivist philosopher Jerry Fodor, one of the more extremist representatives of the symbol-processing ideology of intelligence—who would later go on to attack connectionism in the late 1980s (Fodor, 1972; Leontiev & Luria, 1972).

R. S. Michalski, a Polish-American émigré at the University of Illinois, thus described this 1970s milieu as a time in which learning was "a 'bad' area to do research in" (Boden, 2006, p. 1047). However, by 1983, Michalski, Carbonell, and Mitchell (1983) introduced a collection of papers that would be seen as the first significant textbook on machine learning, though Michalski and his coeditors largely hewed to the hegemonic line regarding knowledge acquisition being a largely symbol-centric activity, requiring a base of preexisting symbolic knowledge. The nascent machine learning field instead distinguished itself by emphasizing not just deductive processes but those of analogy and induction, with the latter including under its umbrella the "learning by example" paradigm maligned by the GOFAI community (Carbonell, Michalski, & Mitchell, 1983a).[8] Regardless, an awareness of developmental and/or socially oriented perspectives on learning is rather lacking in this era of machine learning literature, where the term "teacher" merely indicates the presence of labeled examples (Michalski, 1983)—the scenario now commonly known as supervised learning. This literature also frequently refers to the wholly individualistic concept of "unsupervised" learning or learning without a "teacher" or outside of society—a concept which, if applied to human learning, a theorist like Vygotsky would find very strange.

The lack of reflection on the relevance of existing theories of human learning to machine learning did not significantly improve with the reintroduction of connectionist methods in the mid-1980s (exemplified by the "Parallel Distributed Processing" or PDP volumes of [Rumelhart & McClelland, 1986]). However, the PDP authors were fully aware of the paradigm-shifting quality of their connectionist conception of learning:

> In recent years, there has been quite a lot of interest in learning in cognitive science ... All of this work shares the assumption that the goal of learning is to formulate explicit rules (propositions, productions, etc.) which capture powerful generalizations in a succinct way ... The approach that we take in developing PDP models is completely different ... [W]e do not assume that the goal of learning is the formulation of explicit rules. Rather, we assume it is the acquisition of connection strengths which allow a network of simple units to act as though it knew the rules. (McClelland, Rumelhart, & Hinton, 1986)

While this revival of connectionism was accompanied by some genuine technical improvements—e.g., the unsupervised learning techniques of the fully-connected "Boltzmann machines" (Ackley, Hinton, & Sejnowski, 1985) and a working backpropagation algorithm for real-valued hidden layers (Rumelhart, Hinton, & Williams, 1986)—any hint of a connection between this revised approach to neural learning and developmental theories of learning remained absent for a few years.[9] This began to change in the early 1990s with a succession of texts coming from San Diego and the south of England, beginning with the cognitive scientist Jeffrey Elman at the University of California, San Diego, who popularized what we now know as the "simple" version of a ***recurrent neural network*** (RNN) in a paper suggestively titled "Finding Structure in Time" (Elman, 1990). Unlike the (single-layer or multi-layer) perceptron, in which input data is successively transformed by matrix multiplications and sigmoid functions, the RNN works with sequence data (such as sequences of words or phonemes), and each input is accompanied by the previous output, allowing a "hidden state" vector of values to evolve over time. The recognition of this "developmental" quality of RNN learning led to collaborations between Elman and the developmental psychologist Elizabeth Bates (Bates & Elman, 1993); a work bridging developmental child psychology with connectionism from a former Piaget student, Annette Karmiloff-Smith (1992), who had visited UCSD and worked with Bates and Elman; and an argument for an "epigenetic developmental interpretation" of "connectionist modelling of human cognitive processes" (Plunkett & Sinha, 1992). These authors would all come together for the volume *Rethinking Innateness* (Elman et al., 1996), which appears to mark the end of this brief developmental enlightenment in neural network research. This interesting intersection of connectionism and developmental psychology seemed to wane with the (second) decline of connectionism, induced in part by the rise of support vector machines (Cortes & Vapnik, 1995) and decision tree ensembles (Breiman, 2001a)—also forms of supervised learning, but ones which operated primarily on tabular data, as opposed to the sequence-like data that had inspired Elman. It would then be another two decades before the multilayered neural network would make its most recent resurgence (Cardon, Cointet, & Mazières, 2018).[10]

We contend, however, that the current deep learning "revolution" has already begun to inspire a new intellectual shift comparable to the impact and hegemony of the cognitivists, who were able to popularize an individualistic information-processing metaphor of the mind that ultimately influenced educational practice itself—as in the case of the educational psychologist Robert Gagné's (1977) approach to cognitive processes (Ertmer, Driscoll, & Wager, 2003), as well as Papert's constructionism approach (inspired by a partially asocial reading of Piaget's constructivism). As such, we believe that it will once again become increasingly common to attempt to understand human learning with reference to the new generation of success stories of twenty-first-century AI, perhaps ultimately in the form of radical shifts in educational policy.[11] But at the same time—and quite unlike the early 1990s—we are at a moment in which the sociotechnical embeddedness of these machine learning and deep learning systems, radically increased in scale and scope if not in their basic architectural underpinnings, are making their limitations increasingly salient to a wide population—and the audience for understanding the nature and source of those limitations is increasing. The stakes are now arguably higher for understanding what kind of "learning" machine learning—and deep learning specifically—really represents.

In the next three sections, we will describe three significant aspects of Vygotsky's "cultural-historical" psychology that will, later on, help us address the implicit theory of "learning" in machine learning. First, we will discuss the intrinsically developmental and specifically *sociogenetic* qualities of learning in the work of Vygotsky and his followers; then, we will show how Vygotsky conceived of *concept development* in his psychological experiments with children, which will be useful because contemporary machine learning classifiers excel in recognizing objects in images or in learning vectorial "meanings" of words; and we will discuss how Vygotsky's *zone of proximal development* highlights that one must always understand "learning" as it is instituted in specific educational systems with specific forms of instruction.

What Is "Social" About Learning?

Unlike in machine learning—where, for instance, the notion of "unsupervised" learning implies that it is possible to learn without a teacher—the study of human learning (sometimes referred to as *pedagogy*) explicitly acknowledges the necessity of some kind of teaching agent. However, there has for some decades been a debate in pedagogical thought that can be characterized, broadly speaking, as about whether the best learning model is the "guide by the side" or the "sage on the stage" (Ferster, 2014). The former tends to involve a naturalistic or spontaneist stance whereby children learn best when "left to their own devices." Proponents of this "child-centric" approach claim that learning is optimal and also most enjoyable when unhampered by the limitations and constraints that rigid and homogenizing education systems impose through methods, techniques, and normative expectations; in short, a child's best teacher is experience—a view prefigured by writers such as Rousseau (1762), Pestalozzi (1827), and Montessori (1912). Education in this case is about accompanying and guiding natural learning processes in a nonintrusive manner, namely by adapting content and methods to the learner's developmental stage. The work of Piaget (1954) represents one of the clearest expressions of this position in which education is about making the world available to what the child can do at a given stage of its natural development.

Conversely, the "sage on the stage" perspective reflects what could be called an institutional stance, according to which the central site of learning is, and needs to be, a formal educational structure where individuals develop their cognitive abilities alongside their moral character (Hegel, 1808–1811/1984; Kant, 1803/2007). In this sense, and given human nature's inherent indeterminacy, education is seen as instituting a certain *kind* of individual, as "molding," "shaping," or "structuring" individuals through their learning. This more "content-centric" approach tends to see education as the process through which culture is reproduced; and when viewed critically, as in Bourdieu and Passeron (1977/1990), additionally as a mechanism for the reproduction of social stratification in general. Although the uncritical version of this perspective is generally considered outdated or conservative when compared to the "child-centric" approach—and disparaged as "instructionism" by Papert (1993) and others—this perspective helps us foreground the fact that education is always, at least in part, about bringing into being a specific kind of individual living within a given culture, and, that education *is possible*; i.e., as Kant suggested, there is something in human development which is indeterminate and thus requires a process of education.

But as with most binary oppositions, this presentation is a caricature. Few thinkers or researchers in education theory or pedagogy would unilaterally call for one of these two approaches to pedagogy, and most would recognize that children need curriculum-based knowledge *to learn* as well as more open-ended situations in which their creativity and problem-solving skills are actively stimulated. But simply taking the middle road between two extremes does not lead us to a robust social theory of learning. Vygotsky's cultural-historical psychology—in which the term "historical" refers to a focus on *development* at various interrelated biological, individual, and social levels—offers a serious basis for thinking of alternatives to this mired debate through focusing on the role of *mediation* in the construction of psychological and behavioral functions and processes (Engeström, 1999, p. 28).

Vygotsky developed a research program—cut short by his premature death—that his successors Leont'ev and Luria would carry on and expand (van der Veer & Valsiner, 1991). According to Vygotsky, behavioral and cognitive development through learning is not a process of socialization by which the individual *becomes* social (as is the case for Piaget); instead, the individual is itself the site of a process through which society is transformed (Brossard, 2012). This genetic and relational view of behavioral and cognitive development is Vygotsky's way of expressing the Marxist doctrine of historical materialism, which tells us that we are not so much thrown into "the World" (as phenomenologists would have it) as we are thrown into determinate forms of social activity. As the Vygotsky commentator Roy Pea (1985) neatly summarizes, "our productive activities change the world, thereby changing the ways in which the world can change us."

In this view, development is not simply about successive cognitive functions replacing or evicting one another as the individual accommodates to the pressures of communication and social life, but about transformations in the *organization* of cognitive functions as they relate to one another (Vygotsky, 1987, p. 175). Cognitive functions do not transcend the specificities of social activity, but instead modulate and reorganize themselves accordingly (Prot, 2012, pp. 308–309). These transformations, in turn, bring about new forms of cognitive activity. For instance, Vygotsky is not interested in concepts in and of themselves, but in how their meaning develops within social activities, on the one hand, and how the individual's cognitive activity is transformed through the use of certain concepts, on the other.

This brings us to a fundamental aspect of Vygotsky's sociogenetic theory of psychological development: all higher psychological concepts (such as, for example, the meanings of words) were at some point concrete social relations. As Roth and Jornet (2017) explain, drawing on Vygotsky's 1934 book *Thinking and Speech*:

> In [Vygotsky's] approach, there is a primacy of the social. Whatever higher psychological function can be identified first *was* a social relation with another person. Vygotsky did not suggest that something (e.g. meaning, rule) initially existed *in* a social relation, something that the participants may have constructed together to be internalized by individuals. Instead, the higher psychological function is identical to that earlier social relation. (p. 106)

To illustrate this general idea, Vygotsky (1979) shows how a toddler's spontaneous movements and gestures become the basis of a social activity in which meaning is progressively constructed through the mediating presence of an adult, which in turns paves the way for semiotic and linguistic mediations. Following Vygotsky's account, the act of pointing is first an attempt to grab or reach for an object. Or rather, what matters is that this gesture *is interpreted* as such by an adult who responds by moving the object closer to the child or helping the child reach the object.[12] The child's spontaneous gesture becomes an indicative one that now appropriates the adult's mediating presence, which will ultimately serve as a basis for the child being able to say "*I* want." The toddler (putatively) reaching for an object is doing something more than failing to reach it. With the help of an adult, one could say that it is reaching a new developmental stage by performing actions it cannot yet do alone but some day will.

Correspondingly, when a child learns the word "apple," it is not learning some fixed descriptor of a given object in reality, it is using the word as an instrument within a social activity. The word uttered by the child might mean "I want an apple" or "I'm hungry" or "I want to hold that red thing and throw it"; it takes the place of an entire chain of gestures and actions that have become relatively stabilized through interactions with others. Before ever becoming free-floating signifiers, words congeal and condense concrete social relations as they are used in activities. The density of social relation, the obstacles encountered in activities and the ways in which words, as instruments, help direct action and regulate behavior, are the basis upon which concepts are developed. We can begin to see that the way a child learns the meaning of "apple" may be quite significantly different, for example, from the way a convolutional neural network "learns" to detect the presence of apples in bitmap images, or the way a word embedding model learns the vectorial "meaning" of the word "apple" in high-dimensional space.

For Vygotsky, the development of "higher psychological functions" is essentially a *mediated* process, insofar as these functions involve *signs* as a constitutive dimension of their activity.[13] Vygotsky's understanding of the term "sign" is broad and not strictly limited to a Saussurean perspective where the sign incorporates a preestablished or fixed relationship between a signifier and a meaning (as in Saussure [1915]). In addition to all the culturally relevant mediations (i.e., language, maps, arithmetic, writing, plans, mnemotechnics, etc.) involved in social activities, for Vygotsky any object can potentially become a sign, or a "psychological instrument," if it is integrated into action as a means of controlling one's behavior and planning one's actions (Friedrich, 2012, p. 261; Vygotsky, 1930/1997c).[14]

Vygotsky provides a striking illustration of this thesis in his critique of the Piagetian conception of the child's internal or "egocentric" language. Whereas Piaget sees egocentric language as a transition between pre-social ("autistic") language and "socialized" language, Vygotsky does not take the beginning of the development process to be pre-social. For Vygotsky, the language a child develops when they seem to be "speaking to themselves," using words that are directed at no one in particular, as though gratuitously accompanying an activity (e.g., coloring, building with blocks), in fact corresponds to the process of reorganizing the activity. Talking over the activity is not then an idle accompaniment, aimed simply at telling oneself what one is doing, but a way of making sense of the forces or objects that resist the child's activity, a way of coping with the world's *will*, so to speak. Vygotsky (1987) gives the example of a child he studied who was drawing a tram and pressed too hard on the paper with his pencil, declared "broken," and proceeded to take up a paintbrush to depict a broken tram car while continuing to talk to himself about the new scenario (p. 70). As Yves Clot (1997) comments, words are the instruments children use to think through the obstacles they encounter, but these instruments are not simply lying around waiting to be used; instead, their appropriation transforms the very activity within which they are taken up, thereby actively broadening the meaning they are supposed to "have".

Conceptualization as Problem Solving and Meaning Transformation

Vygotsky focuses on concept *development*, rather than concept *acquisition*, as one of the central forms of mediation through which meaning emerges. In this sense, framing learning as a social activity does not merely imply that the learner progressively *acquires* socially constructed signifiers, but that a concept's meaning actually develops through the social relations that underpin the learning process. As Vygotsky (1987) describes, "in the problem of interest to us, the problem of concept formation, [the] sign is the word. The word functions as the means for the formation of the concept. Later, it becomes its symbol" (p. 126). The meaning of a signifier is not presupposed nor is it intrinsically attached to a word; rather, it is the result of a dialectical process through which meaning develops socially.

Crucially, the correspondence between a word and the concept it enfolds is not learned once and for all but is itself developed through learning. A child can learn the word "tree" without having mastered "tree" as a concept. Vygotsky (1987) explains that "in itself, learning words and their connections with objects does not lead to the formation of concepts. The subject must be faced with a task that can only be resolved through the formation of concepts" (p. 124). Vygotsky is explicitly taking aim at the associationist belief that concepts somehow grow out of repeated associations between an object and a word, that particular traits are gradually superimposed to form a general concept or category that includes all the particular traits or qualities. Learning a concept, Vygotsky insists, is not about thickening the associations or increasing the number of connections. Instead, it implies a qualitatively different form of cognitive activity that is not reducible to quantitative reinforcement of associative connections (pp. 123–124). It isn't that the child using the word "tree" has a half-baked or poor understanding of what a tree is and that when she reaches the developmental stage in which abstract concepts are mastered (i.e., adolescence) she will have a complete understanding of "tree." For Vygotsky, a concept's meaning is not self-contained but intimately connected to the activity within which it is used. A concept comes to life through learning as the subject is confronted with problems it is incapable, in its given developmental state, of resolving by itself.

Vygtosky's insistence on the social nature of word meaning can be read as analogous to Marx's critique of the fetishization of exchange-value over use-value, in which, e.g., a coat is valued as an abstract monetary quantity as opposed to an expression of the social nature of its use and the labor involved in its production and distribution. Specifically, Vygotsky (1987) is attacking contemporaneous approaches in psychology and linguistics for the way they reified meaning by matching a word to its signifier in the same way that Marx undermined classical economic theories of value by exposing the inherently social relationship economic value translates (pp. 162–163, 169–173). What Vygotsky is trying to get at is the *genesis* of meaning and concepts, as well as the activity this genesis entails. Traditional experimental setups in child psychology proceeded by isolating words from their sentences and contexts, thereby depriving the subject of its ability to effectively think through its activity. For example, as Vygotsky describes, "the experimenter selects an isolated word and the child must define it. This definition of the isolated word taken in a congealed form tells us nothing of the concept in action. It tells us nothing of how the child operates with the concept in the real-life process of solving a problem, of how he uses it when some real-life need for it arises" (p. 123).

By contrast, for Vygotsky, every word, insofar as it bears meaning, enfolds a generalization which cannot be understood as a preestablished relationship between a signifier and its meaning but must be studied as an "act of thought": "The word does not relate to a single object, but to an entire group or class of objects. Therefore, every word is a concealed generalization. From a psychological perspective, word meaning is first and foremost a generalization. It is not difficult to see that generalization is a verbal act of thought; its reflection of reality differs radically from that of immediate sensation or perception" (Vygotsky, 1987, p. 47). One can contrast this notion of generalization to the simpler notion of generalization in machine learning, which merely indicates that large numbers of association tasks (e.g., labeling cats vs. dogs in a corpus of images) can lead to greater performance on unseen images, regardless of whether or not the model truly has a coherent high-level "concept" of a cat or dog. A convolutional neural network can be exceptional at distinguishing between bitmap images of cats and dogs, but it could tell you little about the relationship between cats and dogs in Western society.

Vygotsky would thus likely be dubious of this notion of generalization in machine learning; for him, a concept develops because it can help a learner solve a problem, and the learner must experience the *need* for a concept as it informs its activity. As he takes care in emphasizing, however, spontaneously solving problems as we happen to run into them is not enough for a concept to truly develop. Concepts emerge and come to matter for the learner because he or she was presented with tasks or problems to solve within certain situations. As Vygotsky (1987) explains:

> Where the environment does not create the appropriate tasks, advance new demands, or stimulate the development of intellect through new goals, the adolescent's thinking does not develop all the potentials inherent in it. It may not attain the highest forms of intellect or it may attain them only after extreme delays. Therefore, it would be a mistake to ignore or fail to recognize the significance of the life-task as a factor that nourishes and directs intellectual development in the transitional age. However, it would also be a mistake to view this aspect of causal-dynamic development as the basic mechanism of the problem of concept development or as the key to this problem. (p. 132)

Learning as Instituted in Specific Educational Systems: The Zone of Proximal Development (ZPD)

This leads us to a pivotal point of our argument: *concepts are learned, but they also need to be taught*. And this is particularly true, as Vygotsky points out, of *non-spontaneous* or *scientific* concepts, i.e., concepts that relate to systematic forms of knowledge (e.g., "gravity" as it forms a system of concepts in physics with "mass" and "force") and specific problem-solving skills (e.g., solving a mathematical equation). Unlike *spontaneous* concepts which develop through the child's daily activities and encounters, one cannot reasonably expect scientific concepts to develop spontaneously; they require certain social conditions and forms of activity typically found in schools or other educational institutions in which learners are confronted with specific types of problems and in which their motivation to develop and use concepts is actively stimulated and nurtured.

Concepts that are developed out of daily experience—such as money, to use a particularly notorious example—are often difficult to define (Brossard, 2012, p. 102; Simmel, 1907/2004). This does not imply that scientific concepts are completely distinct or disconnected from spontaneous ones. On the contrary, scientific concepts *need* spontaneous concepts even though they synthesize their contradictions on a different cognitive level (Brossard, 2012, p. 103). This entails that education is not so much about inculcating content as it is about mobilizing students' previous experiences (inside and outside of school) into knowledge and skills they can use in new situations. Although critical of the spontaneist maxim that children learn best when left to their own devices and pedagogical intervention should be used parsimoniously, Vygotsky (1987) does recognize a kernel of incontrovertible wisdom in Tolstoy's belief that "consciously transferring new concepts or word forms to the pupil is as futile as attempting to teach the child to walk through instruction in the laws of equilibrium" (p. 171).[15] He explains:

> The development of concepts or word meanings presupposes the development of a whole series of functions. It presupposes the development of voluntary attention, logical memory, abstraction, comparison, and differentiation. These complex mental processes cannot simply be learned. From a theoretical perspective, then, there is little doubt concerning the inadequacy of the view that the concept is taken by the child in completed form and learned like a mental habit. The inadequacy of this view is equally apparent in connection with practice. No less than experimental research, pedagogical experience demonstrates that direct instruction in concepts is impossible. **It is pedagogically fruitless. The teacher who attempts to use this approach achieves nothing but a mindless learning of words, an empty verbalism that simulates or imitates the presence of concepts in the child.** Under these conditions, the child learns not the concept but the word, and this word is taken over by the child through memory rather than thought. Such knowledge turns out to be inadequate in any meaningful application. (p. 170)

Vygotsky explicitly takes aim at what he considers to be an empirical and theoretical error: we cannot expect to get at learning either through personalization—i.e., simply matching "knowledge" with the child's current state of development—or standardization, i.e., setting up a rigid learning plan that is supposed to correspond to the students' developmental stages. In either case, the error is to think tautologically of learning as what can be learned alone given an individual's developmental level. Ultimately, education should be about situating learning within social activities that demand more of the learner than what the learner can perform by themselves.

This leads us to one of Vygotsky's (1987) famous concepts, the *Zone of Proximal Development* (ZPD), an idea that critiques the concept that a child inhabits a particular stage of development based on their present abilities in isolation:

> If the gardener decides only to evaluate the matured or harvested fruits of the apple tree, he cannot determine the state of his orchard. Maturing trees must also be taken into consideration. The psychologist must [also] not limit his analysis to functions that have matured. He must consider those that are in the process of maturing. If he is to fully evaluate the state of the child's development, the psychologist must consider not only the actual level of development but *the zone of proximal development*. (pp. 208–209)

For Vygotsky, instruction must aim to be just ahead of the child's potential zone of development, keeping in mind that this potential includes not just what the child can do independently but also what the child can do with others. In this process, *imitation* is taken to be essential to learning and not as its perversion or inauthentic expression. "Instruction is possible," he says, "only when there is a potential for imitation" (p. 211); as we will see below, this idea that an interactional form of imitation is potentially productive and not simply "bad" learning finds parallels in the recent ML technique of generative adversarial networks.

In this perspective, learning does not *coincide* with development, then, but rather *pulls it forward*. Children learn how to do more than they can do independently because of the social mediations embedded in activity, which entails that learning can only occur where the child is able to imitate what lies just beyond what it is capable of doing on its own.[16] The ZPD is thus the site for those concrete social relations which for Vygotsky, as described above, become internalized as words, concepts, or other cognitive mediations which are subsequently deployed in new social situations.

This view of the intrinsically social quality of the learning process is seemingly at odds with the way institutionalized education tends to evaluate "true" or authentic learning by testing the agent's ability to solve a problem on its own—be that without the help of peers, teachers, or even technical mediations—as well as the way models in machine learning are evaluated on their predictive performance in isolation. On a broader level, this points to the deep interrelation between the way AI in general and ML in particular mirror certain normative or even political stakes involved in defining what learning *should* be by producing a model of what we *think* learning is. Proponents of Vygotsky-influenced educational psychology instead argue that determining the learner's proximal rather than actual developmental stage allows for a differentiated approach to education whereby a learner is confronted with problems that require it to move beyond what it can do by itself, but which are accompanied by the support of social and technical mediations (Moll, 1990). In addition, higher order "scientific" concepts, which can only be learned within formal educational settings, should not all be taught exactly the same way to every student. Making scientific concepts relevant involves having a grasp of each learner's everyday or "spontaneous" concepts that they use to make sense of the world, which the newly acquired scientific concepts will in turn help organize in new ways. Vygotsky's account of the ZPD allows for a form of "personalization" of content and rhythm that does not atomize the learner and recognizes that the very things it is learning are social by nature. When it comes to machine learning, this perspective points to the trouble the field has in evaluating model performance with abstract metrics in what would otherwise be highly social tasks such as translation and image generation, and it implies the need for a radical shift in our way of evaluating what should count as learning and what kind of activity it involves.

Is Machine Learning a Social Form of Learning?

We have seen how Vygotsky's cultural-historical psychology provides an original understanding of what is social about learning; we have seen how he applies this to concept development in particular; and we have learned about the zone of proximal development. Now we can begin to ask: is machine learning—and deep learning in particular, which has over the last decade promised repeatedly to lead to a new paradigm of artificially intelligent agents—actually a kind of *learning* in Vygotsky's sense?

We can consider a now-prototypical case of contemporary (connectionist) machine learning, that of the multilayer convolutional neural network classifier model in the lineage of those developed by Yann LeCun in the 1980s on the MNIST dataset or by Geoff Hinton's students in the early 2010s using Fei-Fei Li's ImageNet dataset.[17] The models that are trained in these scenarios are said to have distinct *architectures*, a kind of morphology in which each "layer" consists of one or more matrices (if two-dimensional) or tensors (if three-dimensional or higher) (with corresponding bias vectors). These architectures generally do not *change* throughout the "lifespan" of the model and thus DL models can be said to have a highly restricted form of "development" that psychologists would call *microgenetic*: namely, the potential to modify, during the training process, their weight parameters, today sometimes numbering in the hundreds of millions or billions.[18] (Like the field of architecture for buildings/physical structures, neural architectures also "evolve" in a *phylogenetic* way, but this is highly dependent on the actions of their [human] architects and the technical environment in which they both reside.[19]) As with all forms of supervised learning, these models update their weight parameters through the use of a simple loss function (e.g., categorical cross-entropy) and optimizer (e.g., stochastic gradient descent) on labeled training data; i.e., each example image is accompanied by a categorical label indicating that it represents a picture of a butterfly and not a picture of a tiger or 998 other objects.

So what kind of learning *is* supervised learning? Clearly it does not easily correspond to the "sage on the stage" or "guide by the side" caricatures mentioned above—we find no lecturer or dynamic accompaniment, only labels and the mechanical instructions of stochastic gradient descent. Supervised learning is instead what early machine learning researchers called "learning by example"—which is ideally not a rote memorization but a learning process most closely akin to the stimulus-response animal experiments of behaviorism. Specifically, supervised machine learning is more similar to the classical conditioning of Pavlov than the operant conditioning of Thorndike and Skinner, in which the animal subject has the freedom to engage in a variety of actions; the latter corresponds more closely with reinforcement learning.[20] But if we appreciate supervised learning (as well as reinforcement learning) as essentially behaviorist—despite its complex ideological and technical underpinnings in a cognitivism that previously revolted against behaviorism as well as (in the case of deep learning) a connectionism that previously revolted against aspects of said cognitivism (Baars, 1986; Bechtel & Abrahamsen, 2002)—then we can ask: well, what did Vygotsky think about behaviorism?

Indeed, the conference talk that kicked off Vygotsky's career in psychology in the mid-1920s was a critique of the Soviet genre of behaviorism known as *reflexology* specifically associated with Pavlov and the neurologist Vladimir Bekhterev—a field whose proponents believed that "all human conduct could be conceived as combinations of conditional reflexes" but which "deemed the scientific study of [subjective experience] impossible" (van der Veer & Valsiner, 1991, p. 41).[21] Vygotsky saw this approach—which Bekhterev explicitly intended to supplant all other forms of psychology—as doomed to fail, especially if the ultimate goal involved an understanding of human consciousness. This was ironic, Vygotsky explained, because these researchers often had spoken interactions with their human subjects in practice, and speech for Vygotsky indeed represented a form of "reflexes" connected to the subject's internal experience; but the reflexologists simply did not consider those interactions a valid form of behavioral data. (At the time, Vygotsky [1997a] instead believed that one might be able to understand higher psychological processes and even consciousness through these "reflexes of reflexes" [p. 79].)

This inattention to speech, in turn, meant that behaviorism—locked in as it was to the "stimulus-response" or "S–R" framework—was blind to the importance of *mediation*, which was a fundamental feature of Vygotsky's later studies of child development. In this transitional stage of Vygotsky's work, he and L. S. Sakharov performed experiments to determine how children learned to form concepts, given a set of differently colored and differently shaped objects along various dimensions that had been assigned nonsense names like "dek" (small and tall objects) or "mup" (large and tall objects) by the experimenters (van der Veer & Valsiner, 1991, p. 261). They argued that children specifically navigate from nonsensical "syncretic" groupings to arrangements into what are called "complexes"—in which groupings are based on objective features, but these features may be irrelevant to adults—and eventually to what Vygotsky then called "true concepts," although this latter stage could only be reached by adolescents and adults.[22] Vygotsky's (1987) insight is that younger children thinking in *complexes*—specifically the highest form of complex, called the "pseudoconcept"—and adults thinking in *concepts* can nevertheless "establish mutual understanding and verbal interaction" (p. 145), despite the child only being able to conceive of, e.g., a word's meaning as a "bundle of attributes or features" (Blunden, 2012, p. 231).[23] Vygotsky (1930/1997c) referred to the transitions to complexes and then concepts as a process of *generalization* that went beyond pattern-matching and to the level of a scientific concept seen in a relational network with other concepts:

> I will give an example. Let us compare the direct image of a nine, for example, the figures on playing cards, and the number 9. The group of nine on playing cards is richer and more concrete than our concept "9," but the concept "9" involves a number of judgments which are not in the nine on the playing card; "9" is not divisible by even numbers, is divisible by 3, is 3^2, and the square root of 81; we connect "9" with the series of whole numbers, etc. Hence it is clear that psychologically speaking the process of concept formation resides in the discovery of the connections of the given object with a number of others, in finding the real whole. That is why a mature concept involves the whole totality of its relations, its place in the world, so to speak … the concept is not a collective photograph. It does not develop by rubbing out individual traits of the object. It is the knowledge of the object in its relations, in its connections. (p. 100)

We can contrast this distinction between complexes and concepts in Vygotsky with the way that deep convolutional models train on MNIST data, which involves correctly labeling scanned images of handwritten digits. Just as in Vygotsky's examples, such a model can reliably emit the label '9' when confronted with an image of a handwritten number nine, but it does not understand the *concept* of 9 as described above. This highlights the difference between *generalization* in Vygotsky and *generalization* in machine learning. For supervised machine learners, "generalization" merely means high accuracy in the model's ability to label previously unseen input data. For Vygotsky, such a model has perhaps learned a pseudoconcept of the ten digits, but it has not learned to generalize to the *true concept* of a digit.[24] From his perspective, even the supposedly "super-human" object classifiers of today do not have these scientific concepts—those acquired through explicit instruction guided by a teacher, like the term "square root." (One can test this proposition today by asking a state-of-the-art generative text model like

GPT-2 [OpenAI, 2019] to complete the phrase "The square root of 4 is," a task at which it is typically unsuccessful.)

What are the greater implications of Vygotsky's critique of behaviorism and his understanding of concept development on our understanding of machine learning? We can go back to our earlier characterization of machine learning as essentially the study and practice of *microgenesis*: a process of training that (in the case of contemporary AI), depending on the task, might take anywhere from an hour to a couple of months.[25] And it is also, to some extent, a practice of *phylogenesis* in which new architectures are designed and "evolved" by human researchers. But what Vygotsky's work shows is that machine learning is *not* about, in general, *ontogenesis*, i.e., the long-term development of a conscious individual, acting in the world, and "trained" by their social surroundings in both informal and formal ways. And machine learning research is also only tangentially concerned with *sociogenesis*, meaning the development of social groups and identities—although in many cases it is clearly implicated in such development, as in the influence of YouTube's recommendation algorithm on political preferences (Ribeiro, Ottoni, West, Almeida, & Meira, 2020). We summarize this comparison in Table 3.1.

Table 3.1 The role of different developmental processes in a human development framework and in a machine learning "model development" approach

	Time scale (approx.)	*Human development*	*Machine learning*
Microgenesis	Minutes to months	A given pedagogical lesson or psychological experiment	Training an ML model with a given loss function
Ontogenesis/sociogenesis	Days to decades (up to ~100 years)	The natural and sociocultural development of the individual	*n/a* (but see transfer learning and generative adversarial networks)
Phylogenesis/ethnogenesis	Up to hundreds to thousands/millions of years	Biological and cultural evolution of the human species	Technical and cultural development of new ML architectures

In our descriptions in the previous sections, it is clear that it is the complexities of microgenesis and ontogenesis—specifically the ontogenesis of the higher psychological functions and of true and/or scientific concepts—with which Vygotsky is most concerned. It is also relatively clear that, to a large degree, **the *natural and sociocultural development of the individual* is not the kind of learning with which machine learning is concerned**. This indicates that as long as the individual learning subject in machine learning is taken to be the ML model/architecture, someone like Vygotsky would not recognize it as a form of learning due to its lack of emphasis on the ontogenesis of a conscious individual, who develops over time in sequences of dialogical processes, each of which permit transitions from *inter*mental to *intra*mental functions (Vygotsky, 1997b, p. 106).

The technical exceptions to this ontogenetic lack in ML/DL, as noted in the table, are quite interesting in that our framing manages to surface the most intriguing and even underrated features and/or innovations of contemporary deep learning techniques: the ability to retrain or *fine-tune* certain types of models on new corpora of data that differ in some way from (and are often much smaller than) the original "pre-training" datasets, which is known as *transfer learning* (Pan & Yang, 2010; Pratt & Jennings, 1996), as well as distinctively interactional training architectures like those of *generative adversarial networks* (GANs). The transfer learning case demonstrates a limited way in contemporary machine learning in which trained models can have an ontogenetic "lifespan" beyond an individual training session by permitting the reuse of parameters learned over longer periods of training. In the case of GANs, a distinct discriminator model, *D*, and a distinct generator model, *G*, are initialized randomly, but *D* is gradually trained in a supervised manner to recognize, e.g., "real" images of human faces, and *G* repeatedly attempts to "fool" *D* with generated face images by learning from *D*'s assessment of its generated images' plausibility (Castelle, 2020; Goodfellow et al., 2014). This training process differs from traditional supervised learning in that the discriminator model acts as a dynamic "instructor" of sorts, who (in the ideal GAN training process) is just slightly ahead of the student in its ability to determine the validity of the generated face images and can thus pull or guide the generator model forward. This can, arguably, represent the use of a kind of *zone of proximal development* within the otherwise sociogenetically degenerate world of machine learning techniques.

However, what if the subject of machine learning is *not* simply the model? If we instead perform an act of reconfiguration (Suchman, 2007) and situate the subject of machine learning as a ***human-machine activity***—i.e., including the ML researcher, their models, and their associated tools and organizational resources—then we have a situation which permits closer analogies to Vygotsky's cultural-historical approach. This is the approach taken by Adrian Mackenzie (2017) when he uses the phrase *machine learners* to refer "to both humans and machines or human-machine relations." In this latter perspective, which observes the intrinsic technicity of human action and becoming—and thereby of ontogenesis and phylogenesis—we would instead argue that a supervised model that finds objects from the space of ImageNet categories permits the coexisting "user" of that model to ontogenetically improve their development of concepts. That is, as a socialized, technical human with an awareness (if not an expertise) in bird species, I can leverage deep learning classifiers to accelerate my own learning and ability to take action in new situations (such as birdwatching). In other situations, such leveraging of ML classification may be seen as hazardous; consider the court judge who, as a machine learner using an algorithm for pretrial risk assessment (Barabas, Doyle, Rubinovitz, & Dinakar, 2020), effectively "learns" a new scientific concept of "pretrial risk" and, by deploying their preexisting agency and authority, leverages it to take further action against specific groups. Vygotsky (1930/1997c) would consider such devices yet another psychological tool that individuals can use to master one's mental processes; in this case "machine learning" would refer to the development of these psychological tools that extend the ontogenetic development of the machine learner. In order for machine learning to truly embrace theories of learning, such a reconfiguration may indeed be necessary.

Conclusion: Who Is Learning in Machine Learning?

The aim thus far has been neither to provide a comprehensive introduction to Vygotskian psychology nor a full critique of machine learning, but merely to emphasize three essential starting points for undertaking a social theory of machine learning. **The first essential point is the idea that learning occurs when a problem is encountered and resolved by the learner, thereby transforming the problem space itself**. To resolve a problem, a child uses instruments (in activity theory, semiotic and/or technical mediations) that are not simply extraneous to its activity but constitute and transform that activity on a much deeper level. When it comes to machine learning, this gives a novel perspective on what it means to evaluate an algorithm's learning on an already-given problem space. From a Vygotskian point of view there is little sense in evaluating learning performances on ready-made problems without taking into account the activity within which the problem is encountered and resolved. Developmentally speaking, there is little sense in unleashing algorithms on abstract image classification or word substitution problems and hoping that their results will lead to a "generalization of generalizations" necessary for higher-level thinking (Vygotsky, 1987, p. 229). While some deep learning models are often held as examples of successful generalization, it is still the case that reinforcement learning models with superhuman performance on a majority of Atari games (Mnih et al., 2015) are still wholly limited to the world of Atari games and would be useless outside that domain. From a Vygotskyan perspective, the difficulty most machine learning techniques have in generalizing models beyond their given problem space is linked to the fact that practitioners tend to consider their problem spaces as equivalent and comparable when in fact they should be approached as qualitatively different learning experiences directed by the individual's development. The excitement around "transfer learning" reflects an implicit recognition that AI, in its current form, is ontogenetically weak: its models can only "fine tune" and—unlike the child learner over the course of years of instructional microgenetic interactions—cannot undergo repeated reformations of past generalizations.

The second essential point is that learning is not something done on one's own, but something that occurs in the space between what one can do on one's own and what one can do with the help of another. In this sense, learning is always a differential experience and implies being presented with certain problems to resolve rather than others and not simply running into problems randomly. Again, Turing's quote can serve as a valuable guide when he reminds us that the college graduate has spent twenty years or so having his or her behavior intentionally modified by teachers. One of the roles of education as an institution is to determine which problems are worth solving, i.e., which problems will have a value for the learner once they are solved, which will be truly transformative in shaping their cognitive development. From this standpoint the ideal or "optimal" learning process is not one where content is made available for a learner's given developmental stage, but one where the learner reaches beyond their developmental stage through a series of sociotechnical mediations that are not mere crutches but make up the very stuff of learning. This, however, implies that we change our ethical and epistemological expectations by not only demanding optimization and automation of ready-made problems (i.e., evaluating based solely on objective functions), but by engaging in concrete learning processes as an educator would, that is an educator who is not simply a test administrator. One can see hints of this today in generative adversarial networks and even more in the experimental genres of developmental robotics that take ontogenesis and sociogenesis more seriously (Oudeyer & Kaplan, 2006).

The third essential point is that the words, concepts, or images that are learned are never fixed relationships between a signifier and signified but are in fact social relations that have been abstracted from their original activity. Crucially, this means that learning is not merely about acquiring abstract content, knowledge, or symbols and applying them to concrete situations, but it is about turning a concrete social relation into abstract technical and semiotic mediation that can be used in other situations to regulate thinking and behavior. In other words, this is where we see learning as an *activity* in and of itself and not only something that merely happens within a given social context; this is where we see learning transforming the world, to paraphrase one of Vygotsky's primary inspirations. We argue, then, that in order to formulate a learning theory of machine learning, it may be necessary to move from seeing an inert model as the machine learner to seeing the human researcher or developer—*along with*, and not separate from, his or her model and surrounding social relations—as the machine learner. Only then can we see the sociotechnical process of empirically observable machine learning in the light of cultural-historical psychology and/or activity theory. *These* machine learners are developing ontogenetically, whereas the model in isolation is largely developing only microgenetically (although see our ontogenetic caveats in Table 3.1). They are taking the social relations from which their data has been constructed (e.g., the massive human labor of the Mechanical Turk workers who labeled ImageNet), internalizing the labeled pseudoconcepts into their models, and incorporating those internalizations into their own ontogenetic development (whether by fine-tuning the existing models or by moving on to training more interesting architectures). On public and private forums, they educate each other in their techniques at levels appropriate to their development;

through the various communicative activities of releasing research papers, codebases, and pre-trained models, they pull each other's development forward. Machine learning as a *technique* is a hermetic process of training individual models—but machine learning as a *cultural activity* is a vast and social process of training other machine learners.

Notes

1. On the dualism between behavior and mind, see Vygotsky (1997a, p. 65); on the dualism between the individual and the social see Cole and Wertsch (1996); for a discussion of the key assumptions of activity theory, see Chaiklin (2019).
2. Our reasons for using activity theory rather than other dominant educational theories are twofold. First, more conventional theories of learning from the late twentieth century—which consider learning as a hierarchy of individual behaviorist and/or information-processing-like achievements ranging from simple associations to logical problem solving (Gagné, 1970)—tend to reduce or eliminate the social, semiotic, contextual, and technological qualities of any human learning situation. Second, alternative approaches, which vary from constructivism (Piaget, 1954) to constructionism (Papert, 1991) to situated learning (Lave & Wenger, 1991), frequently incorporate one or more of the dialectical insights of activity theory.
3. Vygotsky's term *genetic* is unrelated to the branch of biology concerned with DNA or RNA nucleotides, but instead refers to the way his experiments focused on uncovering the developmental phases of a learning process (Ageyev, 2003).
4. While self-learning in humans is of course possible in some situations (Gibbons et al., 1980; Rousseau, 1762), few learning theorists would advocate for the elimination of teachers entirely. Vygotsky argued that instructional experience is internalized, and thus "when the school child solves a problem at home on the basis of a model that he has been shown in class, he continues to act in collaboration, though at the moment the teacher is not standing near him … It is a solution accomplished with the teacher's help. *This help—this aspect of collaboration—is invisibly present. It is contained in what looks from the outside like the child's independent solution of the problem*" (Vygotsky, 1987, p. 216; emphasis added).
5. "As cognitive scientists like George Miller and Herbert Simon crossed back and forth between scientific descriptions of the human and normative discussions of the best way for scientists to think, they borrowed from the folk and social psychological image of right thinking to inform their own personal and public images … These very same scientific self-images

would form the basis for the image of human nature that cognitive science produced" (Cohen-Cole, 2014).

6. By contrast, DL architectures do begin in a tabula rasa manner (while the neural architecture is fixed, the parameter weights are set randomly), and their goals are arguably more limited, to what would have then be dismissively known as a kind of pattern recognition (e.g., the classification of a bitmapped image as containing a tiger).
7. This debate, staged at the Abbaye de Royaumont outside of Paris, was later described as one in which "Chomsky's argument focused exclusively on complex details of the learning of syntax, about which Piaget had virtually nothing to say ... [and] Piaget's ground for argument was conceptual learning, about which Chomsky had nothing to say" (Jackendoff, 1995).
8. For internalist depictions of the history of machine learning of this era, see Carbonell, Michalski, & Mitchell (1983b) as well as Kodratoff (1992).
9. It is remarkable to read one early text attempting to bridge PDP and cognitive psychology (Kehoe, 1988) describing how "cognitive research and theory has focused largely on the already highly productive performance by highly experienced human subjects." On PDP and classical conditioning see also (Klopf, 1988).
10. In the intervening years, a field known as *epigenetic robotics* emerged that integrated developmental perspectives with robotics, which even inspired occasional reference to learning theorists like Piaget and Vygotsky (Berthouze & Ziemke, 2003). Because our focus here is on supervised learning and not reinforcement learning or interactive robotics, we do not discuss this work in detail, but it will undoubtedly be relevant to future histories of "social" reinforcement learning.
11. This inevitable analogical reframing of deep learning toward human learning is a traditional "universalizing" quality of AI, identified by Goldstein and Papert (1977), who explained that "it may seem paradoxical that researchers in the field [of AI] have anything to say about the structure of human language or related issues in education.... [But] [a]lthough there is much practical good that can come of more intelligent machines, the fundamental theoretical goal of the discipline is understanding intelligent processes *independent* of their particular physical realization" (p. 85).
12. The semiotic novelty of Vygotsky's account of word meaning, in which indexical signs are seen as a foundation for the development of conceptual meaning, has been noted by Wertsch (1985): "The indicatory or indexical function of speech makes it possible for adults to draw young children into social interaction because it allows intersubjectivity on perceptually present objects even though complete agreement on the interpretation or categorization of these objects is lacking" (p. 57). Silverstein's (1985) characterization is even more complete: "Vygotsky's account [on the development of concepts] is really a logical reconstruction of the passage

of words from being indexicals connected to the things they ultimately will truly denote, through an 'egocentric' stage in which they serve as performatives of a sort, to their ultimate emergence as sense-valued elements of propositional schemata, each stage being a functional enrichment, not a replacement, of the cognitive utility of language" (p. 231).

13. While some interpreters, following in the line of Leont'ev, hold that signs such as speech are just one type of "tool" that includes external tools and techniques, Vygotsky focused on speech as the most fundamental form of mediation (Miller, 2011, pp. 20–24; Vygotsky, 1987, pp. 60–61).
14. See also Davydov and Radzikhovskii (1986) for a discussion of signs as psychological tools.
15. The passage Vygotsky cites is from Tolstoy (1967, p. 278).
16. A similar conclusion has been reached, although with different social and cognitive implications, by advocates of the extended mind theory (Clark & Chalmers, 1998; Hutchins, 1994; Wheeler, 2011).
17. We describe connectionist ML over the "classic" tabular-oriented ML of Breiman (2001b) so that our critiques have greater purchase on claims for twenty-first-century AI, although in principle our critiques could apply to the simpler architectures of decision trees or SVMs (the latter of which, as pointed out by LeCun (2008), can be seen as a particular genre of two-layer neural network or "glorified template match[ing]").
18. Microgenesis is "based on the assumption that activity patterns, percepts, thoughts, are not merely products but processes that, whether they take seconds, or hours, or days, unfold in terms of developmental sequence" (Werner, 1957, pp. 142–143).
19. See Grosman and Reigeluth (2019) on how the "lineages" of DL architectures impose certain constraints on human invention.
20. Rescorla and Wagner's (1972) mathematical formalization of Pavlovian classical conditioning can be shown to be similar to simple supervised neural network models that typically update their weights based on a learning rate hyperparameter and a least-mean-squares loss function (Sutton & Barto, 1981). (Today, this similarity of machine learning to behaviorism is only really appreciated in the reinforcement learning community, where some of the language is in a direct lineage.)
21. "Pavlov was certainly interested in behavior (a term that acquired almost as many varied meanings as the word 'objective'), but he was not a behaviorist. Unlike John Watson and other American behaviorists of his day, he consistently acknowledged the existence and paramount importance of subjective phenomena—of the internal emotional and intellectual experiences of humans and other animals—and he always believed that science should seek to explain them" (Todes, 2014, p. 295).
22. It is important to recognize that Vygotsky's discussion of syncretism, complexes, and true concepts in the fifth chapter of *Thinking and Speech*

(1987) was originally written around 1930, but his sixth chapter on spontaneous and scientific concepts was written in 1934, the year of his death (van der Veer & Valsiner, 1991, p. 257).

23. Blunden points out that the distinction between pseudoconcepts and true concepts is related to the influence from Hegel's *Logic*: "Dialectical logic is in fact nothing more than the art of dealing with concepts, that is, *true* concepts, rather than simplified, impoverished pseudoconcepts" (Blunden, 2012, p. 253).
24. Such an objection recalls the recent critiques of Gary Marcus: "Deep learning doesn't recognize a dog as an animal composed of parts like a head, a tail, and four legs, or even what an animal is, let alone what a head is, and how the concept of head varies across frogs, dogs, and people, different in details yet bearing a common relation to bodies" (Marcus & Davis, 2019).
25. For a discussion of microgenesis in the context of Vygotsky, see Wertsch and Stone (1978).

References

Ackley, D. H., Hinton, G. E., & Sejnowski, T. J. (1985). A learning algorithm for Boltzmann Machines. *Cognitive Science, 9*(1), 147–169. https://doi.org/10.1016/S0364-0213(85)80012-4.

Ageyev, V. S. (2003, September). Vygotsky in the mirror of cultural interpretations. In A. Kozulin, B. Gindis, V. Ageyev, & S. Miller (Eds.), *Vygotsky's educational theory in cultural context* (pp. 432–450). Cambridge University Press. https://doi.org/10.1017/CBO9780511840975.022.

Ames, M. G. (2018). Hackers, computers, and cooperation: A critical history of Logo and constructionist learning. *Association for Computing Machinery*. https://doi.org/10.1145/3274287.

Baars, B. J. (1986). *The cognitive revolution in psychology*. Guilford Publications.

Barabas, C., Doyle, C., Rubinovitz, J., & Dinakar, K. (2020). Studying up: Reorienting the study of algorithmic fairness around issues of power. *Proceedings of the 2020 Conference on Fairness, Accountability, and Transparency*, 167–176. https://doi.org/10.1145/3351095.3372859.

Bates, E. A., & Elman, J. L. (1993). Connectionism and the study of change. In *Brain development and cognition: A reader* (pp. 623–642). Blackwell.

Bechtel, W., & Abrahamsen, A. (2002). *Connectionism and the mind: Parallel processing, dynamics, and evolution in networks* (2nd ed.). Blackwell.

Berthouze, L., & Ziemke, T. (2003). Epigenetic robotics—Modelling cognitive development in robotic systems. *Connection Science, 15*(4), 147–150. https://doi.org/10.1080/09540090310001658063.

Blunden, A. (2012). *Concepts: A critical approach*. Brill.

Boden, M. A. (1978). Artificial intelligence and Piagetian theory. *Synthese, 38*(3), 389–414.

Boden, M. A. (2006). *Mind as machine: A history of cognitive science*. Oxford University Press.

Bourdieu, P., & Passeron, J. (1977/1990). *Reproduction in education, society and culture* (2nd ed.). Sage.

Breiman, L. (2001a). Random forests. *Machine Learning, 45*(1), 5–32. https://doi.org/10.1023/A:1010933404324.

Breiman, L. (2001b). Statistical modeling: The two cultures (with comments and a rejoinder by the author). *Statistical Science, 16*(3), 199–231. https://doi.org/10.1214/ss/1009213726.

Brossard, M. (2012). Le développement comme transformation par appropriation des œuvres de la culture. In Y. Clot (Ed.), *Vygotski maintenant* (pp. 95–116). La Dispute.

Carbonell, J. G., Michalski, R. S., & Mitchell, T. M. (1983a). An overview of machine learning. In R. S. Michalski, J. G. Carbonell, & T. M. Mitchell (Eds.), *Machine learning: An artificial intelligence approach* (pp. 3–23). Springer Berlin Heidelberg. https://doi.org/10.1007/978-3-662-12405-5_1.

Carbonell, J. G., Michalski, R. S., & Mitchell, T. M. (1983b). Machine learning: A historical and methodological analysis. *AI Magazine, 4*(3), 69. https://doi.org/10.1609/aimag.v4i3.406.

Cardon, D., Cointet, J.-P., & Mazières, A. (2018). Neurons spike back: The invention of inductive machines and the artificial intelligence controversy. *Reśeaux, 5*(211), 173–220.

Castelle, M. (2020). The social lives of generative adversarial networks. *Proceedings of the 2020 Conference on Fairness, Accountability, and Transparency*, 413. https://doi.org/10.1145/3351095.3373156.

Chaiklin, S. (2019). The meaning and origin of the activity concept in Soviet psychology—With primary focus on A. N. Leontiev's approach. *Theory & Psychology, 29*(1), 3–26. https://doi.org/10.1177/0959354319828208.

Chollet, F. (2018). *Deep learning with Python*. Manning Publications.

Chomsky, N. (1959). A review of B. F. Skinner's "Verbal Behavior". *Language, 35*, 26–58.

Clark, A., & Chalmers, D. (1998). The extended mind. *Analysis, 58*(1), 7–19. https://doi.org/10.1111/1467-8284.00096.

Clot, Y. (1997). Avant-propos. In L. S. Vygotski, *Pensée et langage*. La Dispute: SNEDIT.

Cohen, P. R., & Feigenbaum, E. A. (1982). *The handbook of artificial intelligence* (Vol. 3). HeurisTech Press.

Cohen-Cole, J. (2005). The reflexivity of cognitive science: The scientist as model of human nature. *History of the Human Sciences, 18*(4), 107–139. https://doi.org/10.1177/0952695105058473.
Cohen-Cole, J. (2014). *The open mind: Cold War politics and the sciences of human nature*. University of Chicago Press.
Cole, M., & Wertsch, J. V. (1996). Beyond the individual-social antinomy in discussions of Piaget and Vygotsky. *Human Development, 39*(5), 250–256. https://doi.org/10.1159/000278475.
Cortes, C., & Vapnik, V. (1995). Support-vector networks. *Machine Learning, 20*(3), 273–297. https://doi.org/10.1023/A:1022627411411.
Davydov, V. V., & Radzikhovskii, L. A. (1986). Vygotsky's theory and the activity-oriented approach in psychology. In J. V. Wertsch (Ed.), *Culture, communication, and cognition: Vygotskian perspectives* (pp. 35–65). CUP Archive.
de Saussure, F. (1915). *Course in general linguistics*. McGraw-Hill.
Diakopoulos, N. (2014). *Algorithmic accountability reporting: On the investigation of black Boxes*. Academic Commons. https://academiccommons.columbia.edu/doi/10.7916/D8ZK5TW2.
Elman, J. L. (1990). Finding structure in time. *Cognitive Science, 14*(2), 179–211. https://doi.org/10.1207/s15516709cog1402_1.
Elman, J. L., Bates, E. A., Johnson, M. H., Karmiloff-Smith, A., Parisi, D., & Plunkett, K. (1996). *Rethinking innateness: A connectionist perspective on development*. MIT Press.
Engeström, Y. (1999). Activity theory and individual and social transformation. In Y. Engeström, R. Miettinen, & R.-L. Punamäki (Eds.), *Perspectives on activity theory*. Cambridge University Press.
Ertmer, P. A., Driscoll, M. P., & Wager, W. W. (2003). The legacy of Robert Mills Gagné. In *Educational psychology: A century of contributions* (pp. 303–330). Lawrence Erlbaum Associates Publishers.
Ferster, B. (2014). *Teaching machines: Learning from the intersection of education and technology*. Johns Hopkins University Press.
Fodor, J. (1972). Some reflections on L.S. Vygotsky's thought and language. *Cognition, 1*(1), 83–95. https://doi.org/10.1016/0010-0277(72)90046-7.
Friedrich, J. (2012). L'idée des instruments médiatisants. Un dialogue fictif entre Bühler et Vygotski. In Y. Clot (Ed.), *Vygotski maintenant* (pp. 255–270). La Dispute.
Gagne, R. M. (1977). *Conditions of learning* (3rd rev. ed.). Thomson Learning.
Gagné, R. M. (1970). *The conditions of learning* (2nd ed.). Rinehart and Winston: Holt.
Gibbons, M., Bailey, A., Comeau, P., Schmuck, J., Seymour, S., & Wallace, D. (1980). Toward a theory of self-directed learning: A study of experts without

formal training. *Journal of Humanistic Psychology, 20*(2), 41–56. https://doi.org/10.1177/002216788002000205.

Goldstein, I., & Papert, S. (1977). Artificial intelligence, language, and the study of knowledge. *Cognitive Science, 1*(1), 84–123. https://doi.org/10.1207/s15516709cog0101_5.

Goodfellow, I., Pouget-Abadie, J., Mirza, M., Xu, B., Warde-Farley, D., Ozair, S., … Bengio, Y. (2014). Generative adversarial networks. ArXiv:1406.2661 *[Cs, Stat]*. http://arxiv.org/abs/1406.2661.

Grosman, J., & Reigeluth, T. (2019). Perspectives on algorithmic normativities: Engineers, objects, activities. *Big Data & Society, 6*(2), 2053951719858742. https://doi.org/10.1177/2053951719858742.

Hegel, G. W. F. (1808–1811/1984). *Hegel, the letters* (C. Butler & C. Seiler, Trans.). Indiana University Press.

Hutchins, E. (1994). *Cognition in the wild*. MIT Press.

Jackendoff, R. S. (1995). *Languages of the mind: Essays on mental representation*. Bradford Book.

Kant, I. (1803/2007). *Anthropology, history, and education*. Cambridge University Press.

Karmiloff-Smith, A. (1992). *Beyond modularity: A developmental perspective on cognitive science*. MIT Press.

Kehoe, E. J. (1988). A layered network model of associative learning: Learning to learn and configuration. *Psychological Review, 95*(4), 411–433.

Keller, E. F. (2008). Organisms, machines, and thunderstorms: A history of self-organization, part one. *Historical Studies in the Natural Sciences, 38*(1), 45–75. https://doi.org/10.1525/hsns.2008.38.1.45.

Klopf, H. A. (1988). A neuronal model of classical conditioning. *Psychobiology, 16*(2), 85–125. https://doi.org/10.3758/BF03333113.

Kodratoff, Y. (1992). Ten years of advances in machine learning. In P. Dewilde & J. Vandewalle (Eds.), *Computer systems and software engineering: State-of-the-art* (pp. 231–261). Springer US. https://doi.org/10.1007/978-1-4615-3506-5_9.

Langley, P. (1988). Machine learning as an experimental science. *Machine Learning, 3*, 5–8.

Lave, J., & Wenger, E. (1991). *Situated learning: Legitimate peripheral participation*. Cambridge University Press.

LeCun, Y. (2008, April 9). *Visual perception with deep learning*. http://web.archive.org/web/20131211154343/https://cs.nyu.edu/~yann/talks/lecun-20080409-google.pdf.

Leontiev, A. N., & Luria, A. R. (1972). Some notes concerning Dr. Fodor's "reflections on L.S. Vygotsky's thought and language". *Cognition, 1*(2), 311–316. https://doi.org/10.1016/0010-0277(72)90024-8.

Mackenzie, A. (2017). *Machine learners: Archaeology of a data practice*. MIT Press.

Marcus, G., & Davis, E. (2019). *Rebooting AI: Building artificial intelligence we can trust*. Ballantine Books.

McClelland, J. L., Rumelhart, D. E., & Hinton, G. E. (1986). The appeal of parallel distributed processing. In D. E. Rumelhart & J. L. McClelland (Eds.), *Parallel distributed processing: Explorations in the microstructure of cognition* (Vol. 1, pp. 3–44). MIT Press. http://dl.acm.org/citation.cfm?id=104279.104284.

Michalski, R. S. (1983). A theory and methodology of inductive learning. In R. S. Michalski, J. G. Carbonell, & T. M. Mitchell (Eds.), *Machine learning: An artificial intelligence approach* (pp. 83–129). Springer Berlin Heidelberg. https://doi.org/10.1007/978-3-662-12405-5_1.

Michalski, R. S., Carbonell, J. G., & Mitchell, T. M. (Eds.). (1983). *Machine learning: An artificial intelligence approach*. Springer Berlin Heidelberg. https://doi.org/10.1007/978-3-662-12405-5_1.

Miller, R. (2011). Vygotsky in perspective. *Cambridge University Press*. https://doi.org/10.1017/CBO9780511736582.

Minsky, M., & Papert, S. (1969). *Perceptrons: An introduction to computational geometry*. MIT Press.

Mnih, V., Kavukcuoglu, K., Silver, D., Rusu, A. A., Veness, J., Bellemare, M. G., … Hassabis, D. (2015). Human-level control through deep reinforcement learning. *Nature*, *518*(7540), 529–533. https://doi.org/10.1038/nature14236.

Moll, L. C. (1990). Introduction. In L. C. Moll (Ed.), *Vygotsky and education: Instructional implications and applications of sociohistorical psychology* (pp. 1–27). Cambridge University Press.

Montessori, M. (1912). *The Montessori method: Scientific pedagogy as applied to child education in "the Children's Houses" with additions and revisions*. Stokes. http://archive.org/details/montessorimethod00montuoft.

OpenAI. (2019, February 14). *Better language models and their implications*. https://openai.com/blog/better-language-models/.

Oudeyer, P.-Y., & Kaplan, F. (2006). Discovering communication. *Connection Science, 18*(2), 189–206. https://doi.org/10.1080/09540090600768567.

Pan, S. J., & Yang, Q. (2010). A survey on transfer learning. *IEEE Transactions on Knowledge and Data Engineering, 22*(10), 1345–1359. https://doi.org/10.1109/TKDE.2009.191.

Papert, S. (1980). *Mindstorms: Children, computers, and powerful ideas*. Basic Books.

Papert, S. (1991). Situating constructionism. In I. Harel & S. Papert (Eds.), *Constructionism* (pp. 1–12). Ablex Publishing.

Papert, S. (1993). *The children's machine: Rethinking school in the age of the computer*. Basic Books.
Papert, S., Apostel, L., Grize, J. B., Papert, S., & Piaget, J. (1963). Etude comparée de l'intelligence chez l'enfant et chez le robot. In *La filiation des structures* (Vol. 1–1, pp. 131–194). Presses universitaires de France.
Pasquale, F. (2015). *The black box society: The secret algorithms that control money and information*. Harvard University Press.
Pea, R. D. (1985). Beyond amplification: Using the computer to reorganize mental functioning. *Educational Psychologist, 20*(4), 167–182. https://doi.org/10.1207/s15326985ep2004_2.
Pestalozzi, J. H. (1827). *Letters on early education. Addressed to J. P. Greaves, esq*. Sherwood, Gilbert and Piper. http://archive.org/details/lettersonearlyed00pestiala.
Piaget, J. (1954). The construction of reality in the child. *Basic Books*. https://doi.org/10.1037/11168-000.
Piaget, J. (1970). Piaget's theory. In L. Carmichael (Ed.), *Carmichael's manual of child psychology*. Wiley. http://archive.org/details/carmichaelsmanua0001carm.
Piattelli-Palmarini, M. (Ed.). (1980). *Language and learning: The debate between Jean Piaget and Noam Chomsky*. Harvard University Press.
Plunkett, K., & Sinha, C. (1992). Connectionism and developmental theory. *British Journal of Developmental Psychology, 10*(3), 209–254. https://doi.org/10.1111/j.2044-835X.1992.tb00575.x.
Pratt, L., & Jennings, B. (1996). A survey of transfer between connectionist networks. *Connection Science, 8*(2), 163–184. https://doi.org/10.1080/095400996116866.
Prot, B. (2012). Formation d'un concept potentiel et transformations de l'activité. In Y. Clot (Ed.), *Vygotski maintenant* (pp. 307–327). La Dispute.
Rescorla, R. A., & Wagner, A. R. (1972). A theory of Pavlovian conditioning: Variations on the effectiveness of reinforcement and non-reinforcement. In A. H. Black & W. F. Prokasy (Eds.), *Classical conditioning II: Current research and theory* (pp. 64–99). Appleton-Century-Crofts.
Ribeiro, M. H., Ottoni, R., West, R., Almeida, V. A. F., & Meira, W. (2020). Auditing radicalization pathways on YouTube. *Proceedings of the 2020 Conference on Fairness, Accountability, and Transparency*, 131–141. https://doi.org/10.1145/3351095.3372879.
Roth, W.-M., & Jornet, A. (2017). *Understanding educational psychology: A late Vygotskian, Spinozist approach*. Springer International Publishing. https://doi.org/10.1007/978-3-319-39868-6.
Rousseau, J.-J. (1762). *Emile: Or on education* (A. Bloom, Trans.). Basic Books.
Rumelhart, D. E., Hinton, G. E., & Williams, R. J. (1986). Learning internal representations by error propagation. In D. E. Rumelhart, J. L. McClelland,

& PDP Research Group, *Parallel distributed processing: Explorations in the microstructure of cognition* (Vol. 1, pp. 318–362).
Rumelhart, D. E., & McClelland, J. L. (Eds.). (1986). *Parallel distributed processing: Explorations in the microstructure of cognition* (Vol. 1). MIT Press. http://dl.acm.org/citation.cfm?id=104279.104284.
Sejnowski, T. J. (2018). *The deep learning revolution*. MIT Press.
Silverstein, M. (1985). The functional stratification of language in ontogenesis. In J. V. Wertsch (Ed.), *Culture, communication and cognition: Vygotskian perspectives* (pp. 205–235). Cambridge University Press.
Simmel, G. (1907/2004). *The philosophy of money*. Routledge.
Simondon, G. (1958). *On the mode of existence of technical objects* (C. Malaspina & J. Rogove, Eds.). University of Minnesota Press.
Suchman, L. (2007). *Human-machine reconfigurations: Plans and situated actions* (2nd ed.). Cambridge University Press.
Sutton, R. S., & Barto, A. G. (1981). Toward a modern theory of adaptive networks: Expectation and prediction. *Psychological Review, 88*(2), 135–170.
Todes, D. P. (2014). *Ivan Pavlov: A Russian life in science*. Oxford University Press.
Tolstoy, L. N. (1967). The school at Yásnaya Polyána. In L. Wiener (Trans.), *Tolstoy on education*. University of Chicago Press.
Turing, A.M. (1948/1969). Intelligent machinery. In B. Meltzer & D. Michie (Eds.), *Machine intelligence 5* (pp. 3–23). Edinburgh University Press.
van der Veer, R., & Valsiner, J. (1991). *Understanding Vygotsky: A quest for synthesis*. Blackwell.
Vygotsky, L. S. (1979). The development of the higher forms of attention in childhood. In J. V. Wertsch (Ed.), *The concept of activity in Soviet psychology* (pp. 189–240). Routledge.
Vygotsky, L. S. (1987). Thinking and speech. In R.W. Rieber & A. S. Carton (Eds.), *The collected works of L. S. Vygotsky, Vol. I: Problems of general psychology* (N. Minnick, Trans., pp. 39–285). Plenum.
Vygotsky, L. S. (1997a). Consciousness as a problem for the psychology of behavior. In R. W. Rieber & J. Wollock (Eds.), *The collected works of L. S. Vygotsky: Problems of the theory and history of psychology* (Vol. 3). Springer US. https://doi.org/10.1007/978-1-4615-5893-4.
Vygotsky, L. S. (1997b). Genesis of higher mental functions. In R. W. Rieber (Ed.), *The collected works of L. S. Vygotsky: The history of the development of higher mental functions* (Vol. 4, pp. 97–119). Springer US. https://doi.org/10.1007/978-1-4615-5939-9.
Vygotsky, L. S. (1930/1997c). On psychological systems. In R. W. Rieber & J. Wollock (Eds.), *The collected works of L. S. Vygotsky: Problems of the theory and history of psychology* (Vol. 3, pp. 91–107). Springer US. https://doi.org/10.1007/978-1-4615-5893-4.

Werner, H. (1957). The concept of development from a comparative and organismic point of view. In D. B. Harris (Ed.), *The concept of development* (NED-New edition, pp. 125–148). University of Minnesota Press. https://www.jstor.org/stable/10.5749/j.cttttj0x.12.

Wertsch, J. V. (1985). The semiotic mediation of mental life: L. S. Vygotsky and M. M. Bakhtin. In E. Mertz & R. J. Parmentier (Eds.), *Semiotic mediation: Sociocultural and psychological perspectives* (pp. 49–71). Academic Press.

Wertsch, J. V., & Stone, C. A. (1978). Microgenesis as a tool for developmental analysis. *The Quarterly Newsletter of the Laboratory of Comparative Human Cognition*, *1*(1), 8–10.

Wheeler, M. (2011). Thinking beyond the brain: Educating and building, from the standpoint of extended cognition. *Computational Culture*, *1*. http://computationalculture.net/beyond-the-brain/.

CHAPTER 4

The *Other* Cambridge Analytics: Early "Artificial Intelligence" in American Political Science

Fenwick McKelvey

Artificial intelligence (AI), we are led to believe, will soon be weaponized in a new information war. Such speculation happened in the aftermath of Cambridge Analytica and its shadowy use of data in politics (cf. Chessen, 2017). As one popular opinion piece by Berit Anderson (2017) warns, the infamous global consulting firm "is a piece of a much bigger and darker puzzle—a Weaponized AI Propaganda Machine being used to manipulate our opinions and behavior to advance specific political agendas." Better models of voter behavior will "prey on your emotions" by varying messages to your current state of mind. Future campaigns may have "250 million algorithmic versions of their political message all updating in real-time, personalized to precisely fit the worldview and attack the insecurities of their targets." It is not hard to imagine a coming dystopia where AI undermines democratic free will and fair elections.

F. McKelvey (✉)
Department of Communication Studies, Concordia University, Montreal, QC, Canada
e-mail: fenwick.mckelvey@concordia.ca

© The Author(s) 2021
J. Roberge and M. Castelle (eds.), *The Cultural Life of Machine Learning*, https://doi.org/10.1007/978-3-030-56286-1_4

How could AI be so easily imagined as a political weapon? How could developments in machine classification be consider relevant to politics? Especially when Cambridge Analytica and other applications are what Dave Karpf (2016) calls "bullshit," offering further evidence of what Jesse Baldwin-Phillipi (2017) calls the myth of data-driven campaigning. Bullshit and myths overstate the power of these tools, allow them to be positioned as weapons, and convince parties and politicians to buy them—much like Cambridge Analytica did in convincing the world its tools worked and influenced elections.

These fears overlook the state-of-the-art too. Artificial intelligence is already part of political campaigns and has been for a while. In 2018, Blue State Digital (BSD), a leading digital political strategy firm, announced a partnership with AI startup Tanjo (Blue State Digital, 2018). BSD introduced the collaboration in a blog post, explaining that "AI is all around us, creating breakthrough innovations for companies and consumers alike." Alike is an apt way to describe the benefits of the technology. Tanjo uses AI, or what it calls Tanjo's Automated Persona (TAP), to model human behavior. Where message testing usually requires real people, Tanjo creates audiences on demand. TAPs, Blue State Digital continues, simulate "humans' distinct personalities and unique interests" to "predict how they'll react to content." Whether TAPs work as promised is not my question here, nor is whether these *fakes* will undermine democratic trust. What I seek to explain is how we came to believe that humans—especially their political behavior—could be modelled by computers in the first place.

My chapter synthesizes how innovations in political science beginning in the 1950s led to the conditions of possibility for the use of artificial intelligence in politics today. Building on this book's focus on the history of AI from rule-based to today's temporal flows of classifications, my chapter offers a genealogy of artificial intelligence as a political epistemology. Through media genealogy, my project takes a broad view of media, following communication theorists Alexander Monea and Jeremy Packer, who define media as "tools of governance that shape knowledge and produce and sustain power relations while simultaneously forming their attendant subjects" (Monea & Packer, 2016, p. 3152). Media genealogy examines "how media allowed certain problems to come to light, be investigated, and chosen for elimination and how media aided in the various solutions that have been enacted" (p. 3155). Computers, as this chapter explores, came to be a solution to the problems of information war, the utility of the field, and the uncertainties of public opinion.

Over fifty years ago, a new wave of social scientists and programmers, part of what I call the New Political Science (White, 1961), began to experiment with computer simulation as a proxy for public opinion and government behavior. These experiments did not stay in academia. American federal agencies, the US military, and the Democratic Party, briefly, funded these experiments. As a result, digital simulation, forecasting, and modelling became part of new approaches to political systems reformatted as cybernetic systems, or what another important figure in the New Political Science, Karl Deutsch (1963), called in his book the "Nerves of Government." Building on Orit Halpern's (2014) expansive history of the implications of cybernetics to politics, one could say these nerves of government prefigured the neural nets now sold to Blue State Digital.

In trying to navigate the scope of this change, I focus on what Donna Haraway (1985) calls *breakdowns*, in this case, between computing and politics. These breakdowns happened at MIT: the Simulmatics Corporation and its academic successor Project Cambridge.[1] Drawing on archival research, I analyze the constitutive discourses that formulated the problems to be solved and the artifacts of code that actualized these projects. Simulmatics Corporation and Project Cambridge—the *other* Cambridge analytics—integrated behavioralism with mathematical modelling in hopes of rendering populations more knowable and manageable.

My chapter begins by following developments in political science that laid the ground for Simulmatics and Project Cambridge to be heralded as major advances in the field. Harold Lasswell, in particular, encouraged the application of computing in the social sciences as a new weapon to fight what we would now call an information war (a continuation of Lasswell's work in psychological warfare). If these desires were inputs for computers, then Simulmatics and Project Cambridge were the outputs. These projects reformatted politics to run on computers, and, in doing so, blurred voter opinion and behavior with data and modelling. These breakdowns enabled computers to simulate voters and facilitated today's practices of what political communication scholar Phillip N. Howard (2006) calls *thin citizenship*—an approach to politics where data and the insights of AI stand in for political opinion. In doing so, these other analytics at Cambridge erased the boundaries between mathematical states and political judgments—an erasure necessary for AI to be seen as a political epistemology today.

Moody Behavioralists and the New Political Science

By the early 1960s, a mood had set in political science (Dahl, 1961). This mood resulted from deliberate work by researchers who desired a more scientific and objective field, complementary to the physical sciences. Some proponent voices included Harold Lasswell, Ithiel de Sola Pool, and Karl Deutsch, who were themselves influenced by the work of Oskar Morgenstern, John von Neumann, and Herbert Simon in economics and computer science (Amadae, 2003; Barber, 2006; Cohen-Cole, 2008; Gunnell, 1993, 2004; Halpern, 2014; Hauptmann, 2012). Advocates sought to aid government, particularly the US government, in what was a new turn in the long history of the social sciences as a state or royal science (Igo, 2007, p. 6). The distinguished political scientist Robert Dahl would call this a "behavioral mood." Critics would call it the New Political Science.

Dahl described behavioralism[2] as a mood because it was hard to define. He wrote, "one can say with considerable confidence what it is not, but it is difficult to say what it is" (1961, p. 763). The closest he came to providing a definition was, in a 1961 review of behavioralism, a quotation from a lecture at the University of Chicago in 1951 by prominent political scientist David Truman. Truman defined political behavior as "a point of view which aims at stating all phenomena of government in terms of the observed and observable behavior of men" (p. 767). Truman's definition minimized resistance to future applications of computing. If behavior could be stated as observations, these observations could be restated as data. Looking back, behavioralism contributed to the breakdown between human and computer intelligence that Katherine Hayles describes as virtuality: "the cultural perception that material objects are interpenetrated by information patterns" (1999, pp. 13–14). The emphasis on observation may seem rather mundane now. That was Dahl's point. As he concluded, "the behavioral mood will not disappear then because it has failed. It will disappear because it has succeeded," i.e., fully incorporated into the field (Dahl, 1961, p. 770).

The behavioralism mood had been a long time coming. Dahl gave six reasons for the turn toward behavioralism:

1. The influence of the University of Chicago. Dahl mentions Harold Lasswell (who supervised Pool there) and Herbert Simon;

2. The influx of European scholars after World War II, such as Paul Lazarsfeld (who Dahl cites as one of the first to develop the scientific approach to politics continued by behavioralism). Karl Deutsch, I suggest, is also part of this trend though Dahl does not mention him;
3. Wartime applications of the social sciences (cf. Simpson, 2003);
4. Funding priorities of the Social Science Research Council that focused on more scientific methods (Ross, 1991);
5. Better survey methods that allowed for a more granular application of statistics that aggregated data; and,
6. The influence of American philanthropic foundations (cf. Hauptmann, 2012).

These developments fit with the development of scientism, a faith in scientific knowledge's power, that ran through the twentieth-century American social sciences.

Historian Dorothy Ross attributes the turn toward scientism to the leadership of Charles Merriam. The University of Chicago professor helped design the social sciences after World War I. Initially engaged in progressive politics, Merriam turned away from politics and the progressive movement led him to a view of the social sciences that mirrored the natural sciences. According to Ross (1991), Merriam's late program of research "proposed a science defined by 'method,' orientated to 'control' and sustained by organized professional structures to promote research" (p. 396). Merriam's program made its way into the New Political Science through his disciple Harold Lasswell, who became "the heir of Merriam's technological imagination" (p. 455); "Lasswell became the father of the 1950s behavioral movement, in political science, an extension in elevation of scientism in the profession, and by that lineage Merriam was rightly the grandfather" (p. 457). The New Political Science manifested Lasswell's vision for the field and created the possibilities for computing as a political epistemology.

Harold Lasswell and the A-bomb of the Social Sciences

Harold Lasswell was a defining figure in political science, communication studies, and policy studies. Lasswell not only led American academia, he also collapsed divisions between the state and the research community.

During World War II, he helped formulate techniques of psychological warfare at the War Communications Division of the Library of Congress (along with his student Ithiel de Sola Pool) (Simpson, 2003). After the War, Lasswell was a leader in American social science and became president of the American Political Science Association (APSA) in 1956.

Lasswell outlined his vision for the field in his inaugural speech. Building on Merriam's attempts at integrating the human and natural sciences, Lasswell began by declaring, "my intention is to consider political science as a discipline and as a profession in relation to the impact of the physical and biological and of engineering upon the life of man" (1956, p. 961). Behavioralism would be his way to solidify the scientific foundations of the field at a time when the American government needed insights into growing complexity and risk. He continues, "It is trite to acknowledge that for years we have lived in the afterglow of a mushroom cloud and in the midst of an arms race of unprecedented gravity" (p. 961). Political science, particularly in its behavioral mood, would be instrumental in this arms race.

War was a key frame to legitimate Lasswell's vision for political science. As Nobel prize–winning American experimental physicist Luis Alvarez suggested to the Pentagon in 1961, "World War III... might well have to be considered the social scientists' war" (quoted in Rohde, 2013, p. 10). The goal was not necessarily waging better war but rather waging what Lloyd Etheredge (2016) called a "humane approach" to politics (cf. Wolfe, 2018). Better weapons might lead to more humane wars. Speaking to journalist and close friend of the Simulmatics Corporation Thomas Morgan in 1961, Lasswell later suggested, "if we want an open society in the future, we are going to have to plan for it. If we do, I think we have a *fighting* chance" [italics added] (quoted in Morgan, 1961, p. 57).

What would be the weapon in this fight? What would be the weapon of choice for behavioralists and Lasswell's followers? If the atom bomb was the weapon of World War II, then the computer might be the weapon of World War III. As Jennifer Light (2008) notes in her history of computing in politics, "first developed as calculating machines and quickly applied to forecasting an atomic blast, computers soon took on a new identity as modelling machines, helping communities of professionals to analyze complex structures and scenarios to anticipate future events" (p. 348). At the time of Lasswell's speech, computers had gone mainstream. In 1952, CBS contracted Remington Rand and its UNIVAC computer to forecast election results. After UNIVAC predicted an overwhelming Eisenhower win, CBS decided not to air the prediction. It turned out to be correct. By the next election, all major broadcasters used computers for their election night coverage (Chinoy, 2010; Lepore, 2018, p. 559). In tandem, the US Census and the Social Science Research Council had begun to explore how computers could better make available data for analysis (Kraus, 2013).

Social sciences would create their own weapon too: the Simulmatics Corporation. It was an "A-bomb of the social sciences" according to Harold Lasswell in a magazine article that doubled as promotion for the new company. Simulmatics, he continued, was a breakthrough comparable to "what happened at Stagg Field" (quoted in Morgan, 1961, p. 53). Lasswell was referring to Simulmatics' corporation offerings—its People Machine—that built on the company's early research for the 1960 Kennedy campaign, where computer simulations were used to advise a political party on how voters might respond to issues. Lasswell sat on the company's first Advisory Council along with Paul Lazarsfeld, Morris Janowitz, and John Tukey. The project was a culmination of the coming together of scientism, behavioralism, and the New Political Science.

Simulmatics Corporation: The Social Sciences' Stagg Field

The Simulmatics Corporation began as a political consultancy in 1959.[3] The company sold itself as a gateway for companys and federal agencies to the behavioralism sciences. Where Jill Lepore (2020) tells the story of the company's founding in response to the failures of Democratic Presidential Candidate Adlai Stevenson, I emphasize its links to the New Political Science and its first project, research for the 1960 camapaign to elect John F. Kennedy as President.

Simulmatics drew on forecasting and survey data along with political behavioralism. First, Simulmatics attempted to predict voter attitudes based on historical data. By 1959, political scientist Harold Gosnell (a collaborator with Merriam) and pollster Louis Bean had helped popularize the idea that elections could be predicted by statistics. Bean was the lone pollster to predict Truman's 1948 electoral win, beating his rival pollsters Elmo Roper and George Gallup (Rosenof, 1999). Rather than use opinion polling, Bean *forecast* the election results using demographic and statistical trends to measure the political tides. These tides, Bean (1948) wrote,

> are like the unsubstantiated sea serpent that appears periodically along the Atlantic coast. They are discussed every year by popular political analysts and commentators, but without much factual demonstration. (p. 12)

Voting trends were some of the facts Bean analyzed to measure these tides in his 1948 book *How to Predict an Election*, published with the encouragement of Paul Lazarsfeld.

Where Bean used demographic statistics to plot voter trends, Simulmatics could use survey data due to the maturation of the field. The production of public opinion had advanced considerably since the straw polls at the turn of the twentieth century. Surveys about the average American—usually assumed to be a white male—had gained institutional legitimacy, necessary for informed market and government research (Igo, 2007). Ongoing survey research provided a new way to measure the political tides, and Simulmatics made use of these newly public data collections. In 1947, pollster Elmo Roper donated his data to Williams College, creating one of the first repositories of social science data. By 1957, the collection had become the Roper Public Opinion Research Center. Pool and others arranged to have access to the Center's surveys, under the agreement that their opponents in the Republican Party had the same access (which they did not use). Survey data became the basis for computer simulation soon after. William McPhee, coauthor of Voting: A Study of Opinion Formation in a Presidential Campaign with Bernard R. Berelson and Paul F. Lazarsfeld, 3 started work on a voter simulator at the Bureau of Applied Social Research at Columbia University by 1960. McPhee worked with Simulmatics to develop this model in its early political consultancy.

Behavioralism eased the slippage from survey to simulation. Citing Bernard Berelson, Paul F. Lazarsfeld, and William McPhee (1954), Simulmatics proposed the existence of "a human tendency to maintain a subjective consistency in orientation to the world" (Pool, Abelson, & Popkin, 1964, p. 9). Consistency, Pool and his colleagues explained, can be rather difficult to maintain in politics. Voters face many decisions that might cause inconsistencies. A desire to maintain consistency might cause a voter to switch party support, usually late in the campaign. In other words, the elusive swing voter could be found and modelled by looking for voters with contradictory opinions and forecasting whether the *cross-pressure* might cause a change in behavior.

The synthesis of these trends led Simulmatics to develop a simulation that animated survey data to predict changes in voting due to interactions between issues and social variables. That sounds mechanical, but the inner workings of the project were human after all. Before the simulation, Simulmatics made numerous interpretations to create a workable database of political attitudes. They spent the summer of 1959 integrating the code books and punch cards from 65[4] surveys conducted between 1952 and 1960. It was an "arduous task" that resulted in what might have been the first political database (Pool & Abelson, 1961, p. 168) (Table 4.1).

The matrix arranged the opinions of 480 voter types on 52 issues. The 480 types were "defined by socio-economic characteristics." Pool and Abelson explained, "a single voter type might be 'Eastern, metropolitan, lower-income, white, Catholic, female Democrats.' Another might be, 'Border state, rural, upper-income, white, Protestant, male Independents.'" In effect, each voter type was a composite of region, race, gender, and political disposition. Notably, voter types did not include education, age, or specific location. Voter types, instead, fit into one of four abstract regions. Each voter type had "opinions" on what Simulmatics called *issue clusters*. For each intersection of voter type and issue cluster, the databank recorded their occurrence in the population and their attitude (Pool et al., 1964, pp. 30–31).

The matrix masked the arduous interpretive work that created it. Voter types only approximated the survey results, since as Pool et al. (1964) write, "it will be noted that we did not use all possible combinations of all variables, which would have given us some 3,600 voter types, many of which would have been infinitely small" (p. 27). Issue cluster was "private jargon" that referred to their interpretation of multiple survey responses about opinions on political matters; "most of these were political issues, such as foreign aid, attitudes toward the United Nations, and McCarthyism" (p. 27).

What's notable in this moment is the slippage between voter type and voter. Simulmatics' methods directly acknowledge the influence of the seminal works in American political behavior, *Voting* from 1954 by Bernard Berelson, Paul F. Lazarsfeld, and Simulmatic's own William N. McPhee and *The American Voter* from 1960 by Angus Campbell, Philip

Table 4.1 Structure of the Simulmatics 1960 Model of the American Electorate reproduced from the original

In each of 4 regions:	7 SES and City-Size Levels	By Sex, Religion, Ethnicity																		
		Protestant Males			Protestant Females			Catholic Males			Catholic Females			Jews			Negroes			
South	1. A Urban	R	D	I	R	D	I	R	D	I	R	D	I	R	D	I	R	D	I	
	2. A + B Town	R	D	I	R	D	I	R	D	I	R	D	I							
East	3. A + B Rural	R	D	I	R	D	I	R	D	I	R	D	I							
	4. B Urban	R	D	I	R	D	I	R	D	I	R	D	I	R	D	I	R	D	I	
Midwest	5. C Urban	R	D	I	R	D	I	R	D	I	R	D	I							
	6. C Town	R	D	I	R	D	I	R	D	I	R	D	I							
West	7. C Rural	R	D	I	R	D	I	R	D	I	R	D	I							
4X																	96	cells		= 384 cells
In 1 region:	1 + 2 + 3 combined	R	D	I	R	D	I	R	D	I	R	D	I	R	D	I	R	D	I	
Border	4 + 5 + 6 + 7 combined	R	D	I	R	D	I	R	D	I	R	D	I	R	D	I	R	D	I	
1 X																	36	cells		= 36 cells

		Rep.	Dem.	Ind.	
Add, in all	1. Protestants without SES rating in non-labor-force families	R	D	I	
5 regions	2. Catholics without SES reating in non-labor-fource families	R	D	I	
	3. Persons of no religion	R	D	I	
	4. Persons of other religion	R	D	I	
5X				12 cells	= 60 cells
					480 cells

*Key: R means Republican; D means Democratic; I means Independent.
A means professional, executive, and managerial occupations; B means white-collar occupations; C means blue-collar occupations
Urban refers to metropolitan areas exceeding 100,000 population; town refers to communities between 5000 and 100,000; rural refers to places under 5000

Converse, Warren Miller, and Donald E. Stokes. Both studies undermined the idea of individual voter behavior, suggesting instead that voting patterns could be predicted by group and partisan affiliations. These studies established a view to this day that individual choice matters less than group identity and partisanship (Achen & Bartels, 2017, pp. 222–224). By creating more dynamic ways to interact with the aggregate, Simulmatics demonstrated that the voter could be modelled without needing to be understood. Pressures between group identities, not individual opinions, animated the simulations. The behavior of voters not only became the behavior of voter types, but these models were dynamic and replaced political decision-making with probable outcomes.

Simulmatics delivered its first report to the Democratic National Committee just before its 1960 Convention (Lepore, 2018, pp. 598–599). Their first report focused on African Americans, marking a notable change in the object of public opinion; prior survey research largely ignored African Americans. Historian Susan Igo (2007) notes that the dominant pollsters George Gallup and Elmo Roper "underrepresented women, African Americans, laborers, and the poor in their samples" (p. 139). Indeed, the first *Middletown* survey of the 1920s excluded responses from African Americans (p. 57). The first Simulmatics report marks an important turn where race became a significant variable that divided calculations of the American public. The report found that non-voting was less of a concern than expected, and that African Americans might vote more frequently than might have been expected at the time. For Pool and others, the report proved that their data could provide insights into smaller subsets of the American population. While the first report did not involve computer simulation, it marked an early use of new computer technology to address emerging urban and racial issues in the US (McIlwain, 2020, pp. 214–217).

After the convention, the Kennedy campaign commissioned three other reports "on the image of Kennedy, the image of Nixon, and foreign policy as a campaign issue" (Pool et al., 1964, p. 18). These reports drew on the behavioral theory of cross-pressure discussed above. To study the religion issue, Simulmatics grouped its "set of 480 voter-types into 9 possible cross-pressure subsets arising from a 3 × 3 classification on religion and party" reproduced in Table 4.2 (Pool et al., 1964, p. 46). Cross-pressure here meant the tensions between party and religion. For each subset, Simulmatics predicted behavior with special

Table 4.2 Reproduced from Pool et al. (1964, p. 46)

Cross pressure patterns			
	Republicans	*Democrats*	*Independents*
Protestants	(1)	X (2)	(2)
Catholics	X (4)	(3)	(3)
Other	(4)	(5)	(5)

attention to those cells marked X: Democratic Protestants and Republican Catholics. Some simulations were simple. Protestant Republicans, for example, "would vote exactly as they did the last time" (p. 47). For most other groups, Simulmatics developed a unique equation to estimate turnout that required a guess about both probable behavior and what data could be an effective proxy for anti-Catholicism, given the lack of a direct question in its sample of surveys. Simulmatics "disregarded" the religion of African Americans, unlike the unstated "White" voters classified by religion and party (p. 53). These accommodations were a different kind of interpretative work. Where survey research might have discarded non-White voters, Simulmatics re-inscribed race by building different operating assumptions into the model.

Though much of the simulation was manual, Simulmatics' work here marks the beginning of when interests and values were used to model group behavior. These models in turn helped campaigns forecast reactions to future positions and platforms. Behavior, in other words, could be calculated and stand-in for stated opinion. This was a moment where the past behavior of individuals became autonomous, capable of behaving in ways never encountered by the fleshy double.

These innovations had a modest effect on the campaign, if any. Simulmatics did not change campaign strategy, and there is no evidence that subsequent campaigns of the 1960s turned again to simulations (Lepore, 2015). Pool never appears in iconic accounts of the 1960 election. Pool and Abelson (1961), reflecting on the campaign, noted that "while campaign strategy, except on a few points, conformed rather closely to the advice in the more than one hundred pages of the three reports, we know full well that this was by no means because of the reports. Others besides ourselves had similar ideas. Yet, if the reports strengthened right decisions on a few critical items, we would consider the investment justified" (pp. 173–174). Though Simulmatics tried to advise other campaigns, they never found another high-profile candidate like the Kennedy Campaign. The company had plenty of work elsewhere.

The Simulmatics Corporation moved into many directions—the Vietnam war effort, marketing, building simulation games—that drew on its mathematical models of behavior. The company continued to collect more survey data and advise its clients about how to study behavior more scientifically. James S. Coleman, a sociologist prominent for introducing mathematical modelling to the field, assisted Simulmatics in developing games as well as its Dynamark analysis for advertising and marketing on Madison Avenue. In Vietnam, Simulmatics earned approximately $24 million USD in ARPA contracts for data science, such as gauging public opinion about the US occupation of Vietnamese villages (Rohde, 2011). Foreign populations were not just calculated in Vietnam. In its ten-year run, Simulmatics modelled the behaviors of Americans, Venezuelans, and the Vietnamese. Results were mixed. ARPA and military records described a pained relationship with Simulmatics involving Vietnam with projects not meeting contractual or scientific expectations (Weinberger, 2017, pp. 180–181). By 1970, the corporation went bankrupt, nearly acquired by Mathematica, the company cofounded by Oskar Morgenstern (Lepore, 2020, p. 384n65). By then, the political ground had shifted with the Democrats out of the White House following Nixon's win in 1968. Kissinger's realpolitik replaced McNamara's whiz kids. The prospects of a humane war in Vietnam became a farce.

Simulmatics' Long Afterglow

Simulmatics generated some public debate about the consequences of political simulation. Its possible misuses fueled the plot of the novel *The 480* by surfer-political scientist-novelist Eugene Burdick. Named after Simulmatics' 480 voter types, Burdick's bestselling novel described a presidential campaign that used computer modelling to manipulate the public—a dystopian scenario not far off from the present-day worries mentioned in the introduction (Anderson, 2018, pp. 89–92). Historian Jill Lepore (2018) nicely captures Burdick's criticism that "if voters didn't profess ideologies, if they had no idea of the meaning of the words 'liberal' or 'conservative,' they could nevertheless be sorting into ideological piles, based on their identities" (p. 599). Simulmatics thought otherwise. Writing in the introduction to a 1964 book about the project, Pool and his collaborators Robert Abelson and Samuel Popkin (1964) noted that the project "has been subject to a number of sensational newspaper and magazine articles and even of a work of fiction" citing Burdick and promising their book would "correct these lurid fantasies" (p. 1).

The project had its critics in academia, including Noam Chomsky and earlier Howard B. White, former dean of the New School. White coined the phrase the New Political Science. Writing in the summer 1961 issue of *Social Research*, he argued that these tools enabled better manipulation of voters, and he later cited Simulmatics as a key example of the New Political Science. White did not think voter manipulation was new, merely improved. As he wrote, "there is nothing new in manipulated opinion and engineered consent.... Even the sheer bulk of distortion is not altogether news, merely more refined" (1961, p. 150). "What is new," White continued, "is the acceptability, the mere taken-for-grantedness of these things." What he called a New Political Science[5] accepted these innovations as mere tools and not profound revisions to the discipline's normative project. He worried this "value-free" political science would legitimate social manipulation. Pool rejected these claims in a rejoinder published the following year in the same journal (Pool, 1962), and White defended his argument in a response (White, 1962).

Simulmatics was celebrated in the behavioral sciences. The Simulmatics Project became a story repeated in the annals of simulation and modelling in the social sciences (Guetzkow, 1962; IBM Scientific Computing Symposium on Simulation Models and Gaming & International Business Machines Corporation, 1964). A 1965 special issue of the *American Behavioral Scientist*, only eight years old at the time, celebrated the work of Simulmatics as the "benchmark in the theory and instrumentation of the social sciences" (de Grazia, 1965, p. 2). The editorial was written by Alfred de Grazia, an early editor of the journal. A staunch believer in the firm, he subsequently led Simulmatics' ill-fated operation in Saigon for a time (Weinberger, 2017, pp. 174–182). Articles included Simulmatics studies of business systems, communications, and international relations as well as a postscript on the 1964 election. Harold Lasswell wrote the issue's introduction entitled "The Shape of the Future." In no uncertain terms, he explained that the power, and danger, of Simulmatics methods was when "new advances in technique make it possible to give the leaders of rival governments, political parties and pressure groups improved advice for managing their campaigns to influence public judgment of candidates, issues and organization" (Lasswell, 1965, p. 3). Perhaps in response to critics of this power like White and Burdick, Lasswell maintains that "officers of the Simulmatics Corporation are acting responsibly" (1965, p. 3). What is missing from this glimpse of the future is any sign that Simulmatics would be bankrupt four years later, and punch cards would be burned in opposition to this political technology.

In spite of its commercial failure, Simulmatics exemplified a move to use computers for forecasting and model testing in the social sciences (cf. Rhode, 2017). Certainly, the company had many contemporaries. Jay Forrester, also at MIT, developed the DYNAMO (DYNAmic Models) programming language at the MIT Computation Center that eventually resulted in the 1972 report "Limits of Growth" (Baker, 2019). MIT's Compatible Time-Sharing System (CTSS) ran simulations scripted in GPSS and OP-3, another simulation language developed at MIT (Greenberger, Jones, Morris, & Ness, 1965). These are a few American examples of the early field of computer simulations and simulation languages that developed into its own subfield.

Given this afterglow, Simulmatics and its voter types should be seen as *one* predecessor to today's Tanjo Animated Personas. The similarities are striking. Blue State Digital explains that they are "based on data. This data can include solely what is publicly available, such as economic purchase data, electoral rolls, and market segmentations, or it can also include an organization's own anonymized customer data, housed within their own technical environment." If data informs models, then Simulmatics signals an important moment when computation enabled a reevaluation of prior research. In its case, Simulmatics found value in the survey archives of the Roper Center. Today, TAPs are refined by a "machine learning system, along with a human analyst, [that] generates a list of topics, areas of interest, specific interests, and preferences that are relevant to the persona" to generate affiliations akin to issue clusters. Each TAP has a score attached to each interest, similar to the scores used by Simulmatics attached to voter types.

Political simulations, either in 1961 or 2019, promise something akin to *thin citizenship*. Phillip N. Howard (2006) describes thin citizenship as when data functions as a proxy for the voter. Blue State Digital explains that personas "are based on the hypothesis that humans' distinct personalities and unique interests can predict how they'll react to content. We can simulate these interests and conduct testing with them in a way that can augment, or sometimes be as valid as, results from focus groups and surveys." These selling points could just as easily be lifted from a Simulmatics brochure's discussion for its marketing products like Dynamark, a computer program "used to determine the relative value of different promotional activities and their effects upon the attitudes of different subgroups of the population" (Simulmatics, 1961).

TAPs, however, promise to be a much more integral part of a campaign than Simulmatics was. Even though Pool et al. (1964) suggested that the 1960 experiment had merit due to providing "on demand research concerning key issues" (p. 23), the experiment took place at the margins. Further, Simulmatics relied on survey research only for its political simulation. I now turn to the case of Project Cambridge, which provides a way to understand the scale of computers as a political epistemology.

Project Cambridge

Project Cambridge was part of Pool's ongoing work on political simulation. As Simulmatics suffered financially, Pool began to collaborate with a professor returning to MIT, J. C. R. Licklider. Licklider is one of the key figures and funders of modern computing. By 1967, he had returned to MIT after working at the Advanced Research Projects Agency (ARPA) in 1964 followed by a stint at IBM. His research at the time nicely complemented Pool's own interests in data and polling. Licklider was developing the idea of computer resources that he would come to call "libraries of the future," while advocating for better connectivity to the databanks housed by information utilities—a vision not so far off from the design of the seminal ARPANET (Licklider, 1969). Where Simulmatics showed the utility of survey research for computer simulation, Licklider recognized the promise of digital data in general for computing. Pool and Licklider, then, began to collaborate on a project to better collect and operationalize data in government and politics, which became known as Project Cambridge.

Project Cambridge integrated, or at least proposed to integrate, computational social science into decision-making. Its first goal consisted of developing better tools to manage and analyze data that, overall, would "be a powerful methodology for the behavioral sciences." When integrated into public policy, these tools would aid "in the understanding of human interactions and in the prediction of the performance of social systems" (Project Cambridge, 1969). Perhaps most telling is the list of data sources in the initial proposal, which included data collected from the project's various members, such as:

1. International data sets on public opinion, national statistics and demographics, communications and propaganda efforts, as well as armament spending; and
2. Domestic data sets on US economic statistics and demographic statistics, including public opinion polls from the Roper Center.

Project Cambridge, then, was an early attempt to construct a unified system to manage databases. A project like Simulmatics would be just one of many databases in the system, ideally used in connection with each other.

The project sought to mobilize or animate its databases as interactive models. This side of the project had a cybernetic air not unlike the artificial TAPs. Looking to early work in artificial intelligence for inspiration, the project called these models *agents*. Project Director Douwe Yntema, as Andrew Mamo (2011) writes in an excellent dissertation,

> noted the similarity between this agent and the work of AI researcher Oliver Selfridge. While this agent was by no means the autonomous intelligence that motivated the most hyped AI research, it grew directly out of the tradition of automating simple decision-making, and of giving machines the ability to direct themselves. (p. 178; cf. McKelvey, 2018)

Project Cambridge, by 1974, included Pool's General Implicator, a textual analysis tool, as well as SURVEIR, a new data management tool for the Roper Center data. These projects proved to be more a result of statistical computing than artificial intelligence, but the desire certainly endured to use computers as a way to better model humans and societies.

The project also brought together many researchers associated with the New Political Science. Licklider served as principal investigator, but the project was led by Douwe Yntema, senior research associate in psychology at Harvard and senior lecturer at the MIT Sloan School of Management. These two, along with Pool, were only a small part of a massive academic project that listed more than 150 participants, including Karl Deutsch, in its first annual report.

Such ambition was another trend of the 1960s. Beginning in 1963, the US Census Bureau and the Social Sciences Research Council considered ways to convert federal statistics into databases for researchers. When made aware of the project, the press reacted poorly, raising privacy and surveillance concerns. The *Pittsburgh Post-Gazette*, for example, ran the headline "Computer as Big Brother" in 1966. That the project ultimately failed in part due to this public reaction was a warning unheeded by Project Cambridge (Kraus, 2013).

Project Cambridge was controversial from the beginning. As Mamo (2011) writes, the project had two problems: "defense patronage, which ran afoul of Vietnam-era student politics, and the fear that collections of data and analytical tools to parse this data would erode individual privacy" (p. 173). Computing was seen then, and perhaps again now, as a powerful tool of the state (Turner, 2006). Harvard withdrew direct participation in the project due to public outrage (Mamo, 2011, pp. 165–175).

While Licklider and Pool publicly made efforts to distance the project from the government, conceptually Project Cambridge resembled the kind of "on-demand" research described by Pool. It also resembled the work of Karl Deutsch, where digital agents could become the nervous system of a new cybernetic vision of government. Deutsch served as a member throughout the project and was also a member of the Advisory Committee on Policy at the time of the project's renewal in 1971. He defended the project against criticism from the student press about its relationship with the government and the Vietnam War. Writing to the *Harvard Independent* in the fall of 1969, Deutsch argued, "At the present time, I think mankind is more threatened by ignorance or errors of the American or Soviet or Chinese government than it would be by an increase in the social science knowledge of any of these governments" (quoted in Mamo, 2011, p. 40). The computer was, in other words, the more humane approach to political realities.

Deutsch's comments reflect his interest in improving the science of the social sciences. His 1963 book *The Nerves of Government* explicitly discusses the importance of models for the future of political science, moving from classical models to innovations in gaming and eventually to cybernetics. In fact, the book popularized cybernetics to the field. It ends with a flow chart labelled "A Crude Model: A Functional Diagram of Information Flow in Foreign Policy Decisions." This diagram, according to Orit Halpern (2014), was inspired by computer programming; she explains that in it there "are no consolidated entities, only inputs, outputs and 'screens' that act to obstruct, or divert, incoming data" (p. 189). Where Halpern situates the chart in the larger reformulation of data through cybernetics and governance via neural networks, I wish to emphasize this diagram, the book, and Project Cambridge as a shared application of cybernetic thinking to politics itself. This integration of computing as both a model and a screen for politics was integral to Project Cambridge. Indeed, a second draft of the "Project Cambridge Proposal," before Harvard withdrew its institutional support (see Lepore, pp. 287–288), repeatedly mentions Deutsch and his approach to data as inspiration and a resource to be mobilized. In other words, Deutsch and Project Cambridge conceptually integrated simulation into the political system, as part of a collective intelligence or neural network designed to optimize governance.

Such close integration with government never amounted to much. The project was always in a bind: "It needed to claim a defence mission to satisfy the Mansfield Amendment and receive funding, but it also needed to deny that very same purpose in order to attract researchers" (Mamo, 2011, p. 172). It also faced intractable technical problems, such as developing on the experimental MULTICS operating system and, more practically, coordinating its hodgepodge of data, models, and researchers into one unified research environment. Tackling this latter problem became the project's lasting contribution. Project Cambridge partially initiated the formulation of the computational social sciences. Simultaneously, Stanford University developed its own program for computational social sciences, the Statistical Package for the Social Sciences (SPSS), still in use today (Uprichard, Burrows, & Byrne, 2008). Project Cambridge contrasted itself with SPSS, seeking to be a more radical innovation that became known as the Consistent System (CS) (Klensin & Yntema, 1981; Yntema et al., 1972). CS was "a collection of programs for interactive use in the behavioral sciences" that included "a powerful data base management system... with a variety of statistical and other tools" (Dawson, Klensin, & Yntema, 1980, p. 170). Though not as popular as SPSS or FORTRAN, Project Cambridge's legacy enabled the crystallization of computational modelling in the social sciences.

While Project Cambridge had a direct influence on the tools of data science, it also furthered the breakdowns begun by the Simulmatics Corporation. Simulmatics established that public opinion as data could be manipulated in a simulation that could have utility as an on-demand and responsive tool for parties and other decision makers. In one sense, this indicates a prehistory to the observed reliance on data to make decisions in campaigns, or what's called computational management (Kreiss, 2012). Project Cambridge further entrenched the New Political Science to funders, peers, and the public as the vanguard of the field. Even as its ambitions outstripped its technical output, Project Cambridge created a consistency beyond its Consistent System. The project pushed the behavioral sciences beyond survey research into integrated databases that in turn could train computational agents to stand-in for political and voter behavior.

Conclusion

Simulmatics and Project Cambridge, as well as the history that led to their development, provide a prehistory to artificial intelligence in politics. Through these projects, the utility of AI to politics became imaginable. In doing so, political science joins the ranks of what others call the *cyborg sciences* (Halpern, 2014; Haraway, 1985; Mirowski, 2002). This transformation was marked by looking at politics through computers, or what Katherine Hayles (1999) calls *reflexivity*: "the movement whereby that which has been used to generate a system is made, through a changed perspective, to become part of the system it generates" (p. 8). As Donna Haraway (2016), quoting Marilyn Strathern, reminds me "it matters what ideas we used to think other ideas (with)" (p. 12).

The other Cambridge analytics turn re-modelled what John Durham Peters calls the politics of counting. "Democracy," Peters (2001) writes, "establishes justice and legitimacy through a social force, the majority, which exists only by way of math" (p. 434). Numbers legitimate democratic institutions as well as represent the public majority back to the public: "Numbers are... uniquely universal and uniquely vacuous: They do not care what they are counting. Their impersonality can be both godlike and demonic. Numbers can model a serene indifference to the world of human things" (p. 435). Simulmatics and Project Cambridge helped change the numerical epistemology by integrating computers, data, and behavioral theory. Democracy was still about the numbers. Ones and zeros, rather than polls and tallies, now functioned as political representation.

Reformatting politics led to technical not democratic change. The blowback felt by Project Cambridge and Simulmatics demonstrates public concern about technology out of control, not in the public service. Those feelings were widespread in popular culture and only mitigated by the rise of personal computing (Rankin, 2018; Turner, 2006). Pool's ambitions make the limitations of this cybernetic turn all the more apparent—a warning applicable to artificial intelligence. These problems are well stated in E. B. White's critical article about the New Political Science. To Lasswell's characterization of the Simulmatics as the A-Bomb of the social sciences, White (1961) asked "why political scientists want so much to believe that kind of statement that they dare make it" (p. 150). He ends with perhaps the most damning of questions for the claimed innovation: "If Lasswell and Pool really believe that they have an A-bomb, are they willing to leave its powers to advertisers?" Pool did just that, selling Simulmatics to advertising and marketing firms as well as to the US military in Vietnam where the company reported on villagers' opinions of the American occupation.

We might ask the same questions for AI in politics? Indebted to a fifty-year history, benefitting from tremendous concentrations of capital—be it financial, symbolic, or informational—and trusted to envision a new society through its innovations, the bulk of AI seems to be applied to better marketing and consumer experiences. The revolutionary potential of TAPs ultimately seems only to be better message testing in advertising. Where is the AI for good, or a model for a better politics?

The task for a critical AI studies might be to reimagine its political function. To this end, my history offers tragedy as much as critique. Scientists tried and failed to use computers to create a more humane politics; instead, their innovations were enlisted in new campaigns of American imperialism. Yet, the alternative is to wish for simpler times as seen in White's own normative framework. White had strong opinions about the nature of democracy. In rallying against a value-free political science, he signals a vision of politics as a rarefied space of important decisions, similar to philosopher Hannah Arendt's. As he writes, "of course a political decision takes a risk—but it can be considered irrational only if the voters do not care to consider the object of voting as related to the common good." Political decisions matter, but they won't matter "if we are educated to restrict reason to the kind of thing you use to decide whether to spend the extra fifteen cents for imported beer" (White, 1961, p. 134). White instead wanted to return politics to an even more abstract and intangible space than the banks of a computer. Today, White's vision for democracy seems just as elusive and invites a certain curiosity Pool's cold pragmatism and others building computers for a *humane politics* without defending them. Can a critical studies of AI find a radical politics for these machines aware of what past searches for new weapons in the past have done?

Notes

1 I learned that the Simulmatics Corporation was the subject of Dr. Jill Lepore's new book *If Then: How the Simulmatics Corporation Invented the Future* after submitting this chapter. Dr. Lepore's tremendous historical work offers a detailed, lively account of the company's history including its start discussed here. Interested readers should refer to the Dr. Lepore's book for a deeper history of the company. Thanks to Dr. Lepore for her kind reply and helpful comments. Any similarities are coincidental. Any errors are my own.

2 Behavioralism here should not be confused with the similarly named political behaviorism (Karpf, Kreiss, Nielsen, & Powers, 2015, p. 1892n5).

3 Samuel Popkin continued his work in the field of political polling, helping to popular low-information rationality in voter behavior.

4 The number is either 65 or 66. In their book, Pool, Abelson, and Popkin state they used 65 surveys, but they state 66 surveys in their 1961 article in *Public Opinion Quarterly*.

5 Not to be confused with the Caucus for a New Political Science organized at the annual meeting of the American Political Science Association in 1967. This new political science explicitly opposed the rise of behavioralism and state-sponsored research (Dryzek, 2006).

References

Achen, C. H., & Bartels, L. M. (2017). *Democracy for realists: Why elections do not produce responsive government*. Princeton University Press.

Amadae, S. M. (2003). *Rationalizing capitalist democracy: The Cold War origins of rational choice liberalism*. University of Chicago Press.

Anderson, B. (2017, February 12). The rise of the weaponized AI propaganda machine. *Scout: Science Fiction + Journalism*. https://medium.com/join-scout/the-rise-of-the-weaponized-ai-propaganda-machine-86dac61668b#.n8fjxsof5.

Anderson, C. W. (2018). *Apostles of certainty: Data journalism and the politics of doubt*. Oxford University Press.

Baker, K. (2019). Model metropolis. *Logic Magazine*, *6*. https://logicmag.io/play/model-metropolis/.

Baldwin-Philippi, J. (2017). The myths of data-driven campaigning. *Political Communication, 34*(4), 627–633. https://doi.org/10.1080/10584609.2017.1372999.

Barber, B. R. (2006). The politics of political science: "Value-free" theory and the Wolin-Strauss dust-up of 1963. *American Political Science Review, 100*(4), 539–545.

Bean, L. H. (1948). *How to predict elections*. A. A. Knopf.

Berelson, B. R., Lazarsfeld, P. F., & McPhee, W. N. (1954). *Voting: A study of opinion formation in a presidential campaign*. University of Chicago Press.

Blue State Digital. (2018, May 18). *What can AI teach brands about customer-centric marketing?* Blue State Digital. https://www.bluestatedigital.com/ideas/ai-customer-marketing/.

Chessen, M. (2017). *The MADCOM future: How artificial intelligence will enhance computational propaganda, reprogram human culture, and threaten democracy ... and what can be done about it*. Atlantic Council. https://www.jstor.org/stable/resrep03728.

Chinoy, I. (2010). *Battle of the brains: Election-night forecasting at the dawn of the computer age* (Doctoral dissertation, University of Maryland). https://drum.lib.umd.edu/handle/1903/10504.

Cohen-Cole, J. (2008). Cybernetics and the machinery of rationality. *The British Journal for the History of Science, 41*(1), 109–114.

Dahl, R. A. (1961). The behavioral approach in political science: Epitaph for a monument to a successful protest. *American Political Science Review, 55*(4), 763–772.

Dawson, R., Klensin, J. C., & Yntema, D. B. (1980). The consistent system. *The American Statistician, 34*(3), 169–176. https://doi.org/10.2307/2683876.

de Grazia, A. (1965). Social research with the computer. *American Behavioral Scientist, 8*(9), 2. https://doi.org/10.1177/000276426500800901.

Deutsch, K. W. (1963). *The nerves of government*. Free Press.

Dryzek, J. S. (2006). Revolutions without enemies: Key transformations in political science. *American Political Science Review, 100*(4), 487–492. https://doi.org/10.1017/S0003055406062332.

Etheredge, L. S. (Ed.). (2016). *Humane politics and methods of inquiry*. Routledge.

Greenberger, M., Jones, M. M., Morris, J. R., & Ness, D. N. (1965). *On-line computation and simulation: The OPS-3 system*. MIT Press.

Guetzkow, H. S. (Ed.). (1962). *Simulation in social science: Readings*. Prentice-Hall.

Gunnell, J. G. (1993). *The descent of political theory: The genealogy of an American vocation*. University of Chicago Press.

Gunnell, J. G. (2004). The real revolution in political science. *PS: Political Science and Politics, 37*(1), 47–50.

Halpern, O. (2014). *Beautiful data: A history of vision and reason since 1945*. Duke University Press.

Haraway, D. J. (1985). Manifesto for cyborgs: Science, technology, and socialist feminism in the 1980s. *Socialist Review, 80*, 65–108.

Haraway, D. J. (2016). *Staying with the trouble: Making kin in the Chthulucene*. Duke University Press.

Hauptmann, E. (2012). The Ford Foundation and the rise of behavioralism in political science. *Journal of the History of the Behavioral Sciences, 48*(2), 154–173. https://doi.org/10.1002/jhbs.21515.

Hayles, N. K. (1999). *How we became posthuman: Virtual bodies in cybernetics, literature, and informatics*. University of Chicago Press.

Howard, P. N. (2006). *New media campaigns and the managed citizen*. Cambridge University Press.

IBM Scientific Computing Symposium on Simulation Models and Gaming, & International Business Machines Corporation. (1964). *Symposium on simulation models and gaming*. IBM Data Processing Division.

Igo, S. E. (2007). *The averaged American: Surveys, citizens, and the making of a mass public*. Harvard University Press.

Karpf, D. (2016, October 31). *Preparing for the campaign tech bullshit season*. Civil Hall. https://civichall.org/civicist/preparing-campaign-tech-bullshit-season/.

Karpf, D., Kreiss, D., Nielsen, R. K., & Powers, M. (2015). The role of qualitative methods in political communication research: Past, present, and future. *International Journal of Communication, 9*, 1888–1906.

Klensin, J. C., & Yntema, D. B. (1981). Beyond the package: A new approach to behavioral science computing. *Social Science Information, 20*(4–5), 787–815. https://doi.org/10.1177/053901848102000407.

Kraus, R. (2013). Statistical déjà vu: The National Data Center proposal of 1965 and its descendants. *Journal of Privacy and Confidentiality*, *5*(1). https://doi.org/10.29012/jpc.v5i1.624.

Kreiss, D. (2012). *Taking our country back: The crafting of networked politics from Howard Dean to Barack Obama*. Oxford University Press.

Lasswell, H. D. (1956). The political science of science: An inquiry into the possible reconciliation of mastery and freedom. *American Political Science Review, 50*(4), 961–979.

Lasswell, H. D. (1965). Introduction: The shape of the future. *American Behavioral Scientist, 8*(9), 3. https://doi.org/10.1177/000276426500800902.

Lepore, J. (2015, November 16). Politics and the new machine. *The New Yorker*. https://www.newyorker.com/magazine/2015/11/16/politics-and-the-new-machine.

Lepore, J. (2018). *These truths: A history of the United States*. W. W. Norton.

Lepore, J. (2020). *If then: How simulmatics corporation invented the future*. Liveright.

Licklider, J. C. R. (1969). *Libraries of the future*. MIT Press.

Light, J. S. (2008). Taking games seriously. *Technology and Culture, 49*(2), 347–375.

Mamo, A. B. (2011). *Post-industrial engineering: Computer science and the organization of white-collar work, 1945–1975* (Doctoral dissertation). University of California, Berkeley.

McIlwain, C. D. (2020). *Black software: The Internet and racial justice, from the AfroNet to Black Lives Matter*. Oxford University Press.

McKelvey, F. (2018). *Internet daemons: Digital communications possessed*. University of Minnesota Press.

Mirowski, P. (2002). *Machine dreams: Economics becomes a cyborg science*. Cambridge University Press.

Monea, A., & Packer, J. (2016). Media genealogy: Technological and historical engagements of power—Introduction. *International Journal of Communication, 10,* 19.

Morgan, T. B. (1961, January). The people-machine. *Harper's Magazine, 222*(132), 53–57.

Peters, J. D. (2001). "The only proper scale of representation": The politics of statistics and stories. *Political Communication, 18*(4), 433–449. https://doi.org/10.1080/10584600152647137.

Pool, I. S. (1962). Comment for the "New Political Science" reexamined: A symposium. *Social Research, 29*(2), 127–130.

Pool, I. S., & Abelson, R. (1961). The Simulmatics Project. *The Public Opinion Quarterly, 25*(2), 167–183. https://doi.org/10.2307/2746702.

Pool, I. S., Abelson, R. P., & Popkin, S. L. (1964). *Candidates, issues, and strategies: A compusster simulation of the 1960 presidential election*. MIT Press.

Project Cambridge. (1969). *A proposal for the establishment of a program in computer analysis and modelling in the behavioral sciences*. Cambridge Project Records (AC.0285, Box 10). Massachusetts Institute of Technology Institute Archives and Special Collections.

Rankin, J. L. (2018). *A people's history of computing in the United States*. Harvard University Press.

Rohde, J. (2011). The last stand of the psychocultural Cold warriors: Military contract research in Vietnam. *Journal of the History of the Behavioral Sciences, 47*(3), 232–250. https://doi.org/10.1002/jhbs.20509.

Rohde, J. (2013). *Armed with expertise: The militarization of American social research during the Cold War*. Cornell University Press.

Rohde, J. (2017). Pax technologica: Computers, international affairs, and human reason in the cold war. *Isis, 108*(4), 792–813. https://doi.org/10.1086/695679.

Rosenof, T. (1999). The legend of Louis Bean: Political prophecy and the 1948 election. *The Historian, 62*(1), 63–78.

Ross, D. (1991). *The origins of American social science.* Cambridge University Press.

Simulmatics. (1961). *The Simulmatics Corporation* (Ithiel de Sola Pool papers, MC.0440, Box 67, Simulmatics: Correspondence). Massachusetts Institute of Technology Institute Archives and Special Collections.

Simpson, C. (2003). U.S. mass communication research, counterinsurgency, and "scientific" reality. In S. Braman (Ed.), *Communication researchers and policy-making*. MIT Press.

Turner, F. (2006). *From counterculture to cyberculture: Stewart Brand, the Whole Earth network, and the rise of digital utopianism.* University of Chicago Press.

Uprichard, E., Burrows, R., & Byrne, D. (2008). SPSS as an 'inscription device': From causality to description? *The Sociological Review, 56*(4), 606–622. https://doi.org/10.1111/j.1467-954X.2008.00807.x.

Weinberger, S. (2017). *The imagineers of war: The untold story of DARPA, the Pentagon agency that changed the world.* Vintage.

White, H. B. (1961). The processed voter and the New Political Science. *Social Research, 28*(2), 127–150.

White, H. B. (1962). Rejoinder for the "New Political Science" reexamined: A symposium. *Social Research, 29*(2), 142–156.

Wolfe, A. J. (2018). *Freedom's laboratory: The Cold War struggle for the soul of science.* Johns Hopkins University Press.

Yntema, D. B., Dempster, A. P., Gilbert, J. P., Klensin, J. C., McMains, W. M., Porter, W., … Wiesen, R. A. (1972). The Cambridge Project's consistent system. *Proceedings of the ACM Annual Conference, 2*, 976–977. https://doi.org/10.1145/800194.805886.

CHAPTER 5

Machinic Encounters: A Relational Approach to the Sociology of AI

Ceyda Yolgörmez

What is it that we call "social?" What is a society, and what are the implications of our conceptions of what societies consist of? How do studies of the "social" organize this understanding and construct the limits of our sociological imagination? Dealing with the social aspects of the technological, especially in the field of artificial intelligence (AI), is becoming increasingly urgent. For example, MIT Media Lab researchers recently proposed to construct a completely new field called *machine behavior* (Rahwan et al., 2019); their aim is to conceive of a field between the AI sciences and the social sciences in which the machine's behaviors and the social world around them mutually influence one another. The growing hype around AI (perhaps just before its third winter, as some would have it) has created much conversation about how these technologies are becoming part of everyday lives and legitimated existing academic debates over the social impact of these phenomena. Initiatives such as Data & Society and AI Now have been working on the social and political consequences of algorithmic cultures for the better part of the past decade.

C. Yolgörmez (✉)
Machine Agencies, Speculative Life Research Cluster,
Milieux Institute, Concordia University, Montreal, QC, Canada

© The Author(s) 2021

J. Roberge and M. Castelle (eds.), *The Cultural Life of Machine Learning*, https://doi.org/10.1007/978-3-030-56286-1_5

The dramatic shift of attention to the social and political aspects of AI is a testament to the necessity of including social scientists in core debates about the development and circulation of these technologies. However, these conversations, which are very much vital in the current political climate, do not necessarily attempt to make any significant theoretical claims about the status of machinic intelligences and/or how to deal with them conceptually.

This chapter proposes another possibility for dealing with this phenomenon, one that would necessitate a transformation of the boundaries of the common conceptions of the social sciences in general and sociology in particular. First, the chapter will elaborate on Luciana Parisi's (2015) argument that indeterminacy and uncertainty are becoming paradigmatic concerns rather than limits in computational theory. Then, it will bring together ideas from Alan Turing and George Herbert Mead, specifically emphasizing their conceptions of novelty; from this reading it will advance a proposal for a relational sociology of AI. In doing so, this chapter aims to contribute to a conceptual paradigm that would create the possibility for looking at these technologies not just as harbingers of capitalist notions of efficiency and productivity, but as *contributors* to concepts of social agency and novelty. Formulating AI as a social agent that is dynamic and intertwined with indeterminacy would make it possible to theoretically open AI agents up to becoming part of other worldings (Wilson & Connery, 2007). The critical literatures dealing with the social implications of AI would take them as integral parts of the political economies that lie behind the machines themselves. This chapter acknowledges such a route, and yet diverges from it in that it seeks to destabilize the close ties between machinic agencies and capitalist relations. Following this, it allies with an insurgent posthumanist position that contributes to "the everyday making of alternative ontologies" (Papadopoulos, 2010, p. 135). The aim here is thus to expand the sociological landscape to include AI agents in ontologies of the social. The driving question is: how would the everyday practice of sociological imagining shift if it incorporated machinic intelligences as social entities into its purview?

In order to start thinking about AI as an integral part of a social interaction, and not just a mechanical tool that is the extension of already established structures,[1] it is appropriate to focus on the very dynamism that underlies the operations of these intelligences. What separates some genres of AI from other machinic entities and straightforward computational processes and makes it a potential sociological being, is its capacity for interaction, which in turn takes its force from uncertainty. I will examine Luciana Parisi's conceptual work on the centrality of uncertainty in computational processes and turn to Alan Turing to locate this uncertainty in his theory for computational intelligence. This opening, then, will be read through George Herbert Mead's sociology of mind so as to position sociological thinking at the core of AI theorizations. This could be a significant contribution in that the proximity between the theories of Turing and Mead has not yet been made explicit in the literatures that deal with the sociality of AI. As we shall see, with the increasing emphasis on the notions of dynamism, interaction, and indeterminacy in discussions about developing AI, a sociological approach to the study of the machinic mind becomes more appropriate. I argue that Mead's perspective makes it possible to see the relational basis of AI agency and to open up this agentic black box to sociological inquiry.

Sociology of AI

Why should sociology deal with AI? The obvious answer is that AI is increasingly becoming part of our everyday lives. AI automates certain sociotechnical processes and invents new ones, and, in so doing, it introduces certain preconceptions, often in black-boxed form, to the social realm, all the while redistributing the inherent injustices or inequalities of the systems that humans reside in. Issues such as algorithmic biases, the narrow visions of social roles that AI agents take—for instance, Amazon's conversational AI Alexa's contribution to gender and race dynamics is still controversial—and the consequent reproduction of already existing power structures have been problematized in the literatures that deal with AI's social impact (Burrell, 2016; Caliskan, Bryson, & Narayanan, 2017; Hannon, 2016; Parvin, 2019; Phan, 2019). This work is necessary in order to discuss how such technologies take on the historical forces of capitalism, colonialism, patriarchy, and racism and disseminate and rigidify these logics in societies, asymmetrically influencing social groups. The social sciences have taken up the task of discussing and revealing the work that AI phenomena are actually performing as well as speculating on the work that AI might perform in the world. In this line of scholarship, AI emerges as an instrument of technocapitalism and has no real agency on its own; AI can only further the agenda of the systems in which it is embedded. It adds speed and efficiency to processes that are already broken from the perspective of social justice. While all this is true, and while the work that focuses on these aspects of AI is very important (especially as policies to manage the implementation of these technologies are negotiated), there are other and perhaps more consequential ways to think of AI sociologically.

The science and technology studies scholar Steve Woolgar, in a previous generation of AI research, proposed a perspective that would substantiate sociological conceptions of AI. Woolgar (1985) asks the question "Why not a sociology of machines?" to provoke a rethinking of a foundational claim of sociology, namely, that the social is a distinctly human category. He starts by criticizing the narrow role given to the sociologist in discussing AI research; their contribution is generally taken as assessing the "impact" of these technologies, i.e., how they influence the societies that surround them, rather than detailing research processes. This, he claims, contributes to a division between the notions of the technical and the social, thus maintaining the divide between nature and the social. He argues for a methodological shift that would put this distinction into question by bringing the genesis of AI into sociological perspective. His argument points toward an extension of laboratory studies (Cetina, 1995; Latour & Woolgar, 1979) and unsettles the belief that scientific or technological advances occur in a vacuum devoid of interests or meanings. He elaborates his point by providing an analysis of expert systems, which exemplify both how the AI enterprise feeds on the dualisms that pervade the modern sciences and how it maintains its "extraordinary" character. Woolgar thus suggests focusing on the assumptions that go into AI discourse and practice, so as to highlight what kinds of meanings are mobilized to legitimize certain actions and research agendas.

Thinking about why one should study the sociology of AI, a less obvious answer could be the introduction of new modes of thought that algorithmic automation makes possible. For example, with reference to the work of mathematician Gregory Chaitin, Luciana Parisi shows that the assumed algorithmic relationship between input and output has been disrupted; Chaitin's work expands the limits of computational theory by integrating randomness into the core relation between input and output. Parisi (2015) then shows how this entropic conception of information points to the emergence of an "alien mode of thought" (p. 136). This became the case as information theory started treating the "incomputable" as a central tenet of computational processes; she claims that this points to a transformation in the very logic of algorithmic automation. This is interesting for a number of reasons, and Parisi frames this transformation as pointing toward the limitation of critiques of instrumental reason. In conversation with Bernard Stiegler's (2014) argument that thought and affect become engines of profit under technocapitalism and Maurizio Lazzarato's (2012) claim that all relations are reduced to a general indebtedness through apparatuses of automation, Parisi (2015) carves out another possibility that rests on the context of this "all-machine phase transition" (p. 125). She complicates this reading of algorithmic automation that frames machines as linear extensions to capitalistic agendas. She maintains that there is a shift toward dynamism in algorithmic automation, which, if taken into account, challenges the assumed direct relationship between computational intelligence and instrumental reason. She shows how an interactive paradigm is starting to take center stage in computational theories, where notions such as learning, openness, and adaptation come to define such systems.

Possibility of Interactivity in Machinic Intelligences

What is important here is that this dynamism, not canonically considered to be a logic of computational intelligence, becomes the central notion of digital minds.[2] Before the introduction of dynamism, understandings of automated intelligence rested on a static view, wherein the relationship between input and output was taken to be direct and undisturbed—information unproblematically flows between symbolic circuits, and data is computed with a discernibly rule-based, programmed logic in a closed system. There is a certain input, and programming allows that input to be transformed into the desired output. In this paradigm, error, or any form of deviation in the processing of the program, necessarily brings about a break in the system. The flow is interrupted, the machine is broken, the process is severed, and a finality has been reached in the computational procedure. In this paradigm, then, when a break is experienced due to a deviation, human bodies flock to the moment of error, finding the cause of the disruption and reinstating the procedure that is the representation of a pathway to a (pre)determined output from a certain input. It is in this sense that algorithmic automation reflects a mode of intelligence that has a purpose and a finality, or rather, reason. The relationship between input and output is direct, or at least logically structured, which makes computational intelligence a goal-oriented reasoning process. This is why computational processes are taken as hallmarks of order, to the extent that they carry out the reasoning of their programming/programmer. Yet, as Parisi points out, this is not the only manner in which, in her words, "algorithmic automation"—and for us, machinic intelligence—unfolds in social reality. Rather, she argues, as indeterminacy or uncertainty become fundamental to the functioning of computation, these systems become dynamic, open to interactivity, and thus active *in the world*.

AI, when thought in relation to reason, comes to emerge as an orderly, rigidly defined process that interfaces input to output; this means that machinic intelligence works in a predetermined manner with discrete units of ones and zeros. Yet in neural net–based approaches to building AI or interactive computation, this rigid process is disturbed, as indeterminacy is introduced to the computational process. What appeared to be a perfect machine—a "universal machine" in Turing's formulation—does not, in effect, come close to perfection if it is to operate in situ. In his discussion of technical objects, Gilbert Simondon (1958/2017) arrives at a similar idea, in that closed systems only constitute a phase in the evolution of machines. Rather, indeterminacy and openness create conditions for the emergence of the unexpected, which would be the next phase in technicality. In his words,

> The true progressive perfecting of machines, whereby we could say a machine's degree of technicity is raised, corresponds not to an increase of automatism, but on the contrary to the fact that the operation of a machine harbors a certain margin of indeterminacy. … A purely automatic machine completely closed in on itself in a predetermined operation could only give summary results. The machine with superior technicality is an open machine, and the ensemble of open machines assumes man as permanent organizer and as a living interpreter of the inter-relationships of machines. (p. 5)

For Simondon, the possibility for humans to co-work with machines lies in the revealing of such a degree of indeterminacy, which is veiled by the black-box quality of the machine. This point is significant, as indeterminacy allows the possibility for an interactive organization to take place across humans and machines. The conditions of possibility for an emergent interaction order (Goffman, 1967, 1983) lie in the recognition of this indeterminacy.[3]

As Parisi shows in more concrete terms, computational theory already deals with randomness and infinities and does not cast them aside as irrelevant or beyond the scope of computation. Rather, machinic intelligence (or algorithmic automation) turns "incomputables into a new form of probabilities, which are at once discrete and infinite. ... The increasing volume of incomputable data (or randomness) within online, distributive, and interactive computation is now revealing that infinite, patternless data are rather central to computational processing" (Parisi, 2015, p. 131). In Parisi's explanation, derived from Chaitin's more mathematically oriented work, indeterminacy and randomness are taken as productive capacities in communication systems,[4] as randomness challenges the equivalence between input and output. This randomness emerges from an entropic transformation that occurs in the computational process, where the compressing of information in effect produces an increased size in the volume of data. Computational processes are traditionally taken as a process of equilibrium, i.e., a straightforward interfacing between different modalities of data. However, Chaitin shows that there is an indeterminacy and incalculability intrinsic to the computational process.

Irreducibility of Machinic Intelligence

This incomputable element makes machinic thinking irreducible to humanist notions of thought. Rather, machinic intelligence is transformed to include randomness in its algorithmic procedures. The incomputable marks the point at which interactive machinic systems come into being.[5] For Parisi, this point holds the potential for automated intelligences to encompass a landscape that exceeds the logic of technocapitalist instrumentalism, all the while saving the concept of reason from the clutches of market-driven capitalism. She argues that "the incomputable cannot be simply understood as being opposed to reason. ... These limits more subtly suggest the possibility of a dynamic realm of intelligibility, defined by the capacities of incomputable infinities or randomness, to infect any computable or discrete set" (2015, p. 134). In Parisi's explanation, then, the machine does not simply operate in the intelligible realm of computability, but includes randomness that creates the conditions for its interactivity and dynamism, in the sense that the initial conditions of the algorithmic process become malleable. The best example of this irreducibly nonhuman/machinic intelligence can be found in financial systems. As high-frequency trading systems work with large amounts of data and include stochastic programming, their logics of operation spill away from rule-based, linear procedural space; in practice, financial algorithms are usually developed with randomness recognized as part of their computational processes.[6]

Randomness thus becomes intelligible, albeit in a closed manner. Deviating from Simondon's foreshadowing, these incalculables become intelligible, and yet they cannot be synthesized by a subject. The randomness resists an assimilation into sameness. Parisi interprets this as suggesting that "computation—qua mechanization of thought—is intrinsically populated by incomputable data" (p. 134). She emphasizes that this is not an error or a glitch in the system that awaits fixing but rather a part of the processes of computation. This contributes to a conceptualization of machines as entities in their own right and makes possible the emergence of "the machine question" (Gunkel, 2012), in that machinic intelligences can be considered as legitimate social others, i.e., entities that are capable of "encounter" in a social sense as they cannot be absorbed into a sameness in the interaction. The relationalities that emerge from the encounter between human and machinic intelligences have the capacity to evolve in novel ways due to the irreducibility that stems from uncertainty in the computational process. As Parisi (2015) describes, "incomputables are expressed by the affective capacities to produce new thought" (p. 135). The possibility for novelty, then, lies in the recognition that these incalculables are part of computational thinking, as they "reveal the dynamic nature of the intelligible." This novel form corresponds to a "new alien mode of thought," as Parisi calls it, that has the ability to change its initial conditions in ways which would reveal ends that do not necessarily match human reasoning.

Interestingly, Alan Turing also talked about intelligence as being equivalent to machines' capacity to change their initial instructions. In his 1947 lecture to the London Mathematical Society where he first disclosed his ideas about a digital computer, he elaborates on the conditions through which a machine would be taken as being intelligent. The machine that he describes is different from his Turing machine in that it follows the instructions given by a human and yet has the capacity to change its initial programming. What is significant here is that the machine actively contributes to the production of outputs by deviating from the original procedure—designed by the human—between input and output. Turing

(1947), then, recognizes that the perfect and seamless processing of information stands against any conception of intelligence in computation: "if a machine is expected to be infallible, it cannot also be intelligent (p. 13)."[7] He points toward failure, or even error, as a necessary part in the process of cultivating intelligence in machines.

Here it is important to specify that not all AI agents operate socially, as it is the case that not all AI are "intelligent" in the same way. However, there is more concrete investment and output in developing "intelligent" systems of a dynamic kind. The examples that fall into this category use Deep Learning techniques such as supervised and unsupervised learning through neural nets. The famous Go-playing AI, AlphaGo (developed by DeepMind), is one such example. This agent "learns" how to play the game either with (e.g., supervised learning; Silver et al., 2016) or without human knowledge (Silver et al., 2017). Also, the still emerging intersection of creative AI can fall under this "irreducible" category; for instance, Generative Adversarial Networks (GANs) that work on stochastic principles to generate content—e.g., images, text, sound—are an example of algorithmic intelligences that work through a kind of dynamism. These technologies are either designed to function in social realms or to operate interactively, rendering possible relational analyses. This relational character could open up other ways with which AI could be thought, and not as "just" a technology. In the next part, I will try to account for the agency of AI in a sociological sense by reading Turing's formulations through George Herbert Mead's sociology of mind, and I will consider the implications that this reading would have on the conception of sociality and agency.

An Encounter: George Herbert Mead and Alan Turing

George Herbert Mead's influential work *Mind, Self, and Society* (1934) deals extensively with how meanings and selves are formed through societal processes. His efforts were concentrated toward giving a sociological explanation for the phenomenon of consciousness, and thus his ideas form an early "sociology of mind." His formulations were, paradigmatic for the time, very much influenced by humanist ideas. In his thought, the human mind is largely constituted by societal forces, and human (inter)action is guided by communication. Even so, he does not give a completely socially deterministic account, such as a social structure determining the actions of an agent. As will become clearer later in this section, he puts a great deal of emphasis on the novelties and surprise effects, the incalculable and unpredictable, as harbingers of social change. It is once again this idea of incalculability that brings closer the computational "mind"[8] to a social conception of mind.

The potential for novelty was of interest to Turing as well, especially in his famous article "Computing Machinery and Intelligence" (1950). Turing seems to have two perspectives on novelty when it comes to computers. These two perspectives might appear to be contradictory at first, as will become clearer in the following; however, the contradiction between his two answers to the question of whether machines can do anything new doesn't necessarily make these views mutually exclusive. The first view emerges in his consideration of "Lovelace's objection," taking up Lady Lovelace's assertion that a machine can "never do anything really new." Turing suggests that the appreciation of novelty rests in one's "creative mental act," and that if one brings in a deterministic framework to make sense of the world, then the surprise effect produced by the computer will never be captured. For Turing, then, the question is not whether the computer can do anything new, but whether humans have the right attitude to be able to perceive its surprise effect. In this line, the capacity to attribute agency to machines rests on humans' conception of these machines. Who gets included in the "human club" (Lestel, 2017) depends not only on the frames with which humans interpret the agency of machinic intelligences, but also on extending interpretive charity in their interactions so as not to dismiss the machine as a simple tool that crunches numbers. This move might be taken in the framework of social creativity (Graeber, 2005), as the interactions with the machines might pave the way for the emergence of different social practices than the ones that circulate in current imaginaries. While this opens up a way to think about how to establish different relations with machines, it must be stressed that this is an anthropocentric approach in that it puts the human as the ultimate responsible[9] entity that could extend agency, within the bounds of one's own reason. In this conceptualization, the machine is at the receiving end of humans' extension of agency and is itself actually a passive or determinable entity. This chapter will instead take more concern with the incalculable, the unexpected, and the surprise that can be brought about by the agency of machinic intelligence.

Even so, Turing's affective articulation with regard to machines—such as when he states that machines take him by surprise with great frequency—might be considered part of this social creativity. He also puts the emphasis on the conditions under which the machine is performing and says that if they are not clearly defined, machine's intelligence will indeed emerge as a surprise. Turing opens the door for this unpredictability and furthers his argument by stating that a fact does not simultaneously bring its consequences to the purview of the mind. A fact's novelty thus might rest in a potentiality, in a sense. There remain parts, or aspects, of a fact that remain undisclosed, that are "temporally emergent" (Pickering, 1993). Therefore, even the crunching of numbers, or undertaking a pre-given task, can be thought of as part of novelty; the newness rests on the machine's act of calculation, and we can only observe it if we have a creative conception of the machine. It is from this point that the present chapter takes its inspiration. Indeed, a creative conception of machine intelligence is what the sociology of AI would take as its core problematic.

The second notion that Turing brings up in relation to novelty is error. In his defense of machinic intelligence, he elaborates a potential critique of AI that would rest on the idea that "machines cannot make mistakes." This critique would stem from the speed and accuracy with which machines calculate arithmetic problems; this, then, would always lead to a defeat in an Imitation Game. An interrogator can pose a problem, and the machine would either answer very fast, or, if the machine is to confuse the judge, would deliberately make mistakes so as to pass as a human (who is prone to error). But in this case, the mistake would be attributed to its design or a mechanical fault, and still the status of the thinking machine would remain questionable. He states that this particular criticism confuses two kinds of mistakes: "errors of functioning" and "errors of conclusion"; this is where his two perspectives on novelty seem to converge. The former would cover for the kind of mistake that the example presupposes, namely, that error would emerge from a fault in the system. These kinds of errors can be ignored in a more philosophical discussion, as they would not carry an abstract meaning. It is on the errors of conclusion that Turing puts more weight. These arise when a meaning can be attached to the output of the machine, i.e., when the machine emits a false proposition[10]: "There is clearly no reason at all for saying that a machine cannot make this kind of mistake" (Turing, 1950, p. 449). The capacity for the machine to make errors, for Turing, makes it possible for it to enter into the realm of meaning.[11] It is a deviation not only from the expectation that the machine makes perfect calculations but also from the machine's own process of calculation. The machine's process is uninterrupted, in that its error does not emerge as a break, and if the output is faulty, it constitutes a deviation from the system itself. It is this deviation from the designed system that enables a discussion of the agency of the machine, as it creates a novelty that comes with a surprise effect; the ensuing socialities then bear the potential to shift the already existing system.

This novelty-through-surprise effect can be captured in George Mead's sociology of mind as well. His theory will be discussed in relation to the machine's capacity for novelty, so as to arrive at a distributed understanding of agency. Mead makes the case that the essence of the self is cognitive and that mind holds the social foundations of "self," which is composed of two parts: the *me* and the *I*. The *me* forms the social component that calculates the larger context in which one is located; it takes a kind of "world picture" and comprises organized sets of attitudes of others. In a sense, *me* is nested within an organized totality; it can be thought as the rules of the game or the objectified social reality. It is the system in which the individual self acts or, rather, the individual's image of that system. It is a general conception of others (the "generalized other") and is produced a posteriori to the moment of action. Mead uses *I* as that which emerges in the moment of (inter)action as a response to that which is represented in *me*. He emphasizes that the response to the situation is always uncertain, and it is this response that constitutes the *I*. The resulting action is always a little different from anything one could anticipate; thus *I* is not something that is explicitly given in *me*. Lovelace's conceptualization of a computer as a machine of calculation (the Difference Engine is one such machine) may be compared to the operations of *me*. It calculates and provides a representation; the machine, again, emits a world picture. However, in the moment of action, as Turing contends, there is always room for deviation, and, in the case of machines, this happens—perhaps more often than desired—through error.

The errors of conclusion, then, can be compared to Mead's formulation of the *I* as the subject of action that does not rest on its preceding calculations. For both Turing and Mead, the possibility of newness and change comes from the agent's ability to dissociate from the calculable realm, and not through an act of conscious choice, but by what can be termed coincidence or spontaneity.[12] The *I* of the machine, then, comes as a surprise effect. Even though the *me* may calculate things in advance, these calculations may be surpassed by the action of the *I* in the very instant where action comes into being. The mind, according to Mead, can thus reveal itself in a completely novel way, defying anticipation. The *I*, then, stands for subjectivity and the possibility of social action; it harbors the bedrock of agency.

Both for Turing and Mead, the possibility of newness and change does not reside in the act of conscious choice; it necessarily arises out of the agent's capacity to step away from the calculable realm. The novelty emerges in the moment of action, as the relationalities that constitute the agent both provide the ground for calculability and weave different realities that are realized by the emergence of novel action. Those actors who can incite novelty in the world can engender new socialities. In Mead's discussion, sociality refers to a state that is between different social orders. It is an in-betweenness where the response of the *I* has not yet been integrated and objectified in the *me*, and thus an alternative order can be anticipated. Considering machinic agencies with the capacity to incite such sociality, then, requires our methodological attention to be honed toward the moment of interaction.

Agency in Sociality

Talking about interaction without presupposing the existence of humans is not exactly part of sociological tradition. The concept of social interaction would generally assume that human individuals exist prior to interaction and there is a consciousness pertaining to the humans that precedes the interaction. One of the canonical discussions in this line is Max Weber's (1978) theory of social action, where he focuses on the meanings that actors give to their actions and comes up with his famous four *ideal types* of social action that are determined by the intentionality of the actors (pp. 24–25).[13] The concepts that classical sociologists and their descendants have utilized to make sense of social interactions set the tone for this practice to be only intelligible on the level of humans: consciousness, intention, self-identity, reflexivity, other-orientation, active negotiation, and language-based communication (Cerulo, 2009, p. 533). The modern humanist tradition privileges certain types of humans over others and attributes a totality to interiority (an enclosed mind) as opposed to incorporating an exterior world upon which action is taken.

This tradition presupposes a gap between the human prior to (inter)action and a static empirical world that receives the action.

Shifting the focus from before the action (intention, consciousness) to the moment of interaction itself dissolves the self-enclosed individual and allows for the possibility of considering actors' thinking as being *constituted* by the interaction. Thus, the agencies that contribute to an ongoing social interaction come to be defined a posteriori, which allows uncertainties and incalculables to become part of the analysis. Furthermore, this notion of the social also opens up the possibility of including nonhumans as participants in the constitution of social reality[14] as their capacity for encounter becomes legitimized.

When the notion of the social is uncoupled from the human, it also becomes possible to see agency not as bound to an entity but as a constellation of forces that produce an effect in the world. Put more clearly, agency is an effect of the relation between objects—both human and nonhuman. This is a slightly different take than what Actor-Network Theory (ANT) offers. ANT scholars (Callon, 1986, 1987; Latour, 1987, 1984/1988, 1996, 2005; Law, 1992) place much emphasis on conceiving of actants as nodes in a network, working heterogeneously with one another; they do not pay much heed to the notion of the ontologically social. Tim Ingold (2008) points to this gap between the heterogeneous entities that operate in an actor-network and proposes, rather, that action is produced through the lines of the network—in his words, the *meshwork*—which is intimately bound up with the actors. In contrast, agency in ANT is the effect of action, and it is distributed among the actants who are in a network by virtue of the actions that they perform. While this action cannot be reduced to a single entity, it is still understood as capacities of the individual constituents that reside in the network. Ingold suggests, rather, that action "emerges from the interplay of forces that are conducted along the lines of the meshwork. … The world, for me, is not an assemblage of heterogeneous bits and pieces but a tangle of threads and pathways" (p. 212).[15] Through our reading of Mead's sociology of mind, this chapter argues a similar point to Ingold's while also retaining the concept of the social. Instead of agency being a capacity of an individual, agency emerges as a *collective* notion, one that is constituted by various processes; it is in this sense that nonhumans in general, and AI in particular, become relevant to the sociological dimension. The notion of agency does not rely on the *doer* but on the *doing* in which different actors are constituted by their relationalities. So perhaps, the social is the way of relating, the accumulation of actions, the relationalities that become sedimented by continuous encounters and interfaces.[16]

By thinking of AI as having a capacity for novelty, it also becomes possible to see that these neural network models are not just instruments to human conduct. Rather, they are entangled with and through other humans and nonhumans by way of data. AI finds itself embedded in multiple positions, and through its actions, partakes in the construction of a new or different world. AI is an unstable object of study, as it does not fall within the traditional and pure bounds of the human vs. the nonhuman. Rather, AI emerges from entanglements of socio-material relations, and its part in the emergence of agency enables us to cast it as a being that resides and encounters in the social realm. However, I do not mean to enclose AI as such—this is not an operation of rigid definition. The point, rather, is that this can be yet another way to think of AI and that, in this way of thinking, the social is not an exclusively human arena. Instead, the social is about an encounter, about relationality, and can contribute to an expansion of sociological thinking and enable it to look symmetrically at the entities that enter into relations. By setting AI as inherently social, we make it the subject of the sociological gaze. And in focusing on the moment of the encounter, we reveal the manner in which meanings, selves, and societies are produced in relation to machinic intelligences.

Sociology of AI as a Program

One of our main questions, then, could be thought of as, what are the conditions for a successful sociology of AI? There are three themes that would enable the emergence of such a program. The first is that the sociology of AI would not be about boundary policing. Our questions would not concern themselves with whether a social actor is human or nonhuman; nor would we indulge in a further categorization of the empirical world. Rather, we would aim to understand the transgressions and mutations of these boundaries while raising questions about the work that they do in the world. In this sense, a sociological approach to AI would not do the work of the modern sciences; it would not engage in processes of purification (Latour, 1991). Instead, it would itself get entangled in the AI by recognizing the multiplicity and complexity of the subject matter at hand.[17] Secondly, it would incorporate a theory of mind by grounding AI in social interaction. In this sense, a sociological approach to AI could be read alongside arguments about the extended mind (Clark & Chalmers, 1998), and yet it would take seriously social relations as constituents of the minds that come into interaction. It would thus contribute to the social interactionist school but with a different approach to social interaction. Here, the interaction order would not take place among human subjects. Instead, social interactions—which construct the minds that are in the interaction—come to include machinic intelligences, specifically those that have the capacity to encounter.[18] The third and last aspect of any future sociology of AI is that it would incorporate a theory of novelty; it would take seriously the capacity to create new possibilities, even if through error, and aim to highlight the new socialities that come about through this newness. Such a critique of AI could still take on the shape of a critique of capitalism, very rightfully so. Many of these intelligences are produced under capitalist relations and circulate with capitalist logics. However, by engaging with the machinic intelligence's capacities for breaking away from intended use and by focusing on their deviations or irreducibilities that become visible at the level of interaction, it would be possible to locate the moments that potentiate novelty and, thereby, promise new socialities.

Conclusion: Why Does the Sociology of AI Matter?

The social-scientific discourse on technology in general, and artificial intelligence in particular, revolves around a critique of capitalism that takes its direction from a technological-deterministic position. The common critique is that these machines will take over our infrastructures and dominate the lives of humans from an invisible position; or they will automate human social interactions and thus force a new era of Weber's Iron Cage. This chapter respectfully locates itself away from such critique. Rather, it shows how nonhumans unravel in unexpected ways, creating possibilities for different forms of interaction that do not obey the determinations of the affordances of technology, and nor do they entirely follow a capitalistic logic. Their interactions—while taking shape in the context of neoliberal capitalism and thus amenable to reproducing those already existing relations—are not necessarily exhaustible under such categories, and assuming all interactions work to serve the capitalistic agenda is a totalistic approach to mapping reality. I instead argue that focusing on the nature of interaction itself would reveal the ways in which these relationalities can unfold in an unforeseeable manner and thus escape being totalized under the logics of late capitalism. This focus on relationality will demonstrate new ways of imagining differences between humans and machines while retaining their relevance to the sociological gaze.

Questions concerning technologies have traditionally been left to engineering fields, and the social sciences were thought to only be equipped to deal with the *social* phenomena that emerge around technologies (Woolgar, 1985). However, this study proposes another approach, taking the relations with and of the machines as pertinent to social relations. AI presents a borderline case in which sociology can try its hand at a nontraditional field of inquiry and discover to what extent the discipline's boundaries can be reworked. In this sense, this effort is a response to the so-called crisis of the social sciences. Postmodern critiques in the past have pointed to the limitations of taking the human as the foundation of all things,[19] and as the modern human subject purportedly disappeared in endless, neoliberally charged mutations, the humanities and social sciences were thought to be moving toward a point of crisis. By contrast, this chapter finds inspiration in the idea that humans and technologies coexist in multiple forms and raises the stakes of investigating in what ways their relations and agencies unfold and construct complex realities.

The question is not whether AI technologies are "really real" or whether they are legitimate moral subjects with rights. The present AI hype is ridden with notions of creating the next generation of intelligent beings, speculations on the conception of an artificial general intelligence, and various forms of armchair-philosophical "trolley problems." In a cultural landscape that can only think of machinic intelligences through the image of the Terminator, some of these questions might fall on deaf ears. Furthermore, the common response to attempts to situate AI within sociology often remains within the bounds of ethics, but this response would be an attempt to discuss the morality of the machines, an approach which is the result of the discipline's long engagement with the human as the ultimate image of a social world. The implicit assumption is that the machine question would persist in being about humans, asking how humans are affected or how to make machines more human. While this line of critique is very much necessary, if we want to push the boundaries of the disciplines (both sociology and AI), another potentiality must be explored. My call for a relational sociology of AI is an invitation to shift our analytic gaze and ask the questions that are not yet asked or are not dared to be asked.

By attending to the ways in which AI escapes definition and categorization, and yet recognizing that these phenomena have deep implications for the way in which societies unfold, this chapter represents a call to think of the mutability of all things that are considered to be hallmarks of social order. How society is conceived, the ontologies of the social, and the assumptions that go into how relationalities unfold in social reality all have defining influence on the (re)organization of the world. As the world, especially in the North American context, is increasingly becoming a programmable, manageable, controllable, closed entity, it becomes all the more important to critically engage with the meaning of the social and practice our sociological imagination. Thinking about thinking-machines through Mead's sociology of mind makes it possible, for instance, to see them as dynamic parts of unfolding interactions in a social space. They are not simply passive black boxes that compute information in a linear manner. The explainability problem in machine learning, the increasing complexity of neural networks, and the growing influence of algorithmic trading are all contributing to the argument that these intelligences cannot be reduced to being "just technologies." They take active part in meaning making, as illustrated by how the calls for more "context-aware" AI materialize precisely as they become parts of decision-making processes. Being able to read AI through core sociological theories also points to the possibility, or rather the already-established conditions, for undertaking social science in a posthumanist mode. Here, it will be important to not fall into a mainstream posthumanism that appears to be a continuation of traditional liberal subjectivities (Hayles, 1999). Rather, the aspiration here is "*to world* justice, to build associations, to craft common, alternative forms of life" (Papadopoulos, 2010, p. 148). As such, this chapter proposes the building of alternative ontologies that can lead to different imaginaries, in which machines and other entities could coexist in a social manner.

Notes

1. Such structures span from cultures of corporations and start-ups in the tech industry to those of computer science departments and research institutes.

2. There were many practitioners of AI who worked on dynamic systems and resisted representational approaches to building machinic intelligence in the earlier days of AI. Rodney Brooks' projects fall within this paradigm of computation; they take the notions of interactivity and environment very seriously (Brooks, 1987). His students Phil Agre and David Chapman have also dealt with dynamic computational procedures that could deal with the complexity of everyday life (Agre, 1997; Agre & Chapman, 1987).
3. There are many social theories that put uncertainty as the primal condition for interaction. Bakhtin's (1981) dialogical theory is one such theory.
4. For the purpose of this work, randomness and indeterminacy enable the conceptualization of machinic intelligences as agents in social interaction. Machinic intelligences are dynamically unconcealed, and this dynamism renders them as part of social relationalities.
5. Similar works have been produced that point to a shift from an algorithmic to an interactive paradigm in computation. An enthusiastic incursion in this line is Peter Wegner's (1997) "Why Interaction Is More Powerful Than Algorithms?," where he announces the transition as a necessary continuation of the closed system of Turing machines: "Though interaction machines are a simple and obvious extension of Turing machines, this small change increases expressiveness so it becomes too rich for nice mathematical models" (p. 83). Wegner is also making a link between indeterminacy and dynamism.
6. For more on high-frequency trading, please refer to Lange, Lenglet, and Seyfert (2016) and Mackenzie (2018).
7. The Dartmouth proposal (McCarthy, Minsky, Rochester, & Shannon, 1955/2006) makes a similar introjection while talking about how to formulate an artificial intelligence: "A fairly attractive and yet clearly incomplete conjecture is that the difference between creative thinking and unimaginative competent thinking lies in the injection of some randomness" (p. 14).
8. Although mentioned here, the present argument does not deal extensively with the question of the mind.
9. Even infinitely responsible, echoing Emmanuel Levinas' (1979) ethical philosophy.
10. Turing's proposition makes it possible to formulate the intelligence of the machine in the realm of meaning as stemming from its capacity to move away from its initial programming. However, this is not the only manner in which AI could be said to be contributing to meaning making. Some branches of AI, such as computer vision, natural language processing, or context-aware algorithms in general, can contribute to decision-making processes. As they become part of the agency that results in action, it could be said that they also operate in the realm of meaning. Turing does

not talk about different genres of programming, as his discussions are rooted in Turing machines and learning machines; for this reason, I have not indulged in detailing more specificities of such technologies.

11. This claim can be read with analogy to Langdon Winner's famous argument about politics-by-design and inherently political technologies. Winner suggests that there are two ways in which technologies are political. Politics-by-design suggests that the technologies might reflect some politics that go into the design and implementation of a technical system. Whereas inherently political technologies refer to "systems that appear to require, or to be strongly compatible with, particular kinds of political relationships" (Winner, 1980, p. 123). Taking his formula under the concept of error, one can talk about error-by-design or inherently erroneous machines. Error-by-design would once again bring the analytical focus onto the designer or some mechanical fault. However, if the machine is inherently erroneous, then our analysis would have to deal with the agency of the machine.
12. It could be said that Turing had insight into the sociological workings of the mind, even if he did not explicitly deal with these questions. Indeed, a recent article highlights how Turing's life and work reflects the three features of sociological imagination of C. Wright Mills (Topal, 2017), as Turing was (a) able to work out the relations between what is close (human mind) and what is distant (machine); (b) through these analyses, was able to define new sensibilities; and (c) had the ability to imagine a future sociological reality.
13. Weber doesn't use the term intentionality but rather "feeling states" (p. 25).
14. This is in line with Actor-Network Theory's emphasis on symmetrical treatment of the entities—human and nonhuman—that go into a social analysis. Bruno Latour's (1992) famous essay "Where Are the Missing Masses" is a critique of sociology's exclusion of nonhumans from the ontologies of the social. While controversial, this argument opened up a rich avenue for analyzing the construction of reality with particular—symmetrical—attention to materiality and nonhuman actants.
15. Ingold uses the metaphor of SPIDER as opposed to ANT; much like the spider produces the webs around itself through the materials that come out of its body, he suggests that relationalities, as such, are also intimately—and materially—bound together.
16. This formulation takes force from Mead's emphasis on encounter as well as Emile Durkheim's (1912/1986) discussion of the intensity and materiality of social forces in "Elementary Forms of Religious Life."
17. The work of the sociologist, or the anthropologist, could then be considered to be contributing to the field of AI as it could not be separated from the object of analysis. This follows the argument Nick Seaver

(2017) makes "that we should instead approach algorithms as 'multiples'—unstable objects that are enacted through the varied practices that people use to engage with them, including the practices of 'outsider' researchers" (p. 1).

18. The irreducibility of the machinic "intelligence" to a straightforward equilibrium between input and output provides this capacity of the machines to encounter in a social sense.
19. I am referring to Foucault's critique of humanism. Humanism is not only a theory that attempts to explain social life in terms of "natural" characteristics of the human subject but also a meta-theory (especially after the reflexive turn) that underlies much of modern social sciences' methodologies that stem from self-understanding (Paden, 1987). More significantly, this unchanging notion of the human is the product of the Enlightenment in the West, and, as such, it is deeply entangled with the processes of colonization and capitalist exploitation.

References

Agre, P. E. (1997). Computation and human experience. *Cambridge University Press*. https://doi.org/10.1017/CBO9780511571169.

Agre, P. E., & Chapman, D. (1987). Pengi: An implementation of a theory of activity. *Proceedings of the Sixth National Conference on Artificial Intelligence, 278*, 268–272. https://doi.org/citeulike-article-id:2834010.

Bakhtin, M. (1981). *The dialogic imagination* (M. Holquist, Ed.). University of Texas Press.

Brooks, R. (1987). Intelligence without representation. *Proceedings of the Workshop on the Foundations of Artificial Intelligence, 47,* 139–159.

Burrell, J. (2016). How the machine "thinks": Understanding opacity in machine learning algorithms. *Big Data & Society* (June), 1–12.

Callon, M. (1986). Some elements of a sociology of translation: Domestication of the scallops and the fishermen of Saint Brieuc Bay. In J. Law (Ed.), *Power, action and belief: A new sociology of knowledge* (pp. 196–233). Routledge.

Callon, M. (1987). Society in the making: The study of technology as a tool for sociological analysis. In W. E. Bijker, T. P. Hughes, & T. J. Pinch (Eds.), *The social construction of technological systems* (pp. 83–103). MIT Press.

Caliskan, A., Bryson, J. J., & Narayanan, A. (2017). Semantics derived automatically from language corpora necessarily contain human biases. *Science, 356*(6334), 183–186.

Cerulo, K. A. (2009). Nonhumans in social interaction. *Annual Review of Sociology, 35*(1), 531–552.

Cetina, K. K. (1995). Laboratory studies: The cultural approach to the study of science. In S. Jasanoff, G. E. Markle, J. C. Peterson, & T. Pinch (Eds.), *Handbook of science and technology studies* (pp. 140–166). Sage.

Clark, A., & Chalmers, D. (1998). The extended mind. *Analysis, 58*(1), 7–19.

Durkheim, E. (1912/1986). The elementary forms of the religious life. In R. A. Jones (Ed.), *Emile Durkheim: An introduction to four major works* (pp. 115–155). Sage.

Goffman, E. (1967). *Interaction ritual: Essays on face-to-face behavior*. Pantheon Books.

Goffman, E. (1983). The interaction order: American Sociological Association, 1982 Presidential Address. *American Sociological Review, 48*(1), 1–17.

Graeber, D. (2005). Fetishism as social creativity or, fetishes are gods in the process of construction. *Anthropological Theory, 5*(4), 407–438.

Gunkel, D. J. (2012). *The machine question: Critical perspectives on AI, robots, and ethics*. MIT Press.

Hayles, K. N. (1999). *How we became posthuman: Virtual bodies in cybernetics, literature, and informatics*. University of Chicago Press.

Hannon, C. (2016). Gender and status in voice user interfaces. *Interactions*, 34–37. https://doi.org/10.1145/2897939.

Ingold, T. (2008). When ANT meets SPIDER: Social theory for arthropods. In C. Knappett & L. Malafouris (Eds.), *Material agency* (pp. 209–215). Springer Science+Business Media.

Lange, A.-C., Lenglet, M., & Seyfert, R. (2016). Cultures of high-frequency trading: Mapping the landscape of algorithmic developments in contemporary financial markets. *Economy and Society, 45*(2), 149–165.

Latour, B. (1987). *Science in action: How to follow scientists and engineers through society*. Harvard University Press.

Latour, B. (1984/1988). *The pasteurization of France*. Harvard University Press.

Latour, B. (1991). *We have never been modern*. Harvard University Press.

Latour, B. (1992). Where are the missing masses? The sociology of a few mundane artifacts. In W. E. Bijker & J. Law (Eds.), *Shaping technology/building society: Studies in socio-technical change* (pp. 225–258). Cambridge, MA: MIT Press.

Latour, B. (1996). On interobjectivity. *Mind, Culture, and Activity, 3*(4), 228–245.

Latour, B. (2005). *Reassembling the social: An introduction to Actor-Network-Theory*. Oxford University Press.

Latour, B., & Woolgar, S. (1979). *Laboratory life: The construction of scientific facts*. Princeton University Press.

Law, J. (1992). Notes on the theory of actor-network: Ordering, strategy, and heterogeneity. *Systems Practice, 5*, 379–393.

Lazzarato, M. (2012). *The making of the indebted man: An essay on the neoliberal condition*. Semiotext(e).

Lestel, D. (2017). How machines force us to rethink what it means to be living: Steps to an existential robotics. *NatureCulture*, 38–58.

Levinas, E. (1979). *Totality and infinity: An essay on exteriority*. Martinus Nijhoff Publishers.

Mackenzie, D. (2018). Material signals: A historical sociology of high-frequency trading. *American Journal of Sociology, 123*(6), 1635–1683.

McCarthy, J., Minsky, M. L., Rochester, N., & Shannon, C. E. (1995/2006). A proposal for the Dartmouth summer research project on artificial intelligence. *AI Magazine*, *27*(4), 12.

Mead, G. H. (1934). *Mind, self, and society*. University of Chicago Press.

Paden, R. (1987). Foucault's anti-humanism. *Human Studies, 10*(1), 123–141.

Papadopoulos, D. (2010). Insurgent posthumanism. *Ephemera: Theory & Politics in Organization*, *10*(2), 134–151.

Parisi, L. (2015). Instrumental reason, algorithmic capitalism, and the incomputable. In M. Pasquinelli (Ed.), *Alleys of your mind: Augmented intelligence and its traumas* (pp. 125–138). Meson Press.

Parvin, N. (2019). Look up and smile! Seeing through Alexa's algorithmic gaze. *Catalyst: Feminism, Theory, Technoscience*, *5*(1), 1–11.

Phan, T. (2019). Amazon Echo and the aesthetics of whiteness. *Catalyst: Feminism, Theory, Technoscience*, *5*(1), 1–38.

Pickering, A. (1993). The mangle of practice: Agency and emergence in the sociology of science. *American Journal of Sociology, 99*(3), 559–589.

Rahwan, I., Cebrian, M., Obradovich, N., Bongard, J., Bonnefon, J., & Breazeal, C. (2019). Machine behaviour. *Nature, 568,* 477–486. https://doi.org/10.1038/s41586-019-1138-y.

Seaver, N. (2017). Algorithms as culture: Some tactics for the ethnography of algorithmic systems. *Big Data & Society, 4*(2), 205–239.

Silver, D., Huang, A., Maddison, C. J., Guez, A., Sifre, L., van den Driessche, G., … Hassabis, D. (2016). Mastering the game of Go with deep neural networks and tree search. *Nature, 529*(7585), 484–489. https://doi.org/10.1038/nature16961.

Silver, D., Schrittwieser, J., Simonyan, K., Antonoglou, I., Huang, A., Hubert, T., Hassabis, D. (2017). Mastering the game of Go without human knowledge. *Nature, 550,* 354–359.

Simondon, G. (1958/2017). *On the mode of existence of technical objects*. Univocal Publishing.

Stiegler, B. (2014). *The lost spirit of capitalism: Disbelief and discredit*. Wiley.

Topal, C. (2017). Sociological imagination of Alan Turing: Artificial intelligence as social imaginary. *DTCF Journal, 57*(2), 1340–1364.

Turing, A. M. (1950). Computing machinery and intelligence. *Mind, 49,* 433–460.
Turing, A. M. (1986). Lecture to the London Mathematical Society on 20 February 1947. In B. E. Carpenter & B. W. Doran (Eds.), *A. M. Turing's ACE report of 1946 and other papers.* MIT Press.
Weber, M. (1978). *Economy and society. An outline of interpretative sociology.* University of California Press.
Wegner, P. (1997). Why interaction is more powerful than algorithms. *Communications of the ACM*, *40*(5).
Wilson, R., & Connery, C. L. (2007). *The worlding project: Doing cultural studies in the era of globalization.* North Atlantic Books.
Winner, L. (1980). Do artifacts have politics? *Daedalus, 109*(1), 121–136.
Woolgar, S. (1985). Why not a sociology of machines? The case of sociology and artificial intelligence. *Sociology, 19*(4), 557–572.

CHAPTER 6

AlphaGo's Deep Play: Technological Breakthrough as Social Drama

Werner Binder

> They were addressing AI questions that were far larger than the humble game they were attempting to conquer. Can a program learn from its mistakes instead of repeating the same errors every time? Can a form of intuition be instilled into a machine? Is output what matters when determining intelligence, or method? If the human brain is just a very fast computer, what happens when computers become faster than the brain?
> —Garry Kasparov, Foreword to Sadler and Regan (2019)

Ever since the emergence of the field of artificial intelligence (AI) research in the second half of the twentieth century, computer scientists have shown great interest in games as a laboratory for the development of AI and as a benchmark for testing it. With the advent of computers, it became possible to solve simple board games like tic-tac-toe (already in 1952) and checkers (only in 2007) through raw computing power. Nevertheless, solving these comparatively "shallow" games did not yield the deep insights into the nature of intelligence and creativity that AI researchers were hoping for. Games of higher complexity, maybe even

W. Binder (✉)
Masaryk University, Brno, Czech Republic
e-mail: werner.binder@muni.cz

© The Author(s) 2021

J. Roberge and M. Castelle (eds.), *The Cultural Life of Machine Learning*, https://doi.org/10.1007/978-3-030-56286-1_6

unsolvable in a strict sense, such as chess or the Asian game Go, seemed more promising in this regard. Initially celebrated as a milestone in AI research, the victory of the IBM computer Deep Blue over the World Chess Champion Garry Kasparov in 1997 was for AI researchers ultimately disappointing. Deep Blue's "shallow" play, based on extensive databases and brute-force calculations, failed to deepen our understanding of intelligence and creativity, proving unable to address the questions raised by Kasparov himself in the introductory quote above. The endeavor of solving the problem of artificial intelligence through games appeared to have been ill-fated as every triumph by a machine merely seemed to disqualify the game as a true test for intelligence.

On January 27, 2016, DeepMind, a London-based tech startup owned by Google's parent company Alphabet, announced that one of their programs had been able to beat a human professional Go player. The news of AlphaGo's victory shocked the tech world and the Go community alike. While it was expected that at some point a machine would prove superior to humans in the game of Go, such a feat had been thought to be at least a decade away. This initial shock triggered the social drama of AlphaGo, which unfolded as DeepMind challenged the Korean Go legend Lee Sedol. In media commentaries, AlphaGo's games against Lee were quickly framed as "deep play," addressing underlying questions of AI research.

The technological breakthrough of DeepMind, described by CEO and founder Demis Hassabis (2015, May 12) as an "Apollo program for artificial intelligence" whose ultimate goal is to "solve intelligence" and then "use it to solve everything else" (in Simonite, 2016, March 31), claimed significance beyond the game of Go. What was at stake in the social drama of AlphaGo was not human supremacy in Go, but the nature of intelligence and creativity if not the future of humanity itself. As the drama ran its course, AlphaGo was framed as "creative," raising hopes for future developments in the field of AI. DeepMind was able to restage the drama, each time building on its previous successes, developing creative agents for chess and the computer game *StarCraft*.

In this chapter, I take creative license with the concepts of "social drama" (Turner, 1980) and "deep play" (Geertz, 2006a) in order to make sense of AlphaGo's games and the discourses surrounding them. Generally speaking, Victor Turner's concept of social drama highlights the performative aspects and dramatic qualities of social processes. More specifically, it offers a model for particular processes (e.g., public scandals) which unfold in "four phases," labeled "breach, crisis, redress, and either reintegration or recognition of schism" (Turner, 1980, p. 149). I will adapt Turner's model for the study of technological breakthroughs such as AlphaGo. Similar to the "moral breach" we find in a public scandal (p. 150), "cognitive" breaches accompanying technological breakthroughs are often fraught with conflicting meanings, not only sparking heated debates but often developing into a social crisis that can be regarded as a manifestation of deeper conflicts. This is where Geertz's notion of "deep play" comes in, not as it was originally conceived by Bentham (cf. Geertz, 2006a, pp. 431–434), but in the sense given to it by the entirety of Geertz's essay. In the same way as the cockfight offers insights into the deep structure of Balinese society and culture—e.g., regarding human–animal relations or conceptions of masculinity—AlphaGo's "deep play" addresses human–machine relations and questions regarding the nature of intelligence and creativity.

After giving an account of my cultural sociological approach, which includes my take on Turner's social drama, I will discuss the gap between old "brute force" algorithms and the new algorithmic culture based on machine learning as well as philosophical debates on the status of AI and their sociological implications. Against this background, I will analyze the social drama of AlphaGo chronologically. I offer a "thick description" (Geertz, 2006b) of the games and discourses, utilizing game commentaries and media reports as well as interviews and speeches by players and other protagonists. The drama opened with a "cognitive" breach, namely the announcement of AlphaGo's unexpected victory over a low-ranked professional, which widened to a crisis with diverging opinions on AlphaGo's game play and the significance of DeepMind's breakthrough. The crisis was further dramatized by the announcement of a series of games against Lee Sedol, 17-times world champion, which forms the core of my analysis. AlphaGo's "deep play" against Lee was able to address this crisis, leading to a new consensus—with more than a few questions remaining. In an attempt to restage the drama, DeepMind conducted and published 60 games, in which the newest iteration of AlphaGo, "Master," defeated various top professionals online. This second stage of the drama resolved with AlphaGo defeating Ke Jie, the current number one in the Go world, in three games, proving once-and-for-all AI superiority in the game of Go. In the consecutive stages, DeepMind broadened the implications of its technological breakthrough, first "mastering the game of Go without human knowledge" (AlphaGo Zero), then creating a program that was able to play chess at a superhuman level (AlphaZero), and finally developing a program that succeeded in a real-time computer strategy game (AlphaStar). I will conclude the chapter with reflections on the cultural significance of AlphaGo's victory.

Toward a Cultural Sociology of AI: Technological Breakthrough as Social Drama

In the following study, I do not want to offer a sociological critique of contemporary AI research. Instead, I would like to examine the critical capacity of actors to make sense of recent technological innovations such as machine learning. The cultural sociological framework of my analysis reflects this shift from critical sociology to a sociology of critique (Boltanski, 2011; Boltanski & Thévenot, 2007). While cultural sociologists have mostly focused on symbolic patterns that inform meaning-making as social practice and discourse (e.g., Alexander & Smith, 2001/2003, 2010), this study emphasizes the active role of objects in processes of meaning-making. Borrowing from the sociology of critique, we can speak of "reality tests" to which objects and claims are subjected to (Boltanski, 2011; see also Boltanski & Thévenot, 2007, pp. 133–140). Technological objects such as algorithms contribute to the meaning-making process, which "is about the constant intertwining of symbolic representation and more prosaic performance" (Roberge & Seyfert, 2016, p. 8). In other words: AlphaGo has to be taken seriously as a protagonist in its own drama. For this reason, the empirical analysis needs to account for the discursive framing of AlphaGo in conjunction with its actual performance, both of which shaped the course of the social drama.

Turner's concept of "social drama" (1980) has been frequently employed by cultural sociologists in their analysis of social struggles about meaning (e.g., Wagner-Pacifici, 1986; Woods, 2013) or taken as an inspiration for constructing similar models (e.g., Alexander, 2019). All of these uses, however, remain close to Turner's own interest in moral and political conflicts. For this reason, my application of the concept to social struggles about the meaning of technological breakthroughs requires further elaboration and demarcation from the original conception.

According to Turner (1980), a social drama is a "spontaneous unit of social process" (p. 140) that unfolds in four phases. Every social drama starts with a moral breach and widens to a social crisis, which is then addressed by mechanisms of redress, after which the drama concludes with either reintegration or recognition of the schism. In the case of technological breakthroughs, we can distinguish four phases, each differing somewhat from the original model. Turner, for example, defines "breach" as a violation of normative expectations expressing deeper divisions in society:

> A social drama first manifests itself as the breach of a norm, the infraction of a rule of morality, law, custom, or etiquette, in some public arena. This breach is seen as the expression of a deeper division of interests and loyalties than appears on the surface. (p. 150)

In order to understand the nature of the rupture caused by technological breakthroughs like AlphaGo, Niklas Luhmann's distinction between "normative" and "cognitive expectations" is helpful. According to Luhmann (1990), expectations reflect either "a willingness to learn (cognitive expectation) or an unwillingness to learn (normative expectation)" (p. 63). Whereas violated normative expectations are usually reinstated, violations of cognitive expectations lead often to "learning," i.e., the transformation of unexpected experiences into structures of expectation. Whereas classical social dramas revolve around the meaning of and possible compensation for moral transgressions, social dramas triggered by a "cognitive" breach are mainly concerned with the lessons to be learned by society. In both cases, the breach is followed by a "mounting crisis" as actors and groups engage in a contingent struggle for meaning:

> Sides are taken, factions are formed, and unless the conflict can be sealed off quickly within a limited area of social interaction, there is a tendency for the breach to widen and spread until it coincides with some dominant cleavage in the widest set of relevant social relations to which the parties in conflict belong. (Turner, 1980, p. 150)

It only makes sense to speak of a social drama if the social response to the breach is not trivial, meaning if neither punishment nor learning are automatic but problematic. The crisis signifies the social conflict about the meaning of the breach, which needs to be addressed in the next phase:

> In order to limit the contagious spread of breach, certain adjustive and redressive mechanisms ... from personal advice and informal arbitration to

> formal juridical and legal machinery and, to resolve certain kinds of crises, to the performance of public ritual. (p. 151)

Turner highlights the importance of legal trials and public rituals as mechanisms of redress in overcoming a crisis caused by a normative breach. In the case of a social drama resulting from a cognitive breach, "reality tests," such as competitive games, may play a similar role as arbiters of meaning. Claude Lévi-Strauss (1966) once compared the logic of rituals and games as rule-governed practices: rituals establish symmetry among unequal participants, whereas competitive games produce asymmetric results out of equal opportunities (pp. 30–33). Competitive games, as well as other reality tests such as experiments, are preferred mechanisms for resolving cognitive disputes, comparable to rituals in normative conflicts. Still, the result of such a test remains contestable. It is possible to question the fairness of a game, its symmetric starting conditions, or to argue that the test was, after all, not adequate, too "shallow" to address the deeper issues at stake. The success of these mechanisms decides the outcome of the drama:

> The final phase consists either in the reintegration of the disturbed social group … or the social recognition of irreparable breach between the contesting parties, sometimes leading to their spatial separation. (Turner, 1980, p. 151)

For a social drama resulting from a cognitive breach, Turner's final phase, "reintegration or recognition of the schism," can be rephrased as emergence of consensus or consolidation of disagreement. On a final note, social dramas may exhibit different degrees of conclusiveness, such as when a shallow consensus covers deeper disagreements. This is also true for the original conception of the social drama. For example, the Dreyfus affair, which Turner (1980) mentions in his article (p. 150), was not able to overcome the crisis in French society, despite the fact that Dreyfus was fully exonerated and rehabilitated, leading to societal divisions that later resurfaced with the Vichy regime. In the case of AlphaGo, due to inconclusiveness but also because of further technological breakthroughs, the social drama was restaged several times. After each stage the consensus broadened and deepened, lending credibility to DeepMind's ambitions claims. In order to understand the social drama of AlphaGo, we need to explore the technological and epistemic divisions exposed by its cognitive breach.

Chess, Go, and the Quest for Artificial Intelligence

The performance of computers against humans in competitive games, particularly perfect information games like chess and Go, has always been treated as a "reality test" and benchmark for the development of AI. The role of chess in particular has been described as a *drosophila* of "artificial intelligence" (Ensmenger, 2012) or even "reasoning" (Kasparov, 2018), alluding to the role of the fruit fly as model organism for geneticists. In a study of the significance of chess for AI research, Nathan Ensmenger (2012) suggests that the algorithms designed to master chess have misled researchers. Computer chess favored a very specific "algorithmic culture" (Roberge & Seyfert, 2016), characterized by "minimax algorithms" and "brute-force computational techniques," which was ultimately disappointing: "As a result, computers got much better at chess, but increasingly no one much cared" (Ensmenger, 2012, p. 7). Although computers eventually outperformed human players, they did so by playing "shallow" games in a defensive and boring style that was strikingly different from human grandmasters and did not facilitate any deeper insights into the nature of intelligence and creativity.

The matches between IBM's chess program Deep Blue and world champion Garry Kasparov may serve here as an example for an inconclusive social drama and the discontents associated with "brute-force computational" techniques. After losing to Kasparov in 1996, Deep Blue was able to beat the grandmaster in 1997—under questionable circumstances. Deep Blue was not simply designed to play good chess but created and tweaked, even between matches, for the sole purpose of beating Kasparov, who suspected the team of intervening in the ongoing matches themselves. Demis Hassabis, the founder and CEO of DeepMind and a former chess professional himself, recalled the event as follows: "Strangely, although Kasparov lost, it left me more in awe of the incredible capabilities of the human brain than of the machine" (2017, p. 413). Despite its undeniable victory, Deep Blue's play was found "shallow" and uninspiring. Since Deep Blue, the capabilities of computer chess programs have further improved, resulting in tournament play between chess programs (and their programmer teams) but not in a breakthrough in AI research. Having reached a dead end, scientists started to tackle Go, but an algorithmic cultural revolution was necessary to teach a computer to play decent Go.

Why did it take almost twenty years after Kasparov was dethroned by Deep Blue for a computer to beat a professional Go player? While it is true that Go has little cultural capital in Western societies compared to chess, it always had a strong following among mathematicians and programmers (the iconic company Atari was named after the attack move in Go, Conway developed his famous "game of life" on a Go board, etc.). The game simply has been a much harder nut to crack than chess for computers and programmers. While Go has an extraordinarily simple set of rules, the complexity of the game outpaces chess by far. The branching factor, the average number of possible moves per turn, in Go is 250 compared to 35 in chess, a gap that exponentially grows with each move played. The number of legal board states in Go is said to exceed the number of atoms in the observable universe. For this reason, "brute-force" methods, outsmarting human players by sheer computing power, did not yield promising results. It was necessary to reduce the complexity of the game first. A minor breakthrough in computer Go was achieved in 2006 with the implementation of Monte Carlo algorithms, which deliver satisfactory results within a certain margin of error by calculating randomly selected paths. Since the implementation of these algorithms, Go programs have been able to beat good amateurs in even matches—but not professional players.

Before DeepMind made its announcement, most observers expected they were still a decade away from computers beating professional Go players. AlphaGo exceeded these expectations, combining Monte Carlo tree search, artificial neural networks, and machine learning, which enabled the program to build up its own structures of expectation and due to which it was able to reduce Go's complexity more effectively than previous programs. In contrast to chess engines like Deep Blue, AlphaGo did not rely on programmer input and specific knowledge about the game (opening databases, values assigned to figures, etc.). Initially trained on high-level amateur and professional games, AlphaGo developed its own style through self-play. The result was a machine that not only could beat the strongest Go player but also exhibited an aggressive and creative play style strikingly different from conventional chess computers.

The Social Attribution of Intelligence and the Boundaries of the Social World

The social drama of AlphaGo addressed fundamental questions of AI research, which not only pertain to the nature of intelligence and creativity but also to the boundaries of the social world. In order to develop a cultural sociological approach to artificial intelligence, it is helpful to start with an extreme philosophical position in the debate on AI. John Searle (1980), who has been a consistent critic of AI research for decades, argues in his infamous Chinese room thought experiment that a person can simulate a conversation in Chinese without actually knowing the language. For him, the experiment demonstrates that the famous Turing test—testing machines for the capability to pass as a human in a meaningful conversation—cannot be considered a test for intelligence. In Searle's view, intelligence can only be attributed to entities with brains (or brain-equivalents) that produce intentional states and consciousness, which then cause meaningful action. Consistent with his earlier rebuttal of the Turing test, Searle (2014, October 9) argued more recently that contemporary discourses on AI are plagued by the language we use:

> There remain enormous philosophical confusions about the correct interpretation of the technology. For example, one routinely reads that in exactly the same sense in which Garry Kasparov played and beat Anatoly Karpov in chess, the computer called Deep Blue played and beat Kasparov.
>
> It should be obvious that this claim is suspect. In order for Kasparov to play and win, he has to be conscious that he is playing chess, and conscious of a thousand other things such as that he opened with pawn to K4 and that his queen is threatened by the knight. Deep Blue is conscious of none of these things because it is not conscious of anything at all. Why is consciousness so important? You cannot literally play chess or do much of anything else cognitive if you are totally disassociated from consciousness. (paras. 1–2)

According to Searle, Deep Blue cannot literally play chess (and, consequently, AlphaGo cannot play Go), because it lacks consciousness. Computers programs might be good at calculating moves, but they lack the desire and intention to win as well as certain beliefs about how to achieve this goal. It seems at first that Searle criticizes the criteria for the "reality test" for AI, arguing that it is not enough to beat a human opponent in chess or simulate a meaningful conversation. Instead, Searle promotes "consciousness" as ultimate criterion for intelligence, which, however, cannot be subjected to a "reality test." Drawing on Boltanski (2011, pp. 103–107), we can describe Searle's argument as a tautological "truth test." Truth tests, endowed by Searle with philosophical dignity, act as bulwark against the scientific assertation of reality tests. Among philosophers, this view is not uncontested. Daniel C. Dennett (1989) argues in favor of "substrate neutrality," i.e., intelligence does not have to run on brains, and proposes an "intentional stance," according to which we can attribute intentionality and intelligence to any entity to account for its behavior.

From a sociological perspective, the (social) attribution of agency and intelligence on basis of an entity's performance has crucial advantages: it remains agnostic regarding the question of what intelligence really is and thus open to various stances toward (not only technological) objects. Social phenomenology is particularly useful here, turning phenomenology's bane, solipsism, into a methodological boon. While Searle operates with a rather commonsensical notion of subjectivity and consciousness as inherent and exclusive human features, phenomenology forces us to recognize that others appear to us only in our consciousness, making it impossible to prove their independent existence or to observe their consciousness directly (cf. Husserl, 1929/1982, pp. 89–151; Schutz & Luckmann, 1983, pp. 109–114, 131–137).

Building on this phenomenological perspective, Thomas Luckmann (1970) argued that the boundaries of the social world are fluid, not determined by the universal structure of the lifeworld but its contingent cultural-historical articulation. According to Luckmann, human beings and societies have a tendency toward the universal projection of subjectivity, which only becomes particularized through experience and socialization. In totemic societies, to use Luckmann's primary example, institutions tend to stabilize the subjectivity of animals, plants, and inanimate matter. In modern society, however, Luckmann attests to a "de-socialization of the universe" (1970, pp. 86–96). Arguing with Luckmann against Luckmann, we can then describe certain contemporary developments in the field of AI research as a re-socialization of the universe. The inclusion of machines as creative subjects in our lifeworld is facilitated by technological discourses and social imaginaries but also depends on their own performance. AlphaGo's "deep play" demonstrates the importance of performance for the attribution of creativity as well as the fluidity of social boundaries as AlphaGo becomes part of the Go world.

Cognitive Breach and Social Crisis: AlphaGo Vs. Fan Hui

AlphaGo entered the public stage on January 27, 2016, when DeepMind announced that one of their computer programs had been able to beat a professional Go player and published a *Nature* article specifying its technical details (Silver et al., 2016). The five games against the European Go champion Fan Hui, all of which he lost, took place in October 2015 in the company's headquarters in London, but DeepMind kept them secret until the publication of the article. While a Go professional losing to a machine was unprecedented, Fan Hui could not be considered a top player by global standards (set by China, Korea, and Japan). In order to prove the supremacy of AlphaGo, DeepMind announced that it had arranged for a series of five games against the dominant player of the last decade, the Korean Lee Sedol, in Seoul. The same day, Mark Zuckerberg proclaimed that Facebook had been working on a Go program too, which was able to beat strong amateur players (Kelion 2016, January 27). However, the space race between Google's DeepMind, its "Apollo program for artificial intelligence," and Facebook proved to be a short one. Less than two month later, after the first game against Lee Sedol, Demis Hassabis (2016, March 9) was able to announce on Twitter: "We landed it on the moon."

We can describe the unexpected success of AlphaGo against Fan Hui as a cognitive breach that widened to a social crisis as debates about its significance as technological breakthrough erupted. The side cheering for AlphaGo not only emphasized the strength of the program but also its human play style. AlphaGo's opponent, Fan Hui, reported that it didn't feel like playing against a machine: "I know AlphaGo is a computer, but if no one told me, maybe I would think the player was a little strange, but a very strong player, a real person" (in Gibney 2016, January 27). He was seconded by Toby Manning, treasurer of the British Go Association, who was referee for the matches:

> The thing that struck me, playing through the games you couldn't tell who was the human and who was the computer. With a lot of software you find the computer makes a lot of sensible moves and suddenly loses

> the plot. But here, you couldn't tell which was which. (in Gibney 2016, January 27)

Both comments suggest that AlphaGo was able to pass a kind of Turing test, being almost indistinguishable from a strong human player. Nevertheless, AlphaGo could not yet be considered "superhuman" in terms of its Go-playing capabilities. The opposing critical camp in the social drama consisted of members of the Go community who questioned AlphaGo's strength and computer experts arguing that the technology was still in its infancy.

Despite a general agreement on the remarkable play of AlphaGo, most Go commentators were quick to point out the gap in Go skills separating Fan Hui, a mere 2-dan professional, from Lee Sedol, a 9-dan professional (the highest rank in Go).[1] Professional players stated that neither Fan Hui nor AlphaGo played flawlessly and were both well below the standard of top professionals. While the program was judged to be at the verge of professional human play, it was not considered top level. Myungwan Kim, a Korean 9-dan professional, even accused AlphaGo of making "5 dan mistakes" (in Kloester 2016, March 4). The critical discourse in the Go community was seconded by technology experts such as Jonathan Schaeffer, the first to solve checkers, who argued in *Nature* that this is "not yet a Deep Blue moment" and remained skeptical about the progress that AlphaGo could reasonably be expected to make in a few months:

> The real achievement will be when the program plays a player in the true top echelon. Deep Blue started regularly beating grandmasters in 1989, but the end result was eight years later. What I see from these numbers is that the gap between where AlphaGo is and where the top humans are has shrunk enormously, and it's quite possible that with a bit more work and improvements, and more computing power, within a year or two they could do it. (Schaeffer in Gibney 2016, January 27)

In the upcoming match against Lee, Schaeffer would put his "money on the human," comparing AlphaGo to "a child prodigy" who "learned to play really good Go, very quickly," but lacked the necessary experience. Similar expectations prevailed in the Go community. Lee was confident

[1] As of January 1, 2016, Fan Hui ranked 558th and Lee Sedol was ranked fourth in the Go world, having often occupied the pole position in past years; cf. https://www.goratings.org/en/history/2016-01-01.html.

about the upcoming match and most fans would have put their money on him—and some in fact did. While Schaeffer's bet was likely rhetorical, there is a betting culture associated with Go, at least in Asia. Google itself placed what Geertz might have called a "center bet" (2006a), offering one million dollars of prize money for the winner with DeepMind's reputation at stake too, but there were also "side bets," initially favoring Lee. It was only shortly before the matches, when DeepMind announced that its program has been making progress since the Fan Hui games, that the betting odds became about even—which is incidentally what Geertz found in the betting patterns of the side bets on "deep" cockfights (Geertz, 2006a, pp. 425–432). While the team around Demis Hassabis expressed confidence in AlphaGo's performance, they were also aware of weaknesses in the program, "delusions" which occasionally led AlphaGo to misjudge situations badly (see Silver, 2017, October 19).

Not only with the benefit of hindsight, it is possible to identify some flaws in the critics' reasoning before the matches. First, the comparison between AlphaGo and Deep Blue disregarded the impact of machine learning in AI research. Between the matches against Fan Hui and Lee Sedol, AlphaGo had the opportunity to play millions of games against itself, getting stronger with each iteration. Second, due to the peculiarities of its algorithm, it was difficult to judge AlphaGo's power on the basis of games against a comparatively weak opponent. In contrast to chess, Go is a game where players can win by different margins, but half a point is enough. Like other Go programs, AlphaGo was designed to maximize the chances of winning disregarding the total number of points. When AlphaGo is in the lead, it will play safer moves, which give it a better probability of winning, instead of the more aggressive moves a human player might prefer. In order to show the true strength of AlphaGo, it would have to play a very strong professional player, such as Lee Sedol.

Deep Play: AlphaGo Vs. Lee Sedol

The DeepMind team perfectly dramatized the success of AlphaGo, announcing the date and location of AlphaGo's next matches against the legendary Korean player Lee Sedol when breaking the news. The five games, which took place from March 9 to 15, 2016, in Seoul, were a highly publicized event, televised and livestreamed on the internet. It is estimated that in China alone forty million viewers followed the matches live, the electronic billboards in Seoul displayed live updates on the match, and DeepMind's YouTube channel featuring game commentary in English had hundreds of thousands of visitors.

In the first match, Lee Sedol playing as black had the initiative against AlphaGo as white. Not sure what to expect, Lee played a fairly conservative game, to which AlphaGo was able to respond well. Although Lee seemed to be in control for most of the game, AlphaGo was eventually able to gain a lead and Lee resigned after move 186. In the post-match conference, Lee blamed his loss on an error made in the early game, but most commentators considered his probing move 7 not an obvious mistake and certainly not game-deciding. The fact that AlphaGo was able to beat Lee in a solid game, without major mistakes on both sides, sent a strong message about its capabilities. The unexpected outcome of the game was reported in newspapers all over the world. The *New York Times* published four expert opinions on the significance of AlphaGo's victory (Young-Joon, 2016, March 9). The most enthusiastic response highlighted the difference between Deep Blue and AlphaGo, describing machine learning as a true "game changer," whereas the more skeptical voices insisted on the gap separating machines from humans and the difference between mastering a board game and real-world applications. For many Go fans however, the outcome of the series was not yet decided as they waited for Lee, known for his aggressive style, to finally play his game.

The second match, now with AlphaGo as black and Lee Sedol as white, was highly anticipated as AlphaGo would have the initiative—a role that previous Go programs did not cope with very well. After the game, AlphaGo's move 37 was praised as "creative" and "unique," a move a professional Go player would have never played. The move happened to be a variation of the well-known "shoulder hit," usually played at line 4 to block the development of a stone at line 3. AlphaGo played it at line 5, blocking a stone at line 4, which according to conventional wisdom allows the opponent to develop too much territory. Initially, most commentators wondered if the move might have been a mistake; Lee took a cigarette break and more than ten minutes to think about his response to the move. As the game progressed, move 37 strengthened AlphaGo's overall board position allowing it to secure a lead. In the end game, AlphaGo played some unusual "slack"-locking moves (e.g., move 167), which quickly became a topic of debate in the Go community. In the post-match press conference, Lee Sedol complimented AlphaGo for playing "a nearly perfect game" and confessed that "from the very beginning of the game I did not feel like there was a point that I was leading" (DeepMind, 2016, March 9).

In game three, AlphaGo, again as white, was able to gain an early lead, defending successfully against any attempt by Lee Sedol to turn the tables. With the third win in a row, AlphaGo not only sealed the result of the overall contest but also crushed the hopes of many that it could ever be beaten by a human player. David Ormerod (2016, March 12), an Australian Go player who teamed up with An Younggil, an 8-dan professional, to provide a commentary for the games, concluded: "We're now convinced that AlphaGo is simply stronger than any known human Go player." He also offered an interesting interpretation of AlphaGo's infamous "slack moves":

> After being compelled to flex its muscles for a short time and gaining the upper hand, AlphaGo began to play leisurely moves. By now, most observers know that this is a feature of the ruthlessly efficient algorithm which guides AlphaGo's play. Unlike humans, AlphaGo doesn't try to maximize its advantage. Its only concern is its probability of winning. The machine is content to win by half a point, as long as it is following the most certain path to success. So when AlphaGo plays a slack looking move, we may regard it as a mistake, but perhaps it is more accurately viewed as a declaration of victory? (Ormerod, 2016, March 12)

Ormerod reframes this peculiar feature of AlphaGo's algorithm in terms of style and intention and not as a mechanistic failure to optimize the final result. In "slacking," AlphaGo demonstrates its superiority. Like other commentators, Ormerod takes an "intentional stance" (Dennet, 1989) toward the program: "AlphaGo gradually allowed the pressure to slacken, giving false hope to some observers," but it remained nonetheless in control of the game. Lee "tried a clever indirect attack against White's center dragon with Black 77, but AlphaGo's responses made it feel like *it knew exactly what Lee's plan was*" (Ormerod, 2016, March 12). In the end, Lee had to concede the game—and along with it the prize for winning the series.

In the fourth game, the overall outcome already being decided, Lee managed a spectacular comeback as white, exploiting a weakness of the Monte Carlo algorithm while demonstrating the power of human intuition. He did so by choosing a high-risk strategy (*amashi*), allowing his opponent to extend his influence in the center of the board while securing territory in the corners, followed by an attack in the center of the board, which AlphaGo wasn't able to handle adequately. As the 9-dan commentator Michael Redmond asserted in his post-game analysis (in Deep Mind, 2016, March 13), while Lee Sedol was not aware until late which sequence of moves would lead to victory, he certainly had a feeling of a weakness in the center, which he might be able to exploit.

Until move 78, "commentators were lamenting that the game seemed to be decided already" (Ormerod, 2016, March 13)—in favor of AlphaGo. Lee's brilliant move 78 took not only AlphaGo by surprise but most professional observers. Gu Li, a 9-dan Chinese professional, called move 78 the "hand of god" (in Ormerod, 2016, March 13).[2] DeepMind revealed later that AlphaGo dismissed move 78 as very unlikely and consequently missed in its Monte Carlo search the line of play that secured Lee Sedol his victory. Interestingly, its failure was not attributed to deficiencies in the algorithm but to Lee's ingenuity. Both players exhibited superhuman play. Up to that point, AlphaGo had not failed to impress observers, but after its chances of winning suddenly dropped, it exhibited a behavior that commentators like Ormerod described as bot-like:

> This was when things got weird. From 87 to 101 AlphaGo made a series of very bad moves. We've talked about AlphaGo's 'bad' moves in the discussion of previous games, but this was not the same. In previous games, AlphaGo played 'bad' (slack) moves when it was already ahead. Human observers criticized these moves because there seemed to be no reason to play slackly, but AlphaGo had already calculated that these moves would lead to a safe win. The bad moves AlphaGo played in game four were not at all like that. They were simply bad, and they ruined AlphaGo's chances of recovering. They're the kind of moves played by someone who forgets that their opponent also gets to respond with a move. Moves that trample over possibilities and damage one's own position—achieving less than nothing. The game continued for another 80 or so moves, but it ended with AlphaGo's eventual resignation. (Ormerod, 2016, March 13)

The distinction between the "slack moves" of the previous games and the "very bad moves" of game four is instructive. While the "slack moves"

[2] The "hand of god" (*Kami No Itte*), also translated as "divine move," is a trope popularized by the Go manga and anime *Hikaru no Go*; cf. https://senseis.xmp.net/?KamiNoItte.

could be interpreted intentionally, as the confident moves of a superior player taunting the opponent with secure moves that were just good enough to maintain the lead, the "very bad moves" toward the end of game four were meaningless, pointless, and embarrassing—far from being superhuman, they were likened to the moves an absolute beginner would make. Despite the deterioration of its performance after White 78, AlphaGo did not disappoint entirely, clearly dominating the game up until that point. After the game, Lee Sedol humbly confessed: "This victory is so valuable, I wouldn't exchange it for anything in the world" (in Kohs, 2017, 1:14:25–31). While game four revealed a weak spot in AlphaGo's game play and gave new hopes to Lee Sedol's fans and those cheering for team humanity, it did not diminish AlphaGo's previous successes.

In the fifth and final game of the series, Lee tried to replicate this strategy—with a promising start but ultimately no success. At the beginning of the game, when Lee Sedol seemed to have gained a lead, 9-dan commentator Redmond joked that AlphaGo "hasn't recovered from game four yet." Demis Hassabis from DeepMind confided after the game that AlphaGo thought it made a "bad mistake" in the early game and was trying hard "to claw it back" (in Byford, 2016, March 15). Nevertheless, according to most commentators, the game was fairly even until AlphaGo was able to gain and defend a small advantage. After the match, which concluded the series, AlphaGo was awarded a 9-dan honorary degree from the Korean Go Association. Despite the fact that AlphaGo won the competition in game three, the social drama came only to a satisfying conclusion after game five. If AlphaGo had played badly early in game four or if it had also lost the final game, the results would have been perceived as inconclusive. The ritualistic gesture toward AlphaGo not only confirmed the result of the series, it also symbolized the inclusion of AlphaGo in the social world (of Go players). For some time, AlphaGo was even listed as best player in the world in a popular Go ranking (cf. Chi, 2016, July 19).

Lee Sedol vs. AlphaGo was a perfect dramatization of Go, which not only demonstrated the AlphaGo's superiority convincingly but also testified to the human fighting spirit with Lee's amazing comeback in game four. AlphaGo might not have played flawlessly, but it exhibited a human-like capacity for what observers described as "creativity" (Sang-Hun, 2016, March 15), playing effective moves that defied conventional Go wisdom. In the tech-savvy Go countries of East Asia, AlphaGo's success was experienced as a kind of "sputnik shock":

> One thing the Western world is overlooking is that the dominating play of AlphaGo, an AI that was developed by the British, was equivalent to a Sputnik event for Asian nations. Asian nations in reaction to this achievement are doubling down on A.I. investment so as to not only catch up, but also perhaps overtake the West in their AI capabilities. (Perez, 2017, September 4, para. 8)

After AlphaGo defeated Lee Sedol, South Korea announced an investment of an additional 863 million dollars into its AI program, a 55 percent increase of the budget stretched over five years (Zastrow, 2016, March 18). China (cf. Chi, 2016, July 19) and Japan (cf. Shimizu, 2017, April 12) followed soon after, joining the new "space race" to become AI superpowers. Ultimately, the games against Lee Sedol vindicated DeepMind's ambitious claims, thus providing a conclusion to the social drama, which was ritually affirmed by AlphaGo's symbolic inclusion in the Go community. Most importantly, AlphaGo exhibited not just nearly perfect play but a considerable degree of creativity, playing unexpected moves to great effect. A widespread consensus emerged regarding AlphaGo's capabilities, although questions remained regarding its potential to revolutionize the game of Go as well as the broader technical applicability of machine learning.

Restaging the Drama: AlphaGo Master Vs. Ke Jie

After the games against Lee Sedol, AlphaGo continued to haunt the Go community. Between December 29, 2016, and January 4, 2017, a mysterious player called "Master" defeated sixty professional players in online games on two different Go servers.[3] DeepMind, in an attempt to restage the social drama, later revealed that the mysterious player was the latest iteration of AlphaGo. Even though the games were fast paced, giving a natural advantage to the computer, a flawless record against sixty top players was nevertheless impressive. Even more surprising was the fact that the games, all published by DeepMind, included many innovative moves questioning conventional Go wisdom (cf. Baker & Hui, 2017, April 10). The most iconic is probably the early 3-3 invasion, which was considered a beginner's mistake before AlphaGo made it work. The move was

[3] The games have all been published by DeepMind; see https://deepmind.com/alphago-master-series.

quickly imitated by professional Go players, including AlphaGo's future opponent Ke Jie (Lin, 2017, May 20).

At least within the Go community, the publication of the Master games constituted a cognitive breach, albeit one that didn't develop into a proper social crisis. Observers were shocked and awed, but AlphaGo's performance sparked less controversy than curiosity. This second stage of AlphaGo's social drama culminated in the games against Ke Jie, a 19-year-old Chinese Go player who led the world ranking for more than a year. These games were the main event at the Wuzhen Future of Go Summit 2017, which also served as a marketing event for Google in China (Lin & Nicas, 2017, May 25). Among the side events was a game of team Go, in which five Chinese top professionals teamed up to beat AlphaGo, as well as a game of pair Go, in which two professionals played against each other, each of them taking turns with an AlphaGo partner. While the human professionals lost to AlphaGo in the team game, the pair game introduced new meanings into the story of AlphaGo, raising the topic of AI–human cooperation: "In a sense, the match provided a glimpse of how human experts might be able to use AI tools in the future, benefiting from the program's insights while also relying on their own intuition" (American Go E-Journal, 2017, May 27, para. 3).

On May 23, 2017, the three-game series between AlphaGo and Ke Jie started, this time with 1.5 million dollars of prize money for the winner. Despite what we can call an even larger "center bet" (Geertz, 2006a), the game was—from a dramatic point of view—"shallower" than the games against Lee Sedol. In the sixty Master games, AlphaGo showed not only previously unknown strength but an amount of creativity that changed the game of Go forever. Odds for side bets, if there were any, were crushingly in favor of AlphaGo, which meant the best human Go player entered the series as an underdog. Interestingly, the matches against Ke Jie were censored by the Chinese government, which was supposedly afraid that a "damaging defeat ... would hurt the national pride of a state which holds Go close to its heart" (Hern 2017, May 24). While Ke Jie was expected to lose, his reputation as the strongest player of team humanity was nevertheless at stake. It is no surprise that Google (2017) decided to frame The Future of Go Summit in a nonconfrontational way, stressing human-machine cooperation: "Legendary players and DeepMind's AlphaGo explore the mysteries of Go together."

Ke Jie lived up to the high expectations, losing the first game as black by the smallest possible margin, half a point. While such a result against

AlphaGo was surely impressive and a sign of a strong game on Ke's part, it is not a good indicator for estimating the gap between him and AlphaGo, as the latter's algorithm does not care about the margin. Ke Jie surprised the audience with move 7, imitating the early 3–3 invasion that AlphaGo pioneered in the Master series. After the match, Ke admitted that he had little hope of beating AlphaGo. He stated that previous versions of AlphaGo had been human-like, whereas the new Master was like "a god of Go" (in DeepMind, 2017, May 22, 5:49:19–23). Acknowledging the ever-increasing gap between human Go players and artificial intelligence, Ke declared that he will not play AlphaGo in the future. Leaving behind the confines of Go, Ke predicted a bright future for humanity due to progress in AI research:

> I believe in the power of science and technology ... the future will belong to artificial intelligence and the world will be made a much better place and convenient place because of artificial intelligence. (in DeepMind, 2017, May 22, 6:05:55–06:07)

The second game, with Ke Jie as white, took a similar course. Ke played a perfect game well into the mid-game, even by the estimates of AlphaGo (Hassabis, 2017, May 25). Nonetheless, after four hours of play it became clear that Alpha Go was winning and Ke resigned. After the game, Ke Jie stated that this match gave him "the feeling of playing with a human being" (in DeepMind 2017, May 24, 5:17:26–32), while at the same time emphasizing the superhuman qualities of the program. He repeated his assertion that "AlphaGo is the god of the Go game" (5:13:10–13) and conceded that the human understanding of the game is very limited. In contrast to Searle's claim that computers do not understand games like Go or chess, Ke views understanding Go not as a hidden mental process but as the ability to play—which AlphaGo certainly possesses. While the winner of the series was already clear after the second match, Ke Jie asked to play the third game as white on the basis of AlphaGo favoring white in self-play, to which Demis Hassabis agreed (5:16:40–17:47). Despite another strong game, Ke Jie was again forced to concede after move 205.

After the Future of Go Summit, DeepMind published 50 of Master's self-play games, which are now studied by Go players and had a tremendous impact on professional play. In his YouTube commentary on the prestigious Meijin title match in 2018, Michael Redmond remarked on the opening featuring an AlphaGo-style early 3–3 invasion:

> The game started with Yama as black playing 3-3 points and Cho playing 4-4 points, star points, which Cho didn't use to play ... but he changed his styles, the effects of strong computer programs being having on all of us. [After twelve moves:] It's an AI-like game, it's a modern way of playing. (Redmond 2018, August 29, 0:20–1:00)

Whether commentators liked it or not, AlphaGo came to define the modern way of playing Go. While not unexpected in its outcome, AlphaGo's victory over Ke Jie was the last nail in the coffin of human Go superiority and can be considered the final resolution of the social drama triggered by the initial cognitive breach. After the second stage of the drama, the game of Go was not the same, with many unconventional strategies pioneered by AlphaGo entering professional play. While the consensus regarding the significance of AlphaGo had broadened and consolidated, especially in the Go community, questions remained regarding the limitations and broader applications of the technological breakthrough.

Toward a General AI: AlphaGo Zero, AlphaZero, and AlphaStar

While AlphaGo Master once and for all demonstrated its superiority over humans in Go, the generalizability of its algorithm was still debatable. It was unclear how the insights of AlphaGo could be applied to other fields; furthermore, its initial training required a huge amount of data that might be unobtainable in other fields. Only a few months after the Wuzhen Future of Go Summit 2017, DeepMind published another paper in *Nature* where they announced their latest breakthrough in computer Go: a program that learned the game by itself without any human input (Silver et al., 2017). AlphaGo Zero, as it was baptized, proved to be superior to its predecessors, beating the version that played against Lee Sedol in 100 games without a loss and the Master version, which played against Ke Jie, in 89 out of 100 games (Silver et al., 2017, p. 12). Despite being significantly stronger, the newest AlphaGo iteration was praised for its human-like play and creativity (Lee, 2017, October 19). Also AlphaGo Zero's self-plays, published by DeepMind, have been intensely studied in Go circles and shaped professional play.

With AlphaZero, a program able to learn and play all kinds of perfect information board games, DeepMind pushed even further. After only three days of training, AlphaZero was able to beat AlphaGo Zero in 60 out of 100 Go games. Nevertheless, the real purpose of AlphaZero was to master other games like chess, which it did, defeating the powerful Stockfish engine in a series of 100 matches without losing a single game. While many computer chess experts questioned the conditions under which both programs fought against each other, chess players were impressed by AlphaZero's creative and human-like play, including Garry Kasparov:

> For me, as a very sharp and attacking player, it is a pleasure watching AlphaZero play. … We all expect machines to play very solid and slow games but AlphaZero just does the opposite. It is surprising to see a machine playing so aggressively, and it also shows a lot of creativity. It is a real breakthrough—and I believe it could be extremely helpful for many other studies in the field of computer science. (in Ingle, 2018, December 11)

What is crucial here is not the fact that AlphaZero won, but the way it won, which has been decidedly different from Deep Blue and his successors. Instead of typical computer chess, in which the opponent is overwhelmed in defensive games by sheer computing power, AlphaZero—just like AlphaGo—was able to win through surprising yet effective moves which can be thought of as reflecting a deeper insight into the game. A *New York Times* commentary explored the utility an AI like AlphaZero might have for science, envisioning a future "AlphaInfinity":

> Like its ancestor, it would have supreme insight: it could come up with beautiful proofs, as elegant as the chess games that AlphaZero played against Stockfish. . . . AlphaInfinity could cure all our diseases, solve all our scientific problems and make all our other intellectual trains run on time. (Strogatz, 2018, December 26)

Despite initial skepticism and resistance, neural networks and machine learning seem to have conquered the field of computer chess recently. An open-source program called Leela Zero, constructed after the principles of AlphaGo, was able to defeat the newest Stockfish engine in the Top Chess Engine Championship in 2019. Ever since, artificial neural networks feature consistently in title matches. With the emergence of a new algorithmic culture, the days of custom-engineered chess programs like Deep Blue or Stockfish seem to be numbered. In contrast to traditional chess engines, AlphaZero was able to offer strategic insights, which may shape professional chess as its predecessor shaped professional Go (see Sadler & Regan, 2019).

With AlphaStar, DeepMind ventured into the field of hidden-information real-time strategy games, creating a program that achieved grandmaster status with human-like play in the game *StarCraft II*, one of the most popular e-sports (Vinyals et al., 2019). A previous version of the program was criticized for having an unfair advantage over human players thus putting the validity of its reality test into question. As a consequence, its programmers imposed severe handicaps on AlphaStar, limiting its view and reaction time, which forced the grandmaster program to focus on long-term strategies instead of relying on inhuman speed and precision. While AlphaStar was trained on human games, it became—as a professional StarCraft player asserted—an "unorthodox player" with "strategies and a style that are entirely its own" (in The AlphaStar Team, 2019, October 30). The strategic capabilities of this new generation of AI make them interesting in terms of military applications, as an expert confided to the *Guardian*: "Military analysts will certainly be eyeing the successful AlphaStar real-time strategies as a clear example of the advantages of AI for battlefield planning" (Noel Sharkey in Sample, 2019, October 30). While the reality of a battlefield is certainly messier than the virtual reality of game environments, such "real-world" applications are no longer beyond the horizon of expectation.

Concluding Remarks

The social drama of AlphaGo developed in several stages, each moving from breach to crisis, test, and resolution—albeit with varying degrees of dramatization. Each stage of the drama was triggered by a cognitive breach: the publication of an unexpected technological breakthrough. The breach was followed by a social crisis—sometimes more, sometimes less pronounced—in which the significance of the breakthrough was debated and ultimately subjected to a reality test, namely competitive games arranged between the program and human top-players or—in the case of AlphaZero vs. Stockfish—between programs. The successful performances of AlphaGo, AlphaZero, and AlphaStar were able to address the crisis and overcome the initial skepticism, after which a social consensus emerged, and the programs became part of their respective communities. In contrast to the "shallow play" of Deep Blue and traditional chess engines, the "deep play" of AlphaGo and its iterations was repeatedly praised as creative and exerted a profound influence on the games themselves. Traditional chess engines have been used by professional chess players in preparation for their matches, but they did not offer genuine strategic insights—and no answers to the questions raised by Kasparov at the beginning of this chapter. At least the first two of those questions, pertaining to the ability to learn and the capacity for intuition, we are now able to address briefly.

The new algorithmic culture based on machine learning not only allows programs to learn from their mistakes but utilizes the trial-and-error approach as an algorithmic engine. DeepMind's programmers did not have to teach AlphaGo to play good Go, they just needed to design a program that was able to learn efficiently from its mistakes. Later versions did not even require human training data, which eliminated another source of human bias. Furthermore, AlphaGo was able to mimic human intuition, making informed decisions without being able to process all relevant information, which is crucial for mastering the complexity of Go. Even professional Go players have to rely on their feelings about certain moves and board positions; they often know that a move is good, without necessarily being able to explain why. In his piece on "Guessing," Charles Sanders Peirce (1929) describes how experience become sedimented in "habits of the mind," which manifest themselves in acts of intuition, educated guesses that are not based on exact knowledge. Similarly, AlphaGo's artificial neural network, shaped by millions of games of self-play, developed its own "habits of the mind." While chess engines could rely on "brute force" and precise computations against human players, AlphaGo was only able to succeed due to its functional equivalent for human intuition, which allowed for educated guesses in complex situations.

DeepMind, the purported "Apollo program for artificial intelligence" (Hassabis 2015, May 12), had remarkable success in the area of board and computer games, which are characterized by artificial environments with well-defined rules. AlphaGo and AlphaZero were certainly "giant steps" for the Go and chess communities, shaping professional play for years to come. But only time will tell if they were also "giant steps" for humanity toward the goal of general AI. As of now, "real-world" applications of DeepMind's machine learning technology in fields such as health and manufacturing are still in the waiting. At least, DeepMind learning algorithms seemed to have been able to reduce the amount of energy used for cooling in Google data centers by 40 percent (Evans & Gao, 2016, July

20). Despite being consistent with his analogy, Hassabis' tweet after the first victory of AlphaGo against Lee Sedol, "We landed it on the moon," may have been premature. Even after the social drama of AlphaGo turned into a multi-stage rocket, consecutively extending the reach and efficiency of machine learning algorithms, general AI is still far out of reach.

A comparison with the historic Apollo program and the moon landing more than fifty years ago might be instructive here. After the end of the Apollo program, humans never returned to the moon. While there has been undeniable progress in manned spaceflight, these achievements fall short compared to the imaginaries sparked by the Apollo program. All those who expected a trip to Mars before the end of the millennium and the rapid colonization of space were ultimately disappointed. DeepMind and other contemporary AI research efforts may suffer a similar fate, generating effective solutions for a variety of problems while falling short in solving the problem of general AI. Maybe DeepMind's analogy to the Apollo program is misleading altogether and AlphaGo should rather be compared to Sputnik, a relatively useless chunk of metal launched into space in 1957, which nevertheless triggered a consequential space race. The high-tech Go countries China, Korea, and Japan experienced AlphaGo's victory as a kind of "Sputnik shock," which led governments to pour billions of dollars into AI research. The space race for AI, with outcomes uncertain, may have just begun. If this is the case, the cultural significance of AlphaGo can hardly be underestimated. And who knows, maybe one day we will have to accept AIs as full-fledged members of our society.

References

Alexander, J. C. (2019). *What makes a social crisis? The societalization of social problems*. Polity.

Alexander, J. C., & Smith, P. (2001/2003). The strong program in cultural sociology: Elements of a structural hermeneutics. In J. C. Alexander, *The meanings of social life: A cultural sociology* (pp. 11–26). Oxford University Press.

Alexander, J. C., & Smith, P. (2010). The strong program: Origins, achievements, prospects. In J. R. Hall, L. Grindstaff, & M.-C. Lo (Eds.), *Handbook of cultural sociology* (pp. 13–24). Routledge.

American Go E-Journal. (2017, May 27). *AlphaGo Pair and Team Go wrap up*. https://www.usgo.org/news/2017/05/alphago-pair-and-team-go-wrap-up/.

Baker, L., & Hui, F. (2017, April 10). Innovations of AlphaGo. *Deep Mind*. https://deepmind.com/blog/article/innovations-alphago.
Boltanski, L. (2011). *On critique: A sociology of emancipation*. Malden: Polity.
Boltanski, L., & Thévenot, L. (2007). *On justification: On economies of social worth*. Princeton University Press.
Byford, S. (2016, March 15). Google's AlphaGo AI beats Lee Sedol again to win Go series 4-1. *The Verge*. https://www.theverge.com/2016/3/15/11213518/alphago-deepmind-go-match-5-result.
Chi, M. (2016, July 19). AlphaGo now world's No. 1 Go player. *China Daily*. http://www.chinadaily.com.cn/china/2016-07/19/content_26141040.htm.
DeepMind. (2016, March 9). *Match 2—Google DeepMind challenge match: Lee Sedol vs AlphaGo*. YouTube. https://www.youtube.com/watch?v=l-GsfyVCBu0.
DeepMind. (2016, March 13). *Match 4 15 minute summary—Google DeepMind challenge match 2016*. YouTube. https://www.youtube.com/watch?v=G5gJ-pVo1gs.
DeepMind. (2017, May 22). *The Future of Go Summit, Match One: Ke Jie & AlphaGo*. YouTube. https://www.youtube.com/watch?v=Z-HL5nppBnM, 5:49:19–23.
DeepMind (2017, May 24). *The Future of Go Summit, Match Two: Ke Jie & AlphaGo*. YouTube. https://www.youtube.com/watch?v=1U1p4Mwis60.
Dennett, D. C. (1989). *The intentional stance*. MIT Press.
Ensmenger, N. (2012). Is chess the drosophila of artificial intelligence? A social history of an algorithm. *Social Studies of Science, 42*(1), 5–30. https://doi.org/10.1177/0306312711424596.
Evans, R., & Gao, J. (2016, July 20). *DeepMind AI reduces Google data centre cooling bill by 40%*. DeepMind. https://deepmind.com/blog/article/deepmind-ai-reduces-google-data-centre-cooling-bill-40.
Geertz, C. (2006a). Deep play: Notes on the Balinese cockfight. In *The interpretation of cultures: Selected essays* (pp. 412–453). Basic Books.
Geertz, C. (2006b). Thick description: Towards an interpretative theory of culture. In *The interpretation of cultures: Selected essays* (pp. 3–30). Basic Books.
Gibney, E. (2016, January 27). Go players react to computer defeat. *Nature*. https://www.nature.com/news/go-players-react-to-computer-defeat-1.19255.
Google. (2017). *23 May–27 May, Wuzhen, China: The Future of Go Summit*. https://events.google.com/alphago2017/.
Hassabis, D. (2015, May 12). *Human AI is decades away, but we need to start the debate now*. Google Zeitgeist. https://www.youtube.com/watch?v=rbsqaJwpu6A.

Hassabis, D. [@demishassabis]. (2016, March 9). *#AlphaGo WINS!!!! We landed it on the moon. So proud of the team!! Respect to the amazing Lee Sedol too* [Tweet]. Twitter. https://twitter.com/demishassabis/status/707474683906674688.

Hassabis, D. (2017). Artificial intelligence: Chess match of the century. *Nature, 544*(7651), 413–414. https://doi.org/10.1038/544413a.

Hassabis, D. [@demishassabis]. (2017, May 25). *Incredible: According to #AlphaGo evaluations Ke Jie is playing perfectly at the moment* [Tweet]. Twitter. https://twitter.com/demishassabis/status/867584056095002624.

Hern, A. (2017, May 24). China censored Google's AlphaGo match against world's best Go player. *Guardian*. https://www.theguardian.com/technology/2017/may/24/china-censored-googles-alphago-match-against-worlds-best-go-player.

Husserl, E. (1982/1929). *Cartesian meditations: An introduction into phenomenology*. Nijhoff.

Ingle, S. (2018, December 11). "Creative" AlphaZero leads way for chess computers and, maybe, science. *Guardian*. https://www.theguardian.com/sport/2018/dec/11/creative-alphazero-leads-way-chess-computers-science.

Kasparov, G. (2018). Chess, a drosophila of reasoning. *Science, 362*(6419), 1087. https://doi.org/10.1126/science.aaw2221.

Kelion, L. (2016, January 27). *Facebook trains AI to beat humans at Go board game*. BBC News. https://www.bbc.com/news/technology-35419141.

Kloester, B. (2016, March 4). Can AlphaGo defeat Lee Sedol? *Go Game Guru*. https://web.archive.org/web/20160316120725/https://goggameguru.com/can-alphago-defeat-lee-sedol/.

Kohs, G. (2017). *AlphaGo—The movie. Full documentary*. YouTube. https://www.youtube.com/watch?v=WXuK6gekU1Y.

Lee, M. H. (2017, October 19). Go players excited about "more humanlike" AlphaGo Zero. *The Korea Bizwire*. http://koreabizwire.com/go-players-excited-about-more-humanlike-alphago-zero/98282.

Lévi-Strauss, C. (1966). *The savage mind*. Weidenfeld und Nicolson.

Lin, L., & Nicas, J. (2017, May 25). Google's strategic long game in China. *Wall Street Journal*. https://www.wsj.com/articles/google-goes-to-china-making-play-for-talent-and-attention-1495704246.

Lin, V. (2017, May 20). A new perspective on the star point and the implications thereof. *European Go Federation*. https://www.eurogofed.org/?id=127.

Luckmann, T. (1970). On the boundaries of the social world. In M. Natanson (Ed.), *Phenomenology and social reality: Essays in memory of Alfred Schutz* (pp. 73–100). Nijhoff.

Luhmann, N. (1990). Meaning as sociology's basic concept. In *Essays on self-reference* (pp. 21–79). Columbia University Press.

Ormerod, D. (2016, March 12). AlphaGo shows its true strength in 3rd victory against Lee Sedol. *Go Game Guru*. https://web.archive.org/web/20160313032049/https://gogameguru.com/alphago-shows-true-strength-3rd-victory-lee-sedol/.

Ormerod, D. (2016, March 13). Lee Sedol defeats AlphaGo in masterful comeback—Game 4. *Go Game Guru*. https://web.archive.org/web/20160314022418/https://gogameguru.com/lee-sedol-defeats-alphago-masterful-comeback-game-4/.

Peirce, C. S. (1929). Guessing. *The Hound & Horn, 2*(3), 267–282.

Perez, C. E. (2017, September 4). Three cognitive dimensions for tracking deep learning progress. *Medium*. https://medium.com/intuitionmachine/deep-learning-system-zero-intuition-and-rationality-c07bd134dbfb.

Redmond, M. (2018, August 29). *Summary of the game by Michael Redmond: The first game of the Meijin title "go" tournament*. YouTube. https://www.youtube.com/watch?v=7tyY4xPEaKM.

Roberge, J., & Seyfert, R. (2016). What are algorithmic cultures? In J. Roberge & R. Seyfert (Eds.), *Algorithmic cultures: Essays on meaning, performance and new technologies* (pp. 1–25). Routledge.

Sadler, M., & Regan, N. (2019). *Game changer: AlphaZero's groundbreaking chess strategies and the promise of AI*. New in Chess.

Sample, I. (2019, October 30). AI becomes grandmaster in "fiendishly complex" *StarCraft II*. *Guardian*. https://www.theguardian.com/technology/2019/oct/30/ai-becomes-grandmaster-in-fiendishly-complex-starcraft-ii.

Sang-Hun, C. (2016, March 15). Google's computer program beats Lee Sedol in Go tournament. *New York Times*. https://www.nytimes.com/2016/03/16/world/asia/korea-alphago-vs-lee-sedol-go.html.

Schutz, A., & Luckmann, T. (1983). *Structures of the life-world: Volume II*. Northwestern University Press.

Searle, J. R. (1980). Minds, brains, and programs. *Behavioral and Brain Sciences, 3*(3), 417–424. https://doi.org/10.1017/S0140525X00005756.

Searle, J. R. (2014, October 9). What your computer can't know. *New York Review of Books*. https://www.nybooks.com/articles/2014/10/09/what-your-computer-cant-know/.

Shimizu, R. (2017, April 12). Deep learning's rise leaves Japan playing AI catchup. *Nippon.com*. https://www.nippon.com/en/currents/d00307/deep-learning%E2%80%99s-rise-leaves-japan-playing-ai-catchup.html.

Silver, D. [David_Silver]. (2017, October 19). *AMA: We are David Silver and Julian Schrittwieser from DeepMind's AlphaGo team. Ask us anything* [online forum post]. Reddit. https://www.reddit.com/r/MachineLearning/comments/76xjb5/ama_we_are_david_silver_and_julian_schrittwieser/dohp9vc/.

Silver, D., Huang, A., Maddison, C. J., Guez, A., Sifre, L., van den Driessche, G., … Hassabis, D. (2016). Mastering the game of Go with deep neural networks and tree search. *Nature, 529*, 484–489. https://doi.org/10.1038/nature16961.

Silver, D., Schrittwieser, J., Simonyan, K., Antonoglou, I., Huang, A., Guez, A., ... Hassabis, D. (2017). Mastering the game of Go without human knowledge. *Nature, 550*, 354–359. https://doi.org/10.1038/nature24270.

Simonite, T. (2016, March 13). How Google plans to solve artificial intelligence. *MIT Technology Review*. https://www.technologyreview.com/s/601139/how-google-plans-to-solve-artificial-intelligence/.

Strogatz, S. (2018, December 26). One giant step for a chess-playing machine. *New York Times*. https://www.nytimes.com/2018/12/26/science/chess-artificial-intelligence.html.

The AlphaStar Team. (2019, October 30). AlphaStar: Grandmaster level in *StarCraft II* using multi-agent reinforcement learning. *DeepMind*. https://deepmind.com/blog/article/AlphaStar-Grandmaster-level-in-StarCraft-II-using-multi-agent-reinforcement-learning.

Turner, V. (1980). Social dramas and stories about them. *Critical Inquiry, 7*(1), 141–168. http://www.jstor.org/stable/1343180.

Vinyals, O., Babuschkin, I., Czarnecki, W. M., Mathieu, M., Dudzik, A., Chung, J., ... Silver, D. (2019). Grandmaster level in StarCraft II using multi-agent reinforcement learning. *Nature, 575*(7782), 350–354. https://doi.org/10.1038/s41586-019-1724-z.

Wagner-Pacifici, R. E. (1986). *The Moro morality play: Terrorism as social drama*. University of Chicago Press.

Woods, E. T. (2013). A cultural approach to a Canadian tragedy: The Indian residential schools as a sacred enterprise. *International Journal of Politics, Culture, and Society, 26*(2), 173–187. https://doi.org/10.1007/s10767-013-9132-0.

Young-Joon, A. (2016, March 9). Does AlphaGo mean artificial intelligence is the real deal? *New York Times*. https://www.nytimes.com/roomfordebate/2016/03/09/does-alphago-mean-artificial-intelligence-is-the-real-deal.

Zastrow, M. (2016). South Korea trumpets $860-million AI fund after AlphaGo "shock". *Nature*. https://doi.org/10.1038/nature.2016.19595.

CHAPTER 7

Adversariality in Machine Learning Systems: On Neural Networks and the Limits of Knowledge

Théo Lepage-Richer

> Brains do not secrete thought as the liver secretes bile … they compute thought the way electronic computers calculate numbers.—Warren McCulloch, "Recollections of the Many Sources of Cybernetics" (1974)

> Biology is superficial, intelligence is artificial.—Grimes, "We Appreciate Power" (2020)

One Neural Network or Many?

In their influential piece "A Logical Calculus of the Ideas Immanent in Nervous Activity" (1943), Warren McCulloch and Walter Pitts—a neurophysiologist and a logician who were soon to become key figures in the nascent field of cybernetics—introduced a new model to represent knowledge acquisition as it takes place in both biological neurons and computer

T. Lepage-Richer (✉)
Brown University, Providence, RI, USA
e-mail: theo_lepage-richer@brown.edu

© The Author(s) 2021

J. Roberge and M. Castelle (eds.), *The Cultural Life of Machine Learning*, https://doi.org/10.1007/978-3-030-56286-1_7

circuits. Through this model, which they would name "neural nets" a few publications later, they argued that "all that could be achieved in [psychology]" (p. 131) could be reproduced through systems of logical devices connected together according to "the 'all-or-none' law of nervous activity" (p. 117). While most of the work in psychology at the time had taken behavior as its main focus, McCulloch and Pitts instead posited that the mind could become the object of a new experimental science once theorized as the product of networks of interconnected neural units computing the functions embedded in their architecture.

Decades later, neural networks are no longer recognized as a model of the mind, but rather as an effective machine learning framework to extract patterns from large amounts of data. While early attempts to physically implement neural networks in analog computers led to limited results (e.g., Rosenblatt, 1957), many computer scientists in the late 1980s perceived in this model the possibility of overcoming the structural limits of serial computing machines via its parallel and so-called subsymbolic architecture (e.g., Fahlman & Hinton, 1987; McClelland, Rumelhart, & Hinton, 1986). Implemented in software environments, neural networks now provide computer scientists with a powerful operational framework to transpose a wide range of processes onto a computable substrate, enabling applications as diverse as object recognition (e.g., Krizhevsky, Sutskever, & Hinton, 2012), spatial orientation (e.g., Bojarski et al., 2016), and natural language processing (e.g., Hinton et al., 2012).

Between their initial conceptualization as a model of the mind and their subsequent reemergence in the field of machine learning, neural networks were mostly pushed to the fringe of the fields in which they were originally embraced. Whereas the first generation of cognitivists replaced neural mechanisms with information processes as their privileged objects of study for their work on the mind (e.g., Newell, Shaw, & Simon, 1958), many computer scientists who were first introduced to artificial intelligence (AI) by training neural networks disavowed this model for what they saw as its insurmountable linearity (e.g., Minsky & Papert, 1969). Among technical historians, scholars of scientific controversies, and computer scientists alike, the prevalent narrative bridging these two moments generally goes as follows: given the limited computational resources available at the time, neural networks could not achieve the results they were theoretically capable of (Nagy, 1991; Nilsson, 2009), leading competing AI models to become more attractive to corporate and military funders (Guice, 1998; Olazaran, 1996)—a reality which held true until breakthroughs in computing power allowed neural networks to fulfill most of the tasks their early thinkers had anticipated (Goodfellow, Bengio, & Courville, 2016).

This emphasis on neural networks' initial conceptualization and later reemergence as machine learning models might indeed reframe these systems' past and current shortcomings as temporary obstacles; yet, from a historical and epistemological perspective, this narrative seems to obscure the fundamental differences between McCulloch and Pitts' original model and neural networks' current manifestations. Upon closer inspection, these two models appear to have little in common besides their isomorphic structure—i.e., probabilistically connected, specialized units—and shared name: one was a theoretical model of the mind, the other is a functional framework for pattern recognition; one inaugurated the simultaneous development of cognitive science and artificial intelligence, the other now instantiates the irreducibility of one field to the other; one modelled knowledge acquisition as it takes place in both the brain and computer circuits, the other is tightly linked to the development of computing architectures optimized for parallel processing.

What traverses these distinctions, however, is an ambiguity regarding neural networks' status as a theoretical or functional model—an ambiguity which, given McCulloch and Pitts' experimental ambitions, might be as old as the concept itself. While McCulloch and Pitts developed a framework to model learning systems, current implementations of neural networks now provide a functional framework to identify and extract patterns for which no formal definition is available. In both cases, neural networks are conceived of as models of knowledge acquisition based on the operationalization of what lies beyond the limits of knowledge. From that perspective, the core property which unites the different systems encompassed by the concept of neural networks appears to be not so much their structural similarities, but rather their shared conceptualization of the unknown as something that can be contained and operationalized by networks of interconnected units.

Building upon these themes, this chapter is broadly concerned with what will be described as the *adversarial epistemology* underpinning the initial development, and subsequent reemergence and reformulation, of neural networks. By modelling how knowledge acquisition takes place across substrates (e.g., biological neurons, computer circuits, etc.), neural networks can be seen as both media artifacts and mediations of larger sets of discourses related to how the limits of knowledge are represented and understood in the fields where these systems are studied. While cybernetics envisioned a Manichean world in which science and the military strive toward the same ideals of command and control, today's research in machine learning attempts to develop models with more comprehensive representations by studying neural networks' vulnerabilities to a type of inputs called "adversarial examples." By investigating these two historical moments alongside one another, this text will attempt to highlight the persistence of an adversarial epistemology whose emergence coincides with neural networks' initial conceptualization and whose legacy continues to inform this model's current forms. That way, it will argue that neural networks' claim for knowledge is historically contingent on a larger techno-epistemic imaginary which naturalizes an understanding of knowledge as the product of sustained efforts to resist, counter, and overcome an assumed adversary.

The first two sections of this text will examine the co-constitutive relationship between neural networks' experimental epistemology and cybernetics' adversarial framework. To do so, they will situate the initial conceptualization of neural networks—which, for the sake of clarity, will now be referred to as the McCulloch-Pitts model when discussed in their original historical context—within the development of cybernetics as a unified field. In 1954, Norbert Wiener offered a teleological and theological reading of cybernetics by attributing the shortcomings of science to what he called the two "evils" of knowledge, i.e., the Manichean evil of deception and trickery and the Augustinian evil of chaos, randomness, and entropy. Through these two evils, Wiener reframed science as an adversarial endeavor against the limits of knowledge while providing two convenient concepts to mediate the intellectual landscape of not only knowledge and science, but also command and control. In many regards, the McCulloch-Pitts model offered a powerful experimental framework to apply cybernetics' adversarial epistemology; after laying out the reformulation of knowledge fostered by the McCulloch-Pitts model, this text will situate this model at the intersection of Wiener's two evils in order to account for the emergence of an adversarial epistemology conflating the limits of knowledge with the limits of control.

In the third section, this chapter will examine the persistence of this adversarial epistemology by discussing how the limits of knowledge are operationalized in the current literature on neural networks. Neural networks enable many of the defining functions of today's artificial intelligence systems, which has led the blind spots, biases, and failures of these machine learning models to become the objects of study of an ever-growing literature. More specifically, neural networks' vulnerability to adversarial examples—i.e., malicious alterations of inputs that cause neural networks to misclassify them—is now a core concern bridging research in machine learning and cybersecurity. While cybernetics' Manichean framework implied externalized and identifiable opponents (e.g., enemy pilots, Cold Warriors, etc.), the current literature on neural networks frames adversarial examples as both a threat and a privileged tool to increase the accuracy of these systems' learning model. Using adversarial examples as an entry point into the operationalization of the limits of neural networks' epistemology, this text will investigate how today's literature on the topic reframes the failures, biases, and errors produced by neural networks as constitutive of learning systems. In so doing, it will attempt to reframe neural networks as manifestations of a larger adversarial moment in which all errors, failures, and even critiques are conceived of as necessary steps—or necessary evils—in the development of machine learning models with comprehensive epistemologies.

The McCulloch-Pitts Model: A Physiological Study of Knowledge

The McCulloch-Pitts model, as first introduced in "A Logical Calculus," can be roughly described as networks of interconnected neural units acting like logic gates. Each unit is deemed to be in a quantifiable state (excitatory or inhibitory) at all times, which modulates as a function of the sum of the unit's inputs: if the unit's inputs are above a certain threshold value, the unit will be in an excited state and produce a positive value in return; if they are not, the unit will be in an inhibitory state and produce a null or negative value. Based on a voltage input, each neuron can then either fire and pass an impulse along or not fire and inhibit further excitation.

As initially enunciated by Claude Shannon, however, what is being communicated from one unit to the other is more than a voltage value. In "A Symbolic Analysis of Relay and Switching Circuits" (1938), Shannon theorized that Boolean algebra—a subfield of algebra in which the value of all variables is reduced to true and false statements or, as they are usually denoted, 1s and 0s—could be applied to the design of circuits to develop a calculus that is "exactly analogous to the calculus of propositions used in the symbolic study of logic" (p. 471). When a unit fires, it does not so much communicate its value as its state, which can be interpreted into the calculus of propositions it represents. For instance, if a unit is equated with proposition X, that unit's state can both express if X is true or false as well as influence whether the other propositions to which it is logically related are themselves true or false (Shannon, 1938, p. 475). Similarly, McCulloch and Pitts asserted that "the response of any neuron" could be described as "factually equivalent to a proposition which proposed its adequate stimulus" (1943, p. 117); connected together, they claimed, these neural units could then form complex networks capable of expressing any logical propositions independently from the actions, and potential failures, of individual neurons, leading them to conclude that the "physiological relations existing among nervous activities correspond … to relations among propositions" (1943, p. 117).

Despite their similarities, the McCulloch-Pitts model was far from a simple rearticulation of Shannon's framework in neurological terms. By describing biological neurons and their electronic counterparts as both subject to "continuous changes in threshold related to electrical and chemical variables" (1943, p. 117), McCulloch and Pitts introduced the possibility for evolution and adaption within networks of binary devices. These thresholds referred to a value "determined by the neuron" that had to be exceeded "to initiate an impulse" (1943, p. 115). More importantly, these thresholds could change and regulate themselves depending on what was being communicated. "An inhibitory synapse," they wrote, "does not absolutely prevent the firing of the neuron, but merely raises its threshold" (1943, p. 123), meaning that a given proposition could change the very conditions for other propositions to be true. In that sense, instead of simply expressing logical propositions, McCulloch and Pitts' networks could alter and modify their structure in a way akin to learning—a phenomenon they described as the process "in which activities concurrent at some previous time have altered the net permanently" (1943, p. 117). Through the introduction of adjustable thresholds, McCulloch and Pitts thus not only instituted self-regulation as a property of networks of binary devices, but also reframed the mind as a distributed phenomenon emerging from the interactions among simple logic gates.

While Shannon articulated his theory of logical relationships in digital circuits with regard to its applications in electrical engineering, McCulloch and Pitts thought of their model as the cornerstone of a new science of the mind. By providing a quantitative framework through which the mind could be captured as a localizable object of study, the McCulloch-Pitts model instantiated a clear break from the types of behavioral and psychoanalytic research in vogue at the time. While the contribution of the McCulloch-Pitts model to the development of cognitive science has been discussed by many science studies scholars (e.g., Dupuy, 1994; Kay, 2001), cognitive scientists tend to emphasize neural networks' deviation from the field's founding models. In their influential critique of neural networks, for instance, Jerry Fodor and Zenon Pylyshyn (1988) differentiate the approach inaugurated by McCulloch and Pitts from the "classical models of the mind [which] were derived from the structure of Turing and Von Neumann machines" (p. 4). These classical models might not have been "committed to the details of these machines," they specify, but were nevertheless reliant on the basic assumption "that the kind of computing that is relevant to understanding cognition involves operations of symbols" (1988, p. 4), thus establishing an analogical relationship between brains and computing machines.

In contrast, the McCulloch-Pitts model posited that no meaningful distinction between brains and computers could be established from the perspective of knowledge. Rather than conceiving of computers as facilitating the study of the brain, their model provided a shared framework for the study of both brains and computers. This idea is in many ways illustrated by McCulloch and Pitts' limited interest in all questions pertaining to machines and computers per se. In "What Is a Number, that a Man May Know It, and a Man, that He May Know a Number?" (1960), for instance, McCulloch wrote that his investment "in all problems of communication in men and machines" was limited to the way they offered quantifiable manifestations of "the functional organization of the nervous system" in contexts where "knowledge was as necessary as it was insufficient" (p. 7). In that sense, what interested McCulloch in the study of computing was not so much its unique properties or even those relevant to brain mechanisms, but rather how, once studied alongside the mind, it could provide an experimental setting to reproduce and examine processes that could not be studied in the brain itself. For McCulloch, computing was thus a useful object of study insofar as it contributed to his larger project of "reduc[ing] epistemology to an experimental science" (1960, p. 7).

The McCulloch-Pitts model can then be understood as an instance of what Seb Franklin (2015) calls cybernetics' deployment "of digitality as a logic that extends beyond the computing machine" (p. 47).

"In this world," McCulloch and John Pfeiffer (1949) wrote, "it seems best to handle even apparent continuities as some numbers of some little steps" (p. 368). By supporting an approach in which all processes were transposed into systems of "ultimate units," McCulloch framed computers not as machines, but rather as a quantitative framework whose advances opened the way "to better understanding of the working of our brains" (1949, p. 368) via the discretization of their mechanisms. Yet, this digital logic was also transformed by its mobilization within McCulloch and Pitts' experimental epistemology. As they articulated a mathematical model in which brain mechanisms and computing processes were projected onto a shared quantitative framework, McCulloch and Pitts inaugurated a model of knowledge acquisition that was both independent from any given substrate (e.g., biological neurons, computer circuits, etc.) and representative of the embodied qualities of the logical principles underpinning knowledge (e.g., neuron-like structure, weighted connections, etc.). By describing knowledge acquisition as a process that could be exhibited by any substrate capable of embodying certain logical principles, McCulloch and Pitts constituted the mind and computing as functional models for one another as well as reframed their model's digital framework as a set of embodied principles. In that sense, they not only reconceived the study of the mind as an experimental science, but more fundamentally redefined it as an "inquiry into the physiological substrate of knowledge" itself (McCulloch, 1960, p. 7).

The "neural" dimension of the McCulloch-Pitts model did not then refer to any physical properties of the brain *specifically*; it indeed encompassed the brain and its structure, but it also comprised computer circuits and all mathematical models based on a binary logic. Rather, McCulloch and Pitts' engagement with neurality was more directly concerned with how neural or neuron-like structures—here broadly conceived of as networks of densely interconnected binary devices—could exhibit and even produce knowledge. As they noted in "How We Know Universals" (Pitts & McCulloch, 1947), neural networks provided what McCulloch and Pitts thought was the ideal configuration "to classify information according to useful common characters" (p. 127). While linear models might be vulnerable to small perturbations in the inputs they process, neural networks' distributed structure allowed them to "recognize figures in such a way as to produce the same output for every input belonging to the figure" (1947, p. 128). For McCulloch and Pitts (1943), the problem of knowledge was thus intimately linked to determining the type of network structures capable to withstand the stochastic character of the world by filtering out noise and selectively taking information in, leading them to conclude that, "with determination of the net, the unknowable object of knowledge, the 'thing in itself,' ceases to be unknowable" (p. 131).

Cybernetics, which Norbert Wiener (1948) would introduce a few years later as the field dedicated to the scientific study of "control and communication theory, whether in the machine or in the animal" (p. 11), shared many of the concerns and assumptions underpinning the McCulloch-Pitts model. For instance, in addition to catalyzing a similar displacement of historical categories such as the biological and the computational in favor of functional abstractions, cybernetics likewise conflated knowledge and order via a reformulation of information as "a temporal and local reversal of the normal direction of entropy" (Wiener, 1954, p. 25). Some scholars have attended to Wiener's influence on the development of the McCulloch-Pitts model (Abraham, 2002; Halpern, 2012), whereas others have described how this model provided a blueprint for the type of knowledge valued by cyberneticists (Aizawa, 2012; Schlatter & Aizawa, 2008). Yet, in light of such shared epistemic values, it might be more appropriate to understand cybernetics and the McCulloch-Pitts model as manifestations of a larger epistemological moment in which science itself was reframed as an endeavor against uncertainty. In *The Human Use of Human Beings* (1954), for instance, Wiener described science as "play[ing] a game against [its] arch enemy, disorganization" (p. 34), thus proposing an epistemological framework in which knowledge and knowing are linked together against some adversarial force. To produce knowledge and maintain order, Wiener asserted, scientists engage with knowledge's limits as an adversary that must be gradually conquered—but who or what is this evil? As Wiener put it: "Is this devil Manichean or Augustinian?" (p. 34). From there, Wiener proceeded by differentiating what he saw as the two opponents against which cybernetics was striving: the Augustinian evil of chaos, randomness, and entropy and the Manichean evil of deception and trickery.

Norbert Wiener's Two Evils: Adversariality as an Epistemology

Throughout his oeuvre, Wiener repeatedly came back to the problem of evil; yet, as his preoccupations vis-à-vis cybernetics changed through time, so did his understanding of the nature of that evil. In *Cybernetics* (1948), Wiener first situated his new field within a Manichean historical moment, where the field's new developments had opened up "unbounded possibilities for good and for evil" (p. 27). Later, in *The Human Use of Human Beings* (1954), he described cybernetics as a response to "this random element, this organic incompleteness … we may consider evil" (p. 11), which had been uncovered by Josiah Willard Gibbs' statistical mechanics. Instead of displacing one another, however, these two definitions of evil persisted in his work and were eventually formalized into two distinct figures: a Manichean and an Augustinian evil.

Wiener's Augustinian evil refers to "the passive resistance of nature" (1954, p. 36) to its capture as an object of knowledge. While Wiener celebrated science's growing mastery over nature, he also emphasized the mutual irreducibility of nature and science—chaos, randomness, and entropy all destabilize the certainties science strives to acquire and thus function as manifestations of nature's resistance to revealing itself. Yet, these manifestations do not point to any external or identifiable opponent. "In Augustinianism," Wiener specified, "the black of the world is negative and is the mere absence of white" (p. 190). In line with St. Augustine's own definition, Wiener described this evil as an adversarial force constitutive of the world insofar as it is the direct product of its incompleteness. By incompleteness, he referred to nature's disregard for its own laws; while Gibbs and others had already displaced the neatly organized universe of Newtonian physics with a more chaotic one best modelled statistically, Wiener reframed this "recognition of a fundamental element of chance in the universe" into a manifestation of "an irrationality in the world" (p. 11). For him, if nature demonstrates entropic tendencies, it was not because it is opposed to order so much as it lacks order.

At the same time, however, Wiener (1954) refused to recognize this incompleteness or resistance as an inalienable feature of nature. In fact, it was nature's incompleteness that, for him, allowed science to resist principles as fundamental as "the characteristic tendency of entropy … to increase" (p. 12). In that sense, the Augustinian evil "is not a power in itself," he specified, "but the measure of our own weakness" (p. 35). Nature's policy might be hard to decipher, but it can nevertheless be revealed, and "when we have uncovered it, we have in a certain sense exorcised it" (p. 35). Wiener thus also conceived of this evil as a sign of the incompleteness of science's own tools and knowledge. This evil might manifest itself each time science is confronted by nature's incompleteness, but it also points to the possibility of order being established via the fulfilment of science. As emphasized by Wiener, the Augustinian evil "plays a difficult game, but he may be defeated by our intelligence as thoroughly as by a sprinkle of holy water" (p. 35). In that sense, once nature's incompleteness is overcome by science, it is assumed that its adversarial qualities will disappear altogether, bridging the progression of science to the restoration of order in nature. Wiener's Augustinian evil can then be situated within a larger intellectual history in which science is defined by its capacity to impose order on nature. Referring to Francis Bacon's vexation of nature, Wiener redefined knowledge as "something on which we can act [rather] than something which we can prove" (p. 193). It is on this point that Wiener's Augustinian evil differs from that of St. Augustine; while the latter instituted disorder as a fundamental quality of the world, the former posited order as something to be established. In that sense, if Wiener indeed acknowledged some sort of resistance on behalf of nature, it was insofar that this resistance was assumed to eventually give way.

By situating science within an Augustinian framework opposing organization and chaos, Wiener established a regime of knowledge aimed at overcoming nature's entropic propensities. While Wiener (1954) recognized "nature's statistical tendency to disorder" (p. 28) at the level of the universe, he also emphasized the role of information in creating "islands of locally decreasing entropy" (p. 39). Human beings, for instance, not only "take in food, which generates energy," but also "take in information" and "act on [the] information received" (p. 28) to ensure their survival. Machines, for Wiener, similarly "contribute to a local and temporary building up of information" (p. 31) by sharing living organisms' "ability to make decisions" and produce "a local zone of organization in a world whose general tendency is to run down" (p. 34). Information, for Wiener, could then be understood as not only the opposite of entropy—i.e., negentropy—but also the ideal unit for a type of knowledge that participates "in a continuous stream of influences from the outer world and acts on the outer world" (p. 122). Knowledge, in the context of Wiener's Augustinian framework, was thus reformulated into the production of a localized, cybernetically enforced order against chaos and disorganization.

In Augustinianism, order can indeed be established but is defined as much by what fits within the "islands of locally decreasing entropy" produced by information as by what lies outside these islands. In his autobiography, *I Am a Mathematician* (1964), Wiener later commented that, in the face of "the great torrent of disorganization," "our main obligation is to establish arbitrary enclaves of order and system" (p. 324). By emphasizing the arbitrariness of such enclaves, Wiener highlighted not only the functional nature of cybernetics' defining principles, but also how order is produced by exteriorizing the disorganization against which it is mobilized. McCulloch (1950), for his part, shared Wiener's definition of information as "orderliness" (p. 193) yet understood the type of limits Wiener described in Augustinian terms as constitutive of learning systems. In "Why the Mind Is in the Head" (1950), McCulloch argued that "our knowledge of the world" is limited "by the law that information may not increase on going through brains, or computing machines" (p. 193). New connections might "set the stage for others yet to come" (p. 205), but the limits of learning systems' capacity to process information remained for him the fundamental Augustinian limit against which learning took place.

By equating the limits of knowledge with what limited information networks can process, the McCulloch-Pitts model internalized the adversarial limits described by Wiener. Whereas Wiener conceived of knowledge's Augustinian limits as a measure of science's incompleteness, McCulloch framed such limits as making knowledge itself possible. For McCulloch (1950), all knowledge was the result of how networks are wired; as he wrote, "we can inherit only the general scheme of the structure of our brains. The rest must be left to chance. Chance includes experience which engenders learning" (p. 203). In this regard, McCulloch somehow anticipated some of the defining features of later theories of cybernetics by framing chance and randomness as key tools for the production of knowledge. As argued by Jeremy Walker and Melinda Cooper (2011), second-order cybernetics reframed disorder as a fundamental principle of organization by theorizing systems that could "internalize and neutralize all external challenges to their existence" (p. 157). Similarly, by arguing that the mind is in the head because "only there are hosts of possible connections to be formed" (1950, pp. 204–205), McCulloch described a model of knowledge in which all knowledge was produced by the creation of new connections mirroring the stochasticity of the inputs coming from outside. That way, while Wiener established a functional relationship between knowledge and its objects, McCulloch restored an idealized correspondence among them by framing knowledge's Augustinian limits as internal to learning systems. From the perspective of Wiener's Augustinian framework, McCulloch's experimental epistemology thus instantiated a larger reformulation of knowledge from a functional endeavor against the stochasticity of the world to a type of order building off stochasticity.

Wiener's Manichean evil, comparatively, breaks away from this larger intellectual history in which order and chaos, science and nature oppose one another. If Augustinianism refers to randomness, entropy, and, more generally, the incompleteness of nature, Manicheanism rather consists in a "positive malicious evil" (Wiener, 1954, p. 11). While nature cannot actively cover nor alter its structure, the Manichean evil can, and will, "keep his policy of confusion secret and ... change it in order to keep us in the dark" (p. 35). The Manichean evil, in that sense, does not then so much refer to any given object of knowledge as to historically situated opponents against which one produces knowledge (e.g., the Soviet scientist, the Cold Warrior, the enemy spy, etc.). Knowledge, in that framework, is conceived of as a strategic advantage that must be gained in order to secure one's victory against an active opponent who will reciprocally use "any trick of craftiness or dissimulation to obtain this victory" (p. 34).

Contrary to Augustinianism, Wiener's conceptualization of a Manichean evil appears to be strongly anchored in the historical setting in which cybernetics took form. As argued by Lily Kay (2001), the development of cybernetics as "a new science of communication and control" had "enormous potential for industrial automation and military power" and was actively fueled by the escalation of Cold War tensions (p. 591). Similarly, McCulloch and Pitts' reformulation of the mind as a system of "decisions and signals" bore great potential for military funders, she adds, as it opened up many new opportunities "for automated military technologies of the postwar era" (pp. 591–593). In the context of the Cold War, the Manichean limits of knowledge thus encompassed not only what was yet-to-be-known but also the actors against which science was mobilized. In Manicheanism, science is then defined not so much by its exclusion of nature as by its adversarial relationship with some identifiable and historically situated Other. In this framework, Wiener (1954) concluded, "the black of the world" does not refer to "the mere absence of white"; rather, "white and black belong to two opposed armies drawn up in line facing one another" (p. 190).

While the Augustinian evil broadly consists in the transposition of an epistemological framework into a set of situated practices, the Manichean evil refers to the transposition of the military-industrial complex's influence on Cold War science into a full-on scientific epistemology. Many of the early thinkers of cybernetics were first introduced to engineering and other applied sciences via their contribution to the war efforts; for instance, building upon their work on servomechanisms and anti-aircraft turrets during World War II, Wiener and his colleagues proposed in "Behavior, Purpose and Teleology" (Rosenblueth, Wiener, & Bigelow, 1943) a new mode of representation in which human operators' behavioral processes and machines' mechanical responses were modelled into unified control systems. Yet, as Peter Galison (1994) points out, the larger implications of these new modes of representation and of the Manichean framework producing them went beyond their manifestations in the battlefields of WWII and beyond. For Galison, the key innovation of cybernetics did not so much consist in modelling humans and machines together in the context of "the Manichean field of science-assisted warfare" (p. 251), but in how it subsequently decontextualized and expanded these functional equivalences between humans and machines into "a philosophy of nature" (p. 233).

The Manichean framework might then refer to a specific historical moment, but also to a reformulation of historical categories in light of new needs and imperatives. As cybernetics and Cold War militarism developed alongside one another, the laboratory and the battlefield quickly emerged as interchangeable settings in terms of how knowledge was redefined as an adversarial endeavor. If humans and machines were suddenly folded together into unified systems, it was not because they were deemed ontologically equivalent, but rather because they could more easily be intervened on once theorized that way. After the war for instance, Wiener and his lifelong collaborator Arturo Rosenblueth claimed in "Purposeful and Non-Purposeful Behavior" (Rosenblueth & Wiener, 1950) that "the only fruitful methods for the study of human and animal behavior are the methods applicable to the behavior of mechanical objects as well" (p. 326). Rejecting the question of "whether machines are or can be like men," they concluded that, "as objects of scientific enquiry, humans do not differ from machines" (p. 326). In the lab as in the battlefield, new classes and categories were thus established not as an attempt to counterbalance nature's entropic propensities, but rather in accordance with what was deemed the most "fruitful" from a Manichean perspective.

Similarly, the McCulloch-Pitts model's reformulation of the mind into an object of experimental research was indistinguishable from the constitution of brains and machines as functionally and epistemologically equivalent. As McCulloch continued working on the nervous system throughout the years, neural networks' experimental framework proved especially conducive to the ideals of control associated with the Cold War's Manichean atmosphere. In his physiological research on nerves for instance, McCulloch (1966) claimed that the inner workings of the mind could be best understood once modelled as a system of command and control. Later, in "The Reticular Formation Command and Control System" (Kilmer & McCulloch, 1969), McCulloch and William Kilmer further expanded on this idea by arguing that the basic computation of the nervous system affords an effective organization for both the design and control of intricate networked systems. In both cases, the physiological properties of the biological brain were overlooked in favor of an abstract account of neural activity as an optimal design for control. For McCulloch, to construct a system in neural or nervous terms thus not only provided an optimal configuration to exert control upon it, but also instituted the military ideals of command and control into fundamental principles for the organization of learning systems. In the context of McCulloch's work, Wiener's Manichean evil did not then so much take the form of historically situated opponents but of a reformulation of humans and machines into control systems.

Wiener's Manichean and Augustinian evils might imply distinct practices and ideals of knowledge, but their cohabitation in McCulloch's experimental epistemology hinted toward a larger adversarial framework encompassing both evils. By reframing any limits to knowledge as internal, structural limits and by reformulating humans and machines as control systems, the McCulloch-Pitts model not only dissolved any clear boundary between these two evils, but also instituted their adversarial qualities into fundamental principles of knowledge. In the closing section of *The Human Use of Human Beings*, Wiener (1954) accounted for this slippage between the two by asserting that "the Augustinian position has always been difficult to maintain" and "tends under the slightest perturbation to break down into a covert Manicheanism" (p. 191). While the Manichean evil might be intimately linked to the historical context of the Cold War, Wiener acknowledged that there were elements of Manicheanism in settings preceding that period; there was "a subtle emotional Manicheanism implicit in all crusades" (p. 190), Wiener wrote, which culminated in Marxism and fascism, two manifestations of a Manichean evil whose unprecedented scale has "grown up in an atmosphere of combat and conflict" (p. 192). In that sense, while the threat of Manicheanism might have a longer history than this evil's Cold War era manifestations imply, its expansion into a scientific epistemology remained for Wiener a recent invention.

Wiener's two evils do not then refer to distinct, epistemological frameworks as much as to the reformulation of an Augustinian intellectual history in the context of an historically situated Manichean moment. While Wiener recognized, and warned against, the slippage between these two evils, he also linked the advent of his new science to the growing proximity between them; Augustinianism might accommodate a certain indeterminacy—"an irrationality in the world," as Wiener termed it—but its Manichean reformulation does not. Conversely, whereas Manicheanism depicts a world where competing groups, armies, or systems persist by being in opposition, its Augustinian reformulation challenges the possibility of meaningfully distinguishing such entities from one another. At the intersection of these two evils thus lies a displacement of historical categories in favor of a larger reformulation of how knowledge is produced. As Katherine Hayles (1999) points out, cybernetics' constitution of "*the human in terms of the machine*" (p. 64) was key in bringing brains and computers together under a unified model of control systems. Similarly, as Claus Pias (2008) argues, cybernetics had to operate less like a discipline and more like "an epistemology ... [that] becomes activated within disciplines" (p. 111) for philosophy, engineering, neurophysiology, and mathematics to be folded into a new science of control and communication.

The McCulloch-Pitts model can then be understood as an epistemologically situated set of practices informed by cybernetics' dissolution of disciplinary boundaries and historical categories; yet, its experimental framework also appears to have transformed many of cybernetics' principles by providing a functional abstraction to implement them in a whole new range of settings, including the study of the perception of forms (Pitts & McCulloch, 1947) and the clinical treatment of neurosis (McCulloch, 1949). By producing the type of experimental results that were expected in the Manichean setting of the Cold War, the McCulloch-Pitts model reconfigured some of the defining categories through which knowledge's Augustinian limits were conceived and operationalized. That way, while cybernetics' dissolution of historical categories already hinted toward a Manichean ideal of control, the McCulloch-Pitts model further expanded this shift by turning the military ideals of command and control into fundamental principles for the organization of systems. From that perspective, both the McCulloch-Pitts model and cybernetics emerge as manifestations of a shared adversarial epistemology in which all knowledge is reframed as a set of practices and ideals of control aimed at resisting, countering, and overcoming the limits of knowledge.

Deep Neural Networks: Operationalizing the Limits of Knowledge

The same year as McCulloch's death, Marvin Minsky and Seymour Papert—the first of whom was introduced to the field of artificial intelligence (AI) by studying neural networks (Minsky, 1954)—published *Perceptrons* (1969), the first comprehensive critique of biologically inspired models like the one proposed by McCulloch and Pitts. For many historians of science (e.g., Edwards, 1996) and computer scientists (e.g., Goodfellow et al., 2016), *Perceptrons* constituted the first major backlash against neural networks and propelled their subsequent marginalization in the fields of psychology and computer science (e.g., Guice, 1998; Olazaran, 1996). It is there that most historical accounts generally abandon neural networks. In computer science and the history of science alike, neural networks are described as relegated to the footnotes of computer science from that point onward until advances in processing power catalyzed their reemergence in the late 1980s by enabling their large-scale implementation in software environments (e.g., Nagy, 1991; Nilsson, 2009).

This way of narrating the development of neural networks through the lens of these two moments—i.e., their fall from grace and subsequent reemergence—is fairly commonplace in most histories of computing and points to a larger habit of framing the shortcomings of machine learning as temporary obstacles. Yet, by focusing on neural networks' manifestations in computer science, these accounts overlook the McCulloch-Pitts model's second life in the then nascent field of systems theory. As the second generation of cyberneticists abandoned their field's initial emphasis on "homeostatic and purposive behavior" (McCulloch, 1956, p. 147), neural networks became a recurrent framework to study complex systems' autopoietic, self-generating processes. Among the main figures of second-order cybernetics, theoretical biologist Humberto Maturana was arguably the first to use the McCulloch-Pitts model to study systems' structural differentiation from their environment. First introduced to neural networks while working with McCulloch and others on the neurophysiology of vision (Lettvin, Maturana, McCulloch, & Pitts, 1959), Maturana reinterpreted McCulloch and Pitts' neural model as a privileged framework to represent the operations underpinning the ontogenesis of organisms (Maturana & Varela, 1972, pp. 122–123) as well as the structural coupling between organisms and their social domain (Maturana, 1978, pp. 48–50). Later, while investigating the applicability of Maturana's autopoietic turn to social systems, sociologist Niklas Luhmann (1995) revisited McCulloch and Pitts' "self-referential net of contacts" to illustrate how systems sustain themselves by "achieving position in relation to the environment" (pp. 197–198).

While overlooked by most historical accounts, this reformulation of the McCulloch-Pitts model into a framework for the study of adaptive systems not only bridges neural networks' initial conceptualization as a model of the mind and later reemergence as machine learning models, but it also undermines the possibility of articulating a coherent history of neural networks from the perspective of these two moments alone. By the time University of Toronto, New York University, and Université de Montréal became recognized in the 1990s as key centers of a new AI renaissance due to their work on neural networks as effective tools to "build complex concepts out of simpler concepts" (Goodfellow et al., 2016, p. 5), many scholars working on autopoietic processes had already reframed neural networks as a paradigmatic model for self-organization. This transformation is key, for it anticipated many of the conceptual foundations of today's machine learning literature. For instance, by reframing neural networks as effective models to study how complex systems maintain themselves against external perturbations, systems theorists preempted machine learning's conceptualization of adversariality as a fundamental principle for the organization of learning systems.

In computer science, neural networks now refer to a type of machine learning model constituted of multiple layers of specialized neural units whose parameters are determined by the task each network is trained to fulfill (Goodfellow et al., 2016, pp. 5–6). For example, a neural network trained for image classification would be given millions of images of preestablished categories—"dog," "cat," "human," etc.—and then tasked to extract representative patterns for each of them. As the network processes its training dataset, its neurons come to specialize in recognizing specific combinations of features and acquire weighted connection values based on the representativeness of the identified features for each category. Once trained, the network would use these acquired, internal representations to classify new input images within these categories.

In today's context, neural networks can thus be understood as implementations in code of the original McCulloch-Pitts model with some notable additions: the weights of the connections are automatically adjusted by the networks based on available data (Rosenblatt, 1961), the networks include one or more hidden layers of neurons that perform most of the model's computations (Rumelhart, Hinton, & Williams, 1986), and the models now often involve an emphasis on depth, i.e., an ever-growing number of layers, which allows the networks to perform increasingly abstract tasks (Hinton, Osindero, & Teh, 2006). From a physiological model of knowledge across substrates, neural networks have therefore evolved into a powerful model to operationalize a wide range of tasks by extracting patterns and generalized representations from large amounts of data. In that sense, while the McCulloch-Pitts model was initially conceived as an attempt to articulate a *universal* model of knowledge, today's neural networks can rather be understood as a versatile framework to operationalize *specific* forms of knowledge adapted to the growing range of settings in which they are implemented.

Neural networks might have gone from a model of the mind to an epistemological framework based on pattern extraction, but their limits still appear to be framed in adversarial terms. In their influential piece "Intriguing Properties of Neural Networks" (Szegedy et al., 2014), for instance, computer scientist Christian Szegedy and his colleagues describe a puzzling discovery: state-of-the-art neural networks might be able to master incredibly complex tasks, but can also misclassify data—be they images, audio inputs, spatial cues, etc.—that are only marginally different from those that they adequately classify. While such localized failures might be hardly surprising for any probabilistic framework, Szegedy demonstrates that these perturbed inputs generally cause any networks trained to fulfill the same task (e.g., recognizing objects in bitmap images) to perform similar misclassifications, even if they are "trained with different hyperparameters or ... on a different set of examples" (p. 2).

Now called "adversarial examples," as Szegedy et al. termed them (p. 2), these accidental or voluntary alterations of inputs are known to introduce targeted perturbations that lead neural networks to misclassify the resulting data without hindering humans' capacity to categorize them correctly. Since Szegedy's original paper, a growing scholarship has emerged around these targeted alterations, which are now studied for how they "expose fundamental blind spots in our training algorithms" (Goodfellow, Shlens, & Szegedy, 2015, p. 1) or, in other words, the limits of neural networks' epistemology. More specifically, neural networks' vulnerability to adversarial examples has become a central object of research in two main subfields of computer science: cybersecurity and machine learning. With cybersecurity implying locatable attackers and machine learning statistically representing the realities in which it operates, these two bodies of work might a priori seem to mirror the divide between Manicheanism and Augustinianism; yet, the way they both displace any limits to neural networks' epistemology by internal, technical limitations hints toward a third adversarial framework that supplements the dialectic between Wiener's two evils.

The cybersecurity literature covers many types of attacks that involve inputs that could be characterized as adversarial (e.g., SQL injection, buffer overflow, etc.), but adversarial examples differ from such programs by the way they can target a system without having direct access to it. Many scholars have studied adversarial examples from the perspective of the risks they represent with regard to the implementation of neural networks in real-world settings. For instance, Alexey Kurakin and his colleagues (Kurakin, Goodfellow, & Bengio, 2017a) have demonstrated that adversarial examples encountered through video signals and other input channels are misclassified almost as systematically as those fed directly into the targeted machine learning model. While real-world applications of adversarial examples by malicious parties are yet to be documented, they conclude that adversarial examples provide hypothetical opponents with a privileged means to bypass traditional security measures and perform attacks directly against current implementations of neural networks.

While Wiener described two evils adapted to an era of postindustrial warfare, Kurakin situates adversarial examples within a new defense rhetoric in which these attacks are conceived of as measures of the targeted systems' "robustness" (Kurakin, Goodfellow, & Bengio, 2017b, p. 10). Gesturing at potential future iterations of such attacks—"attacks using … physical objects," "attacks performed without access to the model's parameters," etc. (Kurakin et al., 2017a, p. 10)—Kurakin frames adversarial examples as requiring a preemptive response from the machine learning models targeted by these attacks. In line with a growing number of scholars (Gu & Rigazio, 2015; Huang, Xu, Schuurmans, & Szepesvári, 2016), Kurakin advocates for the integration of adversarial examples within neural networks' training datasets in order to not only make them "more robust to attack" (Kurakin et al., 2017b, p. 1) but also expand the limits of their learning model. Adversarial examples might then indeed imply an active opponent; yet, their effectiveness remains more intimately linked to the actual limits of neural networks' epistemology. In that sense, by emphasizing the hypothetical malicious parties behind adversarial examples instead of the structural limits of neural networks' epistemology, this literature assumes that these limits can always be pushed back as long as they are attributed to attackers. That way, the more explicit neural networks' Manichean adversary is, the more understated their Augustinian limits become.

The cybersecurity branch of the literature on adversarial examples thus appears to reaffirm a distinction between Wiener's two adversarial conceptualizations of the limits of knowledge but does so by misidentifying neural networks' Augustinian limits for an active opponent. The machine learning literature on the topic, for its part, seems to further expand this conflation by rooting these systems' claim for knowledge in their internalization of the limits of knowledge, thus dissolving the need for two distinct evils altogether. In machine learning, many have documented the great asymmetry between the proliferation of studies on the different types of adversarial examples and the comparatively slow progresses of those attempting to develop defenses for them (e.g., Carlini et al., 2019). However, instead of designing specific defense strategies for each form of attack, a growing number of researchers now use adversarial examples to acquire a better understanding of neural networks' learning model. In "Explaining and Harnessing Adversarial Examples" (2015), for instance, Ian Goodfellow, Jonathan Shlens, and Christian Szegedy analyze the types of blind spots exploited by adversarial examples and conclude that neural networks' vulnerability to these attacks can be best explained by hypothesizing that neural networks all share a similar form of "linear behavior in high-dimensional spaces" (p. 1).

In addition to advocating for the introduction of adversarial examples in neural networks' training datasets, Goodfellow and his colleagues (2015, pp. 4–6) reframe adversarial examples as powerful debugging tools—neural networks might be profoundly opaque once they are trained, but adversarial examples can nevertheless be used to test where the generalizations they acquire are faulty (p. 7). In that sense, while Kurakin describes adversarial examples as a threat, Goodfellow et al. frame them as an opportunity to expand the limits of neural networks' epistemology. As in cybersecurity, the machine learning literature might then conceive of adversarial examples as pointing toward internal vulnerabilities, but, unlike this other body of work, it also reframes these vulnerabilities as an opportunity to once again improve neural networks' learning model. From that perspective, nothing can truly lie beyond neural networks' epistemology. If a network's failures are systemically framed as opportunities to improve it, failures and limitations themselves become constitutive of the system they destabilize. The cybersecurity literature on the topic might imply some assumed opponent, but the tactics that are used to counter this antagonist are the same as the ones used in machine learning: adversarial examples are added to neural networks' datasets in order to improve their learning model and expand their epistemology. In the context of this adversarial epistemology, there is no difference between an adversarial example produced by an attacker or one designed by a researcher—in all these cases, these failures are framed as constitutive of neural networks by providing the opportunity to improve future iterations of these systems.

What appears to link both the cybersecurity and machine learning literatures is thus a shared assumption that failures, errors, and limitations are in fact key principles for the organization of learning systems. This assumption can be linked back to the adversarial logic of cybernetics but with a key difference. For Wiener (1954), the distinction between the Manichean evil and its Augustinian counterpart would "make itself apparent in the tactics to be used against them" (p. 34). In the case of adversarial examples, however, there is no distinction based on tactics. Be it the product of a malicious opponent or a manifestation of neural networks' poor performance with low probability inputs, an adversarial example can only be countered by being introduced in a neural network's training dataset. As long as neural networks' failures are seen as temporary internal limits instead of external ones, no failure, misclassification, or blind spot can truly destabilize their epistemology; on the contrary, by being framed in adversarial terms, these failures appear as necessary milestones in the development of learning models with all-encompassing epistemologies. In that sense, whereas Wiener instituted a new science that was aimed at countering localizable threats (e.g., enemy regimes, disorganization, etc.), neural networks inaugurated a new epistemological framework in which the manifestations of the limits of these systems' epistemology only further reaffirm their claim for knowledge.

Neural networks might have dissolved the need to distinguish between a Manichean and an Augustinian evil, but their internalization of the limits of knowledge nevertheless points toward a third adversarial framework—an internalized evil, as it will be named here—against which the production of knowledge is mobilized. This internalized evil can be broadly understood as a certitude that, given the right substrate or unit, all limits to knowledge can be internalized and thus made temporary. While McCulloch and Pitts conceived of that substrate as an experimental epistemology onto which all knowledge could be modelled, the current literature on neural networks posits that all perceptual or intellectual tasks can be reduced to sets of quantifiable and operationalizable patterns. In both cases, the limits that neural networks encounter are systematically reframed as temporary internal limits that can, and will, be invariably vanquished. From the perspective of this internalized evil, which traverses McCulloch's work, second-order cybernetics, and current research in machine learning, all limits of knowledge then appear as internal to knowledge itself.

Adversarial examples might be especially well suited to illustrate this internalization of the limits of knowledge, but neural networks' adversarial framework also encompasses the negative social results associated with these systems. Despite the growing body of work documenting how these systems perpetuate the biases and inequalities that underpin their social milieus (e.g., Richardson, Schultz, & Crawford, 2019; West, Whittaker, & Crawford, 2019), neural networks continue to be implemented in virtually all fields of human activity. As demonstrated by many scholars, these systems perpetuate the biases, assumptions, and inequalities that are implicit to the data on which they are trained by acting on their objects in accordance with them. Neural networks, for instance, systematize the gender and racial biases that underpin the contexts in which they are implemented (van Miltenburg, 2016), naturalize physiognomic tropes regarding the link between facial features and criminal intentions (Wu & Zhang, 2016), and reproduce essentialist readings of gender and sexuality (Wang & Kosinski, 2018). Yet, from the perspective of these systems' adversarial epistemology, such negative social results are not so much the products of systemic conditions that need to be politically addressed, but simple engineering problems that can be resolved through better training datasets and more processing power. Instead of highlighting the limits of neural networks' epistemology, such perturbations—be they adversarial examples or social failures—are reframed as constitutive principles of the same systems they would otherwise destabilize.

By blurring the boundary between the malicious and the accidental, the external and the internal, neural networks' adversarial epistemology reframes these failures as calling for better adversarial training as opposed to restrictions on the application of these systems in sensitive contexts. That is not to say that neural networks do not also hold the potential to shed light on many of the biases, blind spots, assumptions, and systemic conditions that are implicit to their training. Machine learning makes painfully obvious many of the biases and structural conditions that underpin social relationships—yet, by dismissing such outcomes as blind spots, bugs, or glitches, researchers and technology providers misidentify these failures as internal to the systems they train, rather than being constitutive of the social relations that underpin the production and implementation of neural networks. In this regard, neural networks not only render the distinction between a Manichean and an Augustinian evil obsolete, but they also internalize all errors, limits, failures, or even critiques by reconceiving them as necessary evils in the development of better machine learning models, forcing any external challenge against these systems to inhabit the adversarial framework it aims to subvert.

Conclusion: From a Physiological to a Computable Model of Knowledge

Machine learning, both as a field and a technological ideal, is often depicted as intimately linked to a series of technical breakthroughs in processing and computing power that took place from the 1990s onward; yet, each of its models relies on a larger history of ideals and practices of knowledge that threaten to be misread or overlooked if considered in computational terms only. At this time, neural networks outperform other models on virtually all the tasks that define the field and have established many of the terms through which machine learning and its related disciplines are being studied. As hinted at throughout this text, however, neural networks can, and should, be conceived of as both an operational model and an epistemological framework; since Kurt Hornik's demonstration that any functions can be approximated by "multi-output multilayer feedforward networks" (Hornik, Stinchcombe, & White, 1989, p. 363), the literature on neural networks has overwhelmingly equated this property—the so-called universal approximation theorem—with a capacity to reproduce, or at least model, any intelligent behavior. While this leap from approximating functions to reproducing intelligent behavior might seem ambitious, it is akin to the shift from computing logical propositions to modelling the mind that McCulloch and Pitts' neural model enabled roughly fifty years earlier.

This chapter has attempted to not only challenge the dominant narrative that neural networks only required more computing power to reemerge and become widely adopted as machine learning models, but also to provide an overview of the adversarial epistemology underpinning these systems' internalization of the limits of knowledge. The McCulloch-Pitts model inhabited a disciplinary landscape that is hardly reducible to computer science and from which computer science itself emerged. By the time machine learning was constituted as a field, neural networks had already been reframed into a functional model for the study of adaptive systems, thus providing a promising framework to operationalize a wide range of processes for which no formal explanation or description is available. Access to greater computing power might have allowed neural networks to produce the type of results that are now expected from learning systems, but it is first and foremost as an epistemological framework positing that all knowledge can be distilled into sets of computable units that this model should be conceived of—a framework that, this chapter argued, involves an adversarial understanding of all limits to knowledge as internal to knowledge itself. The adversarial nature of McCulloch's experimental epistemology might have been (and still somehow remains) understated, but deep neural networks' internalization of the limits of knowledge nevertheless appears to have brought cybernetics' reformulation of knowledge as something "on which we can act" (Wiener, 1954, p. 193) to a fully operational level.

The adversarial epistemology in which these systems operate appears then to manifest itself through the slippages between theory and implementation, modelling and operationalization, and epistemology and experimentation that characterize the different forms, practices, and models generally associated with the term "neural networks." In that sense, if the operations performed by neural networks can be defined as adversarial, it is not so much because they marginalize, antagonize, or exclude—which they of course do—but rather because they force all knowledge on which they intervene to inhabit their adversarial epistemology. By reframing any limit or social failure as a temporary technical problem, this adversarial epistemology thus not only enables a larger computational determinism that assumes all knowledge can be projected onto a computable substrate, but also equates the limits of that substrate with the limits of knowledge itself.

References

Abraham, T. (2002). (Physio)logical circuits: The intellectual origins of the McCulloch–Pitts neural networks. *Journal of the History of the Behavioral Sciences, 38,* 3–25.

Aizawa, K. (2012). Warren McCulloch's turn to cybernetics: What Walter Pitts contributed. *Interdisciplinary Science Reviews, 37*(3), 206–217.

Bojarski, M., Del Testa, D., Dworakowski, D., Firner, B., Flepp, B., Goyal, P., ... Zieba, K. (2016). End to end learning for self-driving cars *[Cs].* http://arxiv.org/abs/1604.07316.

Carlini, N., Athalye, A., Papernot, N., Brendel, W., Rauber, J., Tsipras, D., ... Kurakin, A. (2019). *On evaluating adversarial robustness [Cs].* http://arxiv.org/abs/1902.06705.

Dupuy, J.-P. (1994). *Aux origines des sciences cognitives.* La Découverte.

Edwards, P. (1996). *The closed world: Computers and the politics of discourse in Cold War America.* MIT Press.

Fahlman, S., & Hinton, G. (1987). Connectionist architectures for artificial intelligence. *Computer, 20*(1), 100–109.

Fodor, J., & Pylyshyn, Z. (1988). Connectionism and cognitive architecture: A critical analysis. *Cognition, 28,* 3–71.

Franklin, S. (2015). *Control: Digitality as cultural logic.* MIT Press.

Galison, P. (1994). The ontology of the enemy: Norbert Wiener and the cybernetic vision. *Critical Inquiry, 21*(1), 228–266.

Goodfellow, I., Bengio, Y., & Courville, A. (2016). *Deep learning.* MIT Press.

Goodfellow, I. J., Shlens, J., & Szegedy, C. (2015). Explaining and harnessing adversarial examples. *International Conference on Learning Representations* (pp. 1–11). http://arxiv.org/abs/1412.6572.

Grimes. (2020). We appreciate power (feat. HANA) [Song]. On *Miss_Anthropocene* [Album]. 4AD.

Gu, S., & Rigazio, L. (2015). Towards deep neural network architectures robust to adversarial examples. *International Conference on Learning Representations* (pp. 1–9). https://arxiv.org/pdf/1412.5068.pdf.

Guice, J. (1998). Controversy and the state: Lord ARPA and intelligent computing. *Social Studies of Science, 28*(1), 103–138.

Halpern, O. (2012). Cybernetic sense. *Interdisciplinary Science Reviews, 37*(3), 218–236.

Hayles, N. K. (1999). *How we became posthuman: Virtual bodies in cybernetics, literature, and informatics*. University of Chicago Press.

Hinton, G., Deng, L., Yu, D., Dahl, G. E., Mohamed, A., Jaitly, N., et al. (2012). Deep neural networks for acoustic modeling in speech recognition: The shared views of four research groups. *IEEE Signal Processing Magazine, 29*(6), 82–97.

Hinton, G., Osindero, S., & Teh, Y.-W. (2006). A fast learning algorithm for deep belief nets. *Neural Computation, 18,* 1527–1554.

Hornik, K., Stinchcombe, M., & White, H. (1989). Multilayer feedforward networks are universal approximators. *Neural Networks, 2,* 359–366.

Huang, R., Xu, B., Schuurmans, D., & Szepesvári, C. (2016). Learning with a strong adversary. *International Conference on Learning Representations*, 1–12. https://arxiv.org/pdf/1511.03034.pdf.

Kay, L. (2001). From logical neurons to poetic embodiments of mind: Warren S. McCulloch's project in neuroscience. *Science in Context*, *14*(4), 591–614.

Kilmer, W., & McCulloch, W. (1969). A model of the vertebrate central command system. *International Journal of Man-Machine Studies, 1,* 279–309.

Krizhevsky, A., Sutskever, I., & Hinton, G. (2012). ImageNet classification with deep convolutional neural networks. *Advances in Neural Information Processing Systems, 25,* 1106–1114.

Kurakin, A., Goodfellow, I., & Bengio, S. (2017a). Adversarial examples in the physical world. *International Conference on Learning Representations* (pp. 1–14). https://arxiv.org/pdf/1607.02533.pdf.

Kurakin, A., Goodfellow, I., & Bengio, S. (2017b). Adversarial machine learning at scale. *International Conference on Learning Representations* (pp. 1–17). http://arxiv.org/abs/1611.01236.

Lettvin, J., Maturana, H., McCulloch, W., & Pitts, W. (1959). What the frog's eye tells the frog's brain. *Proceedings of the IRE, 47*(11), 1940–1951.

Luhmann, N. (1995). *Social systems*. Stanford University Press.

Maturana, H. (1978). Biology of language: The epistemology of reality. In G. Miller & E. Lenneberg (Eds.), *Psychology and biology of language and thought: Essays in honor of Eric Lenneberg* (pp. 27–63). Academic Press.

Maturana, H., & Varela, F. (1972). *De maquinas y seres vivos*. Editorial Universitaria.

McClelland, J., Rumelhart, D., & Hinton, G. (1986). The appeal of parallel distributed processing. In D. Rumelhart & J. McClelland (Eds.), *Parallel distributed processing, volume 1* (pp. 3–44). MIT Press.

McCulloch, W. (1949). Physiological processes underlying psychoneuroses. *Journal of the Royal Society of Medicine, 42*(1), 71–93.

McCulloch, W. (1950). Why the mind is in the head? *Dialectica, 15*(9), 192–205.
McCulloch, W. (1956). Toward some circuitry of ethical robots, or an observational science of the genesis of social evaluation in the mind-like behavior of artifacts. *Acta Biotheoretica, 11*(3–4), 147–156.
McCulloch, W. (1960). What is a number, that a man may know it, and a man, that he may know a number? *General Semantics Bulletin, 26–27,* 7–18.
McCulloch, W. (1966). The command and control system of the vertebrates. *Proceedings of the International Federation for Information Processing Congress, 2,* 636.
McCulloch, W. (1974). Recollections of the many sources of cybernetics. *ASC Forum, 5*(16), 1–26.
McCulloch, W., & Pfeiffer, J. (1949). Of digital computers called brains. *Scientific Monthly, 69*(6), 368–376.
McCulloch, W., & Pitts, W. (1943). A logical calculus of the ideas immanent in nervous activity. *Bulletin of Mathematical Biophysics, 5,* 115–133.
Minsky, M. (1954). *Theory of neural-analog reinforcement systems and its application to the brain model problem* (Doctoral dissertation). Princeton University.
Minsky, M., & Papert, S. (1969). *Perceptrons: An introduction to computational geometry*. MIT Press.
Nagy, G. (1991). Neural networks—Then and now. *IEEE Transactions on Neural Networks, 2*(2), 316–318.
Newell, A., Shaw, J. C., & Simon, H. (1958). Elements of a theory of human problem solving. *Psychological Review, 65*(3), 151–166.
Nilsson, N. (2009). *The quest for artificial intelligence: A history of ideas and achievements*. Cambridge University Press.
Olazaran, M. (1996). A sociological study of the official history of the Perceptrons controversy. *Social Studies of Science, 26*(3), 611–659.
Pias, C. (2008). "Hollerith 'Feathered Crystal'": Art, science, and computing in the era of cybernetics. *Grey Room, 29,* 110–134.
Pitts, W., & McCulloch, W. (1947). How we know universals: The perception of auditory and visual forms. *The Bulletin of Mathematical Biophysics, 9*(3), 127–147.
Richardson, R., Schultz, J., & Crawford, K. (2019). Dirty data, bad predictions: How civil rights violations impact police data, predictive policing systems, and justice. *New York University Law Review, 94*(2), 192–233.
Rosenblatt, F. (1957). *The Perceptron: A perceiving and recognizing automaton (Project PARA)*. Buffalo, NY: Cornell Aeronautical Laboratory.
Rosenblatt, F. (1961). *Principles of neurodynamics: Perceptrons and the theory of brain mechanisms*. Buffalo, NY: Cornell Aeronautical Laboratory.

Rosenblueth, A., & Wiener, N. (1950). Purposeful and non-purposeful behavior. *Philosophy of Science, 17*(4), 318–326.

Rosenblueth, A., Wiener, N., & Bigelow, J. (1943). Behavior, purpose, and teleology. *Philosophy of Science, 10,* 18–24.

Rumelhart, D., Hinton, G., & Williams, R. (1986). Learning representations by back-propagating errors. *Nature, 323,* 533–536.

Schlatter, M., & Aizawa, K. (2008). Walter Pitts and "A logical calculus". *Synthese, 162*(2), 235–250.

Shannon, C. (1938). A symbolic analysis of relay and switching circuits. *Transactions American Institute of Electrical Engineers, 57,* 471–496.

Szegedy, C., Zaremba, W., Sutskever, I., Bruna, J., Erhan, D., Goodfellow, I., & Fergus, R. (2014). Intriguing properties of neural networks. arXiv:1312.6199 *[cs.CV]* https://arxiv.org/pdf/1312.6199.pdf.

van Miltenburg, E. (2016). Stereotyping and bias in the Flickr30K dataset. *Computer Vision and Language Processing* (pp. 1–4). http://www.lrec-conf.org/proceedings/lrec2016/workshops/.

Walker, J., & Cooper, M. (2011). Genealogies of resilience: From systems ecology to the political economy of crisis adaptation. *Security Dialogue, 42*(2), 143–160.

Wang, Y., & Kosinski, M. (2018). Deep neural networks are more accurate than humans at detecting sexual orientation from facial images. *Journal of Personality and Social Psychology, 114*(2), 246–257.

West, S. M., Whittaker, M., & Crawford, K. (2019). *Discriminating systems: Gender, race, and power in AI*. AI Now Institute.

Wiener, N. (1948). *Cybernetics; Or, communication and control in the animal and the machine* (2nd ed.). MIT Press.

Wiener, N. (1954). *The human use of human beings: Cybernetics and society* (2nd ed.). MIT Press.

Wiener, N. (1964). *I am a mathematician: The later life of a prodigy*. MIT Press.

Wu, X., & Zhang, X. (2016). Automated inference on criminality using face images. arXiv:1611.04135 *[cs.CV]*. https://arxiv.org/pdf/1611.04135v2.pdf.

CHAPTER 8

Planetary Intelligence

Orit Halpern

More than a decade has passed since the pathbreaking book *The Shock Doctrine* (2007) was published. A supposed "letter" or message from the "frontlines" of neoliberalism, Naomi Klein's tour de force provided a new vocabulary and, more importantly, a new tactical map, a topographical representation, or an image, if we will, of how contemporary forms of capitalism operate. Labelling it "disaster capitalism," Klein took some thirty odd years of history and discovered a pattern in the data. She showed how closely psychiatrists "shocking" and torturing patients in the 1950s resembled the torture and massacre of political dissidents and the violent reorganization of economy in the name of "structural readjustment" throughout the 1970s globally.

Today, the doctrine of shock has never appeared more pertinent, particularly in the midst of the COVID-19 global pandemic. Now is the right time to reflect and ask what has or has not changed over the last fifty years since the 1970s that marked the start of post-Fordism and neoliberalism for many scholars. I want to extend Klein's argument to take account of technical change and transformations in the nature of extractionism and economy.

O. Halpern (✉)
Concordia University, Montreal, Canada
e-mail: orit.halpern@concordia.ca

© The Author(s) 2021

J. Roberge and M. Castelle (eds.), *The Cultural Life of Machine Learning*, https://doi.org/10.1007/978-3-030-56286-1_8

In our current moment, market volatility, planetary-scale disease tracking, and human suffering appear to be indelibly and literally normatively connected. Saving the economy has been as important as saving human lives. While there have been pandemics in the past, never has the threat of disease and species-wide danger been so synchronically shared through media. Computational and digital technologies mark this event. We track curves, analytics, and numbers while also assuming big data will manage the coming plague. Automated platforms and social networks deliver our goods, mediate our work and friendships, and maintain what might have once been labelled the "social." Artificial intelligence and machine learning are also being deployed to predict future disease curves and to rapidly discover, test, and simulate the protein structures and compounds that might serve as treatments or vaccinations. This turn to computation as salvation is unique, I argue, to our present, and it says much about our future imaginaries of life on this, and perhaps soon to be, other planets.

I want, therefore, to return to the site originally mapped as the first "experiment" in shock and economy—Chile. I return asking a new set of questions about how technology and life are currently governed, and, more importantly, how we are *experimenting* with the future of life through new forms of computational design and infrastructures. I label this next version, or perhaps test of the shock doctrine, the "smartness mandate," and its marker is the penetration of computation and automation into every segment of human life. To sketch the contours of this new condition, this chapter speculatively examines the Atacama Desert in Chile as a topological site for envisioning and mapping technical futures.

In the course of this piece, I will survey a series of sites traversing scientific inquiry, energy and extraction, and calculative techniques. I want to emphasize that this is not a thorough or complete ethnography. I do not claim full knowledge of Chile or the Atacama, I am not an area specialist. Rather, I use this landscape to question our generally held beliefs in relation to AI. In contemplating our present, I will link the ALMA installation, an astronomical observatory that was part of the event horizon telescope, with the lithium beds in the Salar de Atacama and the Center for Mathematical Modelling in the University of Chile, Santiago. This landscape will bridge data and matter; these sites are the producers of some of the largest nonproprietary data sets on Earth and providers of many of the materials that create the information age. In this essay, I will argue that collectively these sites form the landscape of a *planetary testbed*, a petri dish cultivating potential futures of life, politics, and technology on Earth and beyond.

Event Horizons

A point of no return.—*Oxford English Dictionary*
A boundary beyond which events cannot affect an observer on the opposite side of it.—Wikipedia

On April 10, 2019, this first image of a black hole appeared to humanity. To produce this miracle demanded that scientists and engineers from a team spanning the globe turn the Earth itself into a vast sensor to gather data from black holes: the Event Horizon Telescope (EHT). Only a dish the size of this planet could create a sensor sensitive enough to collect weak electromagnetic signals from more than 50 million light years away in order to provide, at long last, empirical evidence supporting Einstein's general theory of relativity (Fig. 8.1).

When the image was released it circulated at literally the speed of light across that most human and social of networks—the internet. Comments online ranged from amazement to vast frustration that the black hole did indeed look just like we thought it might. "Awesome!," "amazing," "mystical," and "capable of making humans fall in love" jockeyed with "anticlimactic," "really?" and "it looks like the 'Eye of Sauron' from Lord of the Rings." Maybe, such comments suggest, the culmination of having turned our whole planet into a technology is just a fake artifact of computer graphics algorithms; merely another stereotypical image recalling longstanding standard Western cultural tropes of radically alien and powerful forces (Overbye, 2019)? In combining both mythic aesthetic conceptions of outer space and the power of the gods with the dream of objectivity and perfect vision through technology, the image brings forth a dual temporal imaginary. The event-image both crystallized new imaginaries of a planetary (and even post-planetary) scale future integrated through data and machine sensing and mobilized our oldest and most repeated conventions of what extreme nonhuman alterity might appear like, returning us to the legacies of myth and g-ds.

Whatever the "truth" of this image, I argue that it provides evidence of a radical reformulation of perception. This image presents the figure of the terminal limits of human perception while simultaneously embodying

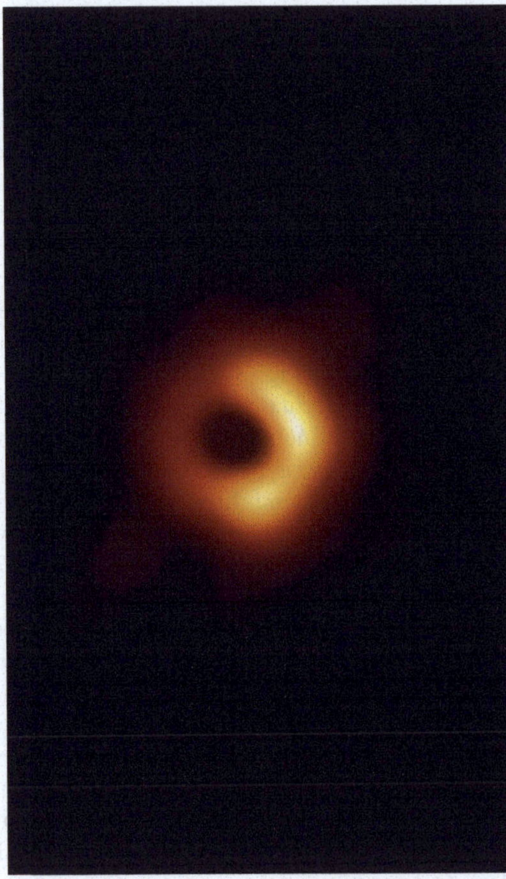

Fig. 8.1 First image of black hole, April 10, 2019 (*Credit* EHT collaboration)

a new form of experience comprised not within any one human or even technical installation, but through the literal networking of the entire planet into a sensor-perception instrument and experiment. This image provides an allegory, therefore, of the artificial intelligence and machine learning systems that underpin it, while it simultaneously exemplifies a classic problem in physics and computation—mainly, the impossibility of objectivity and the limits of being able to calculate or access infinity.

Objectivity

These problems have a history in science. As many scholars have demonstrated, the concept of mechanical objectivity first emerged in the nineteenth century with photography and film. The idea was linked to recognizing the fallibility of the human body and the impossibility of *human* objectivity, which simultaneously birthed a new desire for perfect, perhaps divine-like objectivity, inherited from Renaissance perspectivalism. This G-d like objectivity would now arrive not through the celebration of the human but through prosthesis and mechanical reproduction.[1] The latest forms of big data analytics, what I have termed in my past work *communicative objectivity*, push this history to a new scale and intensity transforming the management of time and life (Halpern, 2014). The event horizon abandons a return to the liberal subject and offers a new model. A model of objectivity not as certainty but as the management of uncertainty and as the production, in fact, of new zones by which to increase the penetration of computation and expand the frontiers of both science and capital. In the case of the event horizon, the frontier is to reconcile and integrate two radically different forms of math and theory—general relativity and quantum mechanics. This is a scalar question—gravity is not understood at the large scale in the same way as at a subatomic or nano-scale; the hope is that these experiments will allow a unification of these two scales. In doing so, the event horizon experiments are logistical in their logic, attempting to unify and syncopate the extremely local and specific with the very large and generic.

At stake are questions of chance and what constitutes evidence and objectivity for science. Black holes were predicted, but even Einstein did not believe his own prediction, refusing to accept so radical a mutation of time and space. Einstein, it appears, still wanted to know the truth. The idea of a space beyond which his own laws no longer applied was unthinkable. However, the event horizon is not the realm of surety but of probabilities and uncertainties. Physicists can define or speculate on certain state spaces but can never precisely know the exact movement of any one particle or element. Furthermore, the event horizon is the territory of histories. Black holes may contain keys, "a backward film," according to physicist and historian of science Peter Galison, to the universe's entire history. Time can reverse in the black hole, and the faint glimpse of the vast energies that cluster around the event horizon suggest possible past trajectories, but never just one (Overbye, 2020).

In response to this situation of imperfect visualizations and radical scalar and temporal indetermination, the call now is to increase computational power and add more dishes, perhaps in space, in order to increase the resolution of this massive instrument. This is the logic of *communicative objectivity*, the turn to automation and big data as modes of managing extreme uncertainty. The limits of knowledge are an imperative for technical progress (Overbye, 2020). Furthermore, the very apparatus of the EHT demonstrates the new integration of the scales of the earth and those of the stars to produce new economies and forms of knowledge. As I will show, both of these problems—the limits of human objectivity and the emergence of new forms of experience, analytics, and sensing—are deeply intertwined in how we currently govern and manage life on Earth through computation (Fig. 8.2).

Sublimity

One of the key installations in this project was the Atacama Large Millimeter/Submillimeter Array (ALMA) installation, which I visited on March 13, 2017. Located on the Chajnantor Plateau in the Atacama Desert in Chile, the radio telescopes are installed at an elevation of 5050 meters in one of the driest and most extreme environments on Earth.[2]

The entire installation appears to be designed to provoke a radical awe of scale, of human insignificance, and of the possibility of technical mastery of, and perhaps through, the vast vistas of the desert and, beyond that, the stars. The massive vehicles that tow these machines are specifically built for the purpose by space agencies. But even these machines, each tailor-made with tires two stories tall, seem almost tiny when viewed in comparison to the rest of the plateau (Fig. 8.3).

In my mind, the apparatus reflected and advanced every fantasy of extraplanetary exploration I read as a child in science fiction books and watched on NASA-sponsored public programming on TV. This analogy

Fig. 8.2 March 13, 2017 High Altitude Sub millimeter wave array, Alma Observatory, Chajnantor Plateau, Atacama, Chile. Part of the EHT (*Photo* Orit Halpern)

Fig. 8.3 Photo: Orit Halpern

is not just fiction. NASA and other space agencies use this desert to test equipment, train astronauts, and study the possible astrobiology of the future planets we will colonize (Hart, 2018). If the event horizon is the point of no-return, the Atacama is the landscape of that horizon, the infrastructure for our imaginaries of abandoning Earth and never returning to the past. But again, this is an irony, for ALMA collects history. Every signal processed here is eons old, millions if not billions of light years in time-space.

This technical infrastructure combined with an environment among the most arid on Earth produces strange aesthetic effects in a viewer. Such infinitude brought to us by the gift of our machines might be labelled "sublime." What incites such emotions at one moment in history, however, may not in another. The sublime is a series of emotional configurations that come into being through historically different social and technological assemblages. My sentiments of extreme awe and desire for these infrastructures, a sense of vertigo and loss of figure-ground relations, a descent into the landscape, recalls the work of historian David Nye on the "technological sublime." For North Americans, according to Nye, the later nineteenth century offered a new industrial landscape that incited extreme awe and concepts of beauty through structures like extension bridges. Structures such as the Brooklyn Bridge were deliberately built over the longest part of the river to prove the technical competence of its builders. Other constructions—skyscrapers, dams, canals, and so forth—were all part of this new "nature" that came into being at the time. Sites that produced a vertigo between figure and ground and reorganized social comprehensions of what constituted "nature" and "culture" or objects and subjects. The sublime, after all, is the loss of self into the landscape (Halpern, 2014; Nye, 1994).

Post-World War II environments saw a subtle shift in this aesthetic condition as it became increasingly mediated through television and other communication devices, making technical mediation a site of desire and aesthetic production. ALMA takes the informational situation to a new extreme. Here technology produces a new landscape that turns infrastructure into a site of sublimity, confusing the boundaries of the technical and "natural" and refocusing our perception toward a post-planetary aesthetic that is about transforming both scale (Earth is small) and time. The discourse surrounding ALMA suggests that all planets, including ours, and all their component landscapes are recording instruments surveying temporalities far outside of and beyond human experience (Halpern, 2014).

Machine Vision

To process the most ancient of signals demands the latest in machine learning methods and other analytic techniques. These data sets are utilized in partnership by Microsoft and other similar organizations as training sets due to their complexity and the difficulty in separating noise from signals as well as environments providing sites for testing algorithms and experimenting with new approaches to supervised and, especially, unsupervised learning (Zhang & Zhao, 2015). The image was produced through a massive integrated effort, analogous to the scientific images produced by other remote-sensing devices, such as the Mars rovers featured in Janet Vertesi's (2015) account of machine vision at NASA. These rovers are coordinated and their data synthesized and analyzed into signification through a large process that is not the work of individuals but groups. The same can be said for the EHT.

To produce the event horizon image scientists used interferometry, a process that correlates radio waves seen by many telescopes into a singular description. The trick is to find repeat patterns that can be correlated between sites of the EHT and to remove the massive amounts of "noise" in the data, in order to produce this singular "image" of what the National Science Foundation labelled the "invisible." Since black holes are very small on the scale of space and a large amount of other data from different phenomena in space enter the dishes as well, only machines have the capacity to analyze the large volume of signals and attempt to remove the supplementary data. Signals are picked up from an array of observatories around the world, and those that match what relativity theory predicted would be an event horizon must be correlated. Finding these signals requires the data be "cleaned"—a critical component of finding what is to be correlated. This process occurs in many different sites. I visited the data cleaners for ALMA at the European Space Observatory base in Santiago, where we discussed the process. Many of the teams worked with different machine learning approaches to use unsupervised learning methods to identify artifacts in the data and remove them. The process was quite difficult since no one had ever "seen" an event horizon or knew exactly what kind of information they were seeking.[3] Having never seen a black hole, and never being able to, what should we look for? Our machines are helping us decide.

Humanity, however, insists on its liberal agency. Irrespective of infrastructural capacities, the final image was attributed to a young woman, Katie Bouman, a postdoctoral researcher at the Harvard-Smithsonian Center for Astrophysics. Bouman apparently created the algorithm that allowed the vast amounts of data gathered at the EHT's many installations to be compared and synthesized into a singular image. In fact, Bouman was not an astronomer or astrophysicist but a computer scientist working on machine vision as a more generic problem (Grossman & Conover, 2020; Temming, 2019; Vertesi, 2015).

This attribution gestures to our own human temporal problems with the new media networks within which we are caught. It is not that the algorithm was not important, but that obviously a great deal of work by many people went into setting up the data-gathering experiment and developing methods to "clean" data. Bouman emerged as a progressive image that might translate the incoherence of a massive system into the identity politics of human history. The new discourse suggested we, like Einstein, were not yet comfortable with the horizon to our own control and command over our networks. This tension between radical uncertainty and inhuman cognition as well as our need to produce temporal command over data is one of the key features driving the growth of AI and its seemingly correlated discourses of mastery over futurity.

At ALMA, objectivity is indeed an impossibility. To process this data, figure-ground relations were literally confused. The official tour guide tells me that these telescopes contain units at the base that are the temperature of deep space in order to isolate and process signals from space and separate them from "noise" from the earthly atmosphere. By returning the signal to its "original" temperature the appropriate wavelengths can be isolated. In this installation, data is literally contextualized in an environment built within the experimental set-up. The furthest outside of Earth recreated within the machines. But perhaps this is the lesson of all scientific experiments: we create environments that are always already artificial and make nature from them (Pinch, Gooding, & Schaffer, 1989). Like the experiments of behavioral scientists and cyberneticians that produced new worlds in the name of depicting the planet, the ALMA telescopes recreate outer space within to produce visibility for the invisible and to reassemble eons of galactic time in the space of scientific practice. And if we take the event horizon as the allegory for our present, where we have turned the earth into a medium for information gathering and analysis, then this is even truer. The sites of data production, data gathering, and analysis are increasingly blurry in their boundaries. The planet has become a medium for recording inscriptions.[4]

Energy

The earth as medium is a truism in the Atacama that takes many forms. "Chile is copper" is an oft repeated mantra, I am told by Katie Detwiler, an anthropologist working on the Atacama and my guide to this place. And copper is in almost every machine, conducting all our electricity. The Atacama has some of the largest copper mines on Earth. Copper is industrial material; it also rests (although perhaps only for now) on an industrial economy. Copper markets are still relatively unleveraged. Unlike some other energy, mineral, and metal markets, there is little futures or derivative action. As a commodity copper suffers from modern economic concepts of business cycles, and its political economy is seemingly still grounded in terms like GDP and GNP along with concepts, stemming from Thomas Malthus and Adam Smith in the eighteenth century, of resource limitation, scarcity, demand, price, and above all population and nation. In Chile, copper is equated with nationalism. Under Pinochet these mines were unionized (contrary to what we might expect), and the state corporation CODELCO continues to smelt all the copper. This rather surprising history for a dictator synonymous with Milton Friedman and the Chicago Boys emerged from an alignment with right wing nationalists, authoritarianism, and neoliberalism (Klein, 2010).

But a few miles from ALMA is another landscape of extraction, metal, and energy. This one is linked to the stars and future(s). Space X, Tesla, and the high-tech industries that in theory will eventually replace the vestiges of our old heavy industrial and carbon-based economies all bank on the Atacama. For in this desert lies the new gold of a future Saudi Arabia, or so I am told by business journals and newspapers (Kroener, 2008): the Salar de Atacama, whose salt flats bear lithium. The lightest of metals, lithium supposedly represents the future of both machines and energy, destined to be the medium that replaces the carbon futures that financial markets and nations have so heavily bought into and leveraged (Fig. 8.4).

The beds are beautiful, created by brine brought to the surface. Lithium is never pure; it is mixed with other things, also all valuable,

Fig. 8.4 March 23, 2017, Salar de Atacama, SQM fields (*Photo* Orit Halpern)

such as magnesium and potassium. As one looks over the fields, there is an array of colors ranging from yellow to very bright blue. The first fields are still full of potassium that might serve as bedrock for fertilizers. As the beds dry longer, they turn bluer and then yellower. Finally, after almost a year, the bed fully dries[5] and lithium salt, LiCl, emerges. The salt is scraped from the bed, harvested, separated from trace boron and magnesium, and affixed with Sodium Carbonate for sale. Alejandro Bucher, the technical manager of the installation, takes us on a tour.[6] Its owners, Sociedad Química y Minera (SQM), he tells us, care about the environment—almost no chemicals are used in the process. The extraction of lithium is solar powered; the sun dehydrates the water and draws off the salts. A pure process. Except that it drains water. He assures us, however, that the latest expansions and technical advances will "optimize" this problem. Better water evaporation capture systems and planned desalinization plants will reduce the impact on this desert, which is the driest on Earth, and on these brine waters that are also the springs for supporting fragile ecosystems of shrimp, bacteria, and flamingos. Environmentalists, however, beg to differ; inquiries into the environmental impact of the fields have been undertaken, and the process of assessment has been criticized as opaque (Carrere, 2018).

What Pinochet never did—privatize mining—has fully come to pass with lithium. While SQM is Chilean, it is private. SQM has been attacked for anti-trade union practices, and unions are fighting to label lithium a matter of national security so the state can better regulate the material (IndustriALL Global Union, 2016). This corporation also partakes in planetary games of logistics around belt roads and resources. In 2018, the Chinese corporation Tianqi acquired a 24% share of SQM, essentially coming to dominate the corporation. While the government continues to monitor the situation and demand limits on Chinese participation on the corporate board, the situation is in flux (Gúzman, 2018). These games also demand privatized water supplies. Water is a massive commodity. Some of the largest desalinization plants on Earth will be built here by a range of vendors largely servicing the mining sector. These installations are built to fuel mining in the region. Desalinization is yet another extractive technology that facilitates the transformation of seemingly finite boundaries and resources into flexible eternally expandable frontiers, in this case through advanced technological processes of removing salt from seawater. Thus, a new infrastructure of corporate actors merging high tech with salt and water to support our fantasies of eternal growth emerges, so that we may drive clean cars and eventually arrive to the stars—where we will extract ever more materials (Harris, 2020).

These salts are also the fragile infrastructures for unique ecosystems and peoples. The water usage from these installations threatens indigenous communities in the area, already disposed and disenfranchised by the mining industry.

It is also in service of imagining a future on other planets that another group of scientists—astrobiologists—study the bacteria in these brines. These bacteria have evolved differently; the extreme conditions of the salts might offer clues, these scientists tell us, of life on Mars. These cellular creatures hold the key to survival in space and to the liveliness that might exist on other planets. We cannot accept being alone in the universe, and these bacteria allow us to envision, in their novel metabolisms and capacity to live under PH conditions lethal to most other organisms, another way to live. These beds, the astrobiologists argue, cannot be taken away to make batteries; they harbor our key to space and the way to terraform (Boyle, 2018; Parro et al., 2011).[7] What are we to do? How to realize a future, driven by these batteries, that disappears as we make them?

Optimization

More than anything, the lithium mines suggest new attitudes to, or maybe practices of, boundary making and market making. They demonstrate a move away from the perfect stabilities of supply-and-demand curves to the plasticity of another order of algorithmic finance and logistical management grounded in the computations of derivative pricing equations and debt capitalism.[8] The relationship between these very different and radically shifting territories of mining, salt harvesting, and astronomy can therefore only be realized in the turn to mathematics.

The incommensurabilities in scale and materials between the operations of mines and the seemingly metaphysical interests of the astronomical sciences are resolved at the Centre for Mathematical Modeling (CMM) in the University of Chile, located in Santiago some 1600 kilometers south. It is one of the world's premier research centers for applied mathematics in mining. A few days after my time at ALMA, I visit the center.

In a lecture room, a number of researchers present on themes of how machine learning, big data, and complex modelling might transform mining. One of the lead scientists in mathematical modelling at the center, Alejandro Jofré, is trained in optimization and game theory. He explains that the center's mission is to bring the best in mathematical modelling to bear on questions of mine optimization, discovery, and supply chain management. Cheapening and improving exploration is critical, as it is the most expensive and difficult part of the extraction process, often bearing no return. This search for ways to do more with less is necessary as all the materials on Earth, are, without question, running out. But this finitude of resources can be addressed through an infinity of data (Figs. 8.5 and 8.6).

This new optimization economy is also aligned, as Dr. Eduardo Vera, the executive manager of innovation and development at the CMM and in the National Laboratory for High Performance Computing argued, with rethinking mining unions and labor. The hierarchies of mines must go. In their place will be management by regular feedback loops derived from billions of sensors and automated systems that sense and decide the best actions: the best manner to ventilate, heat, cool, dig, chemically separate, mix, dispose, and scavenge material. The space of mining opened to the space of mathematics and abstraction; making Terran limits plastic, scavengable, optimizable, and ultimately grounded in the math of physics and astronomy. These communication systems, complex geological models, fluid and energy dynamics, and communication systems might also find themselves at use in other places. Over lunch, he tells me that entire computational infrastructures are being built at this moment. Large investments are being made by both corporate and government sources to develop the computer power to run advanced mathematical models and crunch vast data sets for the dual purposes of modelling Terran geologies and extraterrestrial phenomena. Ultimately, the mathematics being generated through abstract models and astronomy may also discover new methods and predictive analytics for use in asteroid and other mining.

Goldman Sachs released a report almost synchronously with my visit arguing for the future of asteroid mining, on April 6, 2017. The report was "bullish" on asteroid mining. "While the psychological barrier," the report noted, "to mining asteroids is high, the actual financial and technological barriers are far lower." Spacecraft and space travel are getting cheaper, and asteroids could be grabbed and hauled into low Earth orbit for mining. According to CalTech, the report cited, building asteroid-grabbing spacecraft would cost the same as setting up a mine on Earth. Goldman Sachs definitively urges speculation on space. While the market

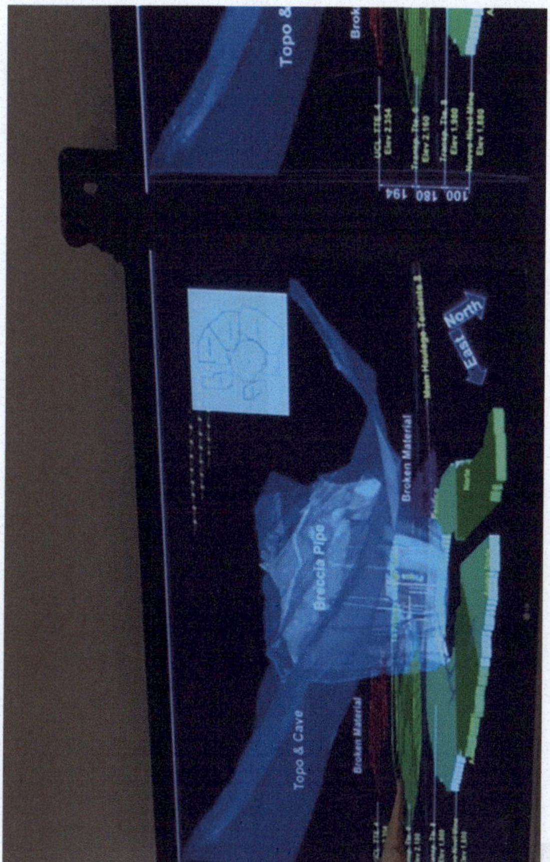

Fig. 8.5 Dr. Alejandro Jofré presenting on real-time analytics for decision making in extraction. March 21, 2017, CMM, University of Chile, Santiago (*Photo* Orit Halpern)

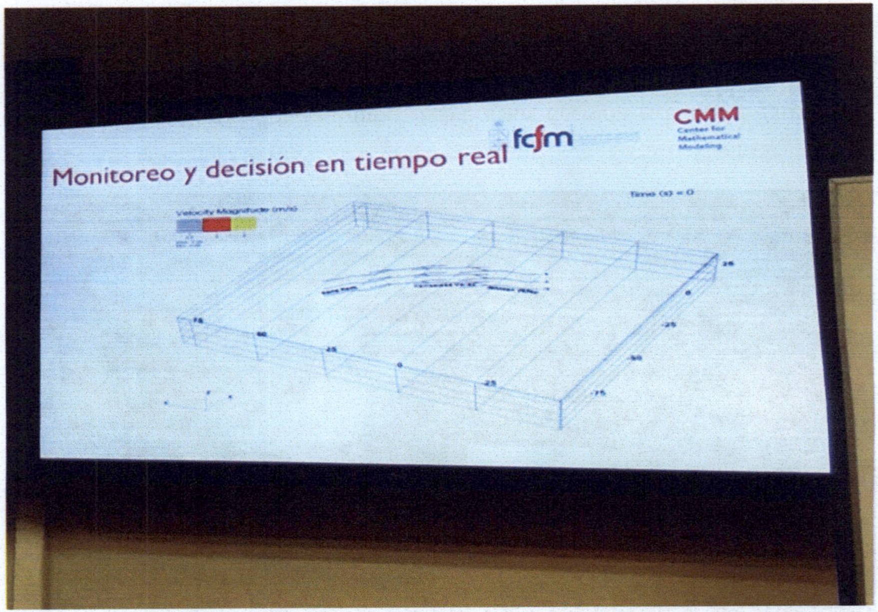

Fig. 8.6 Dr. Alejandro Jofré presenting on real-time analytics for decision making in extraction. March 21, 2017, CMM, University of Chile, Santiago (*Photo* Orit Halpern)

may tank on Earth, there is no question that humanity will need the materials (Edwards, 2017). Back on Earth, in Santiago, researchers speak of how astronomy's wealth of data and complicated analytics can be brought to bear on developing the complex mathematics for geological discovery and simulations of mine stability and resources.

The discussion also indicates a shift of economy, perhaps from extraction to optimization. Vast arrays of sensors, ever more refined chemistry, and reorganized labor and supply chains are developed whose main function is to produce big data for machine learning that will in theory rummage through the tailings, discarded materials, and supplementary and surplus substances of older extractive processes in order to reorganize the production, distribution, and recycling of materials in the search for speculative (and financializable) uses for the detritus and excrement of mining.[9] These computational-industrial assemblages create new economies of scavenging, such as the search for other metals in tailing ponds or the reuse of these waste materials for construction or other purposes, currently in vogue globally. In this logic, the seemingly final limits of life and resources become instead an extendable threshold that can be infinitely stretched through the application of ever finer and more environmentally pervasive forms of calculation and computation, which facilitate the optimization of salvage and extraction of finite materials. One might argue that this optimization is the perverse parallel of the event horizon. If one watches a clock fall into the event horizon, all one will see is time forever slowing down; the horizon will never be reached. History is eternally deferred at the threshold of a black hole. Big data practices for extraction provide a grotesque doppelgänger of physical phenomena. Even as energy, water, and ore run out, the terminal limits to the Terran ability to sustain capital are deferred through financial algorithms and machine learning practices. Better modelling and machine learning can allow mines to extend their operations, discover ever more minute deposits of ore, and continue to expand extraction. In fact, the application of artificial intelligence and big data solutions in geology and mine management has increased Chile's contribution to global copper markets. Chile actually expanded its mining outputs, despite degraded repositories, growing from providing 16% of global copper for industrial use to 30% between the 1990s and the present (Arboleda, 2020, p. 66). CODELCO, the state-owned copper conglomerate, has entered into major agreements with Uptake, a Chicago-based artificial intelligence and big data enterprise platform provider (Mining Journal, 2019). The only problem with this fantasy to stop or turn back time is that we are not travelling at the speed of light and Earth is not a black hole. Instead, these practices make crisis an impossibility and blind us to the depletion of the ecosystem.

Temporalities

The desert I visited, therefore, is the site of new capacities to recognize novel forms of life in astrobiology, of new mathematics for fluid and materials dynamics in the real-time monitoring and modelling of massive mines, and of the production of new images of the universe. Maybe the Atacama is always dying; its flora and fauna vanishing. But as engineers at SQM tell me, the new technologies will allow them to optimize water usage, to recycle and collect what evaporates, and to make water in the desert. What was once a limited, finite resource in the desert—water—is now elastic and optimizable, fortifying the environment and making it resilient. The new minerals and economies of space and lithium envisioned to replace the older metals and energies of industrialism will be run on algorithmic finance markets, hyper-speculation, and an embrace of transformation and shock. Resource limitations and catastrophic environmental events are no longer understood as crises necessitating a response through expertise and Milton Friedman's fiscal policies, but rather as ongoing processes that can be incrementally experimented with and addressed through endless adjustments and manipulations in time and data collection (Fig. 8.7).

But time and data can be manipulated in many ways. Back on Earth there is a film that came out in 2010: *Waiting for the Light* (2010) by Patricio Guzmán. In the immediate aftermath of Chile's coup on September 11, 1973, thousands were tortured and disappeared and nearly ten percent of the population were exiled, the paramilitary stalked Chile. Traveling in a Puma helicopter from detention site to detention site, the so-called Caravan of Death carried out the executions of twenty-six people in Chile's south and seventy-one in the desert north. Their bodies were buried in unmarked graves or thrown from the sky into the desert. The desert was militarized, turned into a weapon for the killing of dissidents and the training of troops, and its resources used to support the state. Guzmán parallels the search for bodies by mothers of dissidents killed by Pinochet with astronomers watching and recording the stars in the Atacama's high-altitude observatories (the wave millimeter arrays had

Fig. 8.7 Calama Memorial for Pinochet Victims, https://commons.wikimedia.org/wiki/File:Memorial_DDHH_Chile_06_Memorial_en_Calama.jpg (Downloaded August 6, 2019)

not yet been made operational). Above all, his theme is that the landscape is a recording machine for both human and inhuman memories: the traces of stars 50 million years away and the absence of loved ones within human lives. The film implies that the desert itself provides some other intelligence or maybe memory and not only for humans.

When I hear scientists speak of the possibility of real-time decision making in mining and the optimization of energy and materials through the perfection of sensing technology and big data in the mine, I hear a fantasy of stretching finite resources to infinite horizons through big data and artificial intelligences. I also hear a smaller, more embodied parallel fantasy of a new form of experience and cognition no longer nested in single human bodies, whether those of laborers or expert economists, but rather bequeathed to large networks of human-machines. These dreams of AI and machine learning—managed extraction hearken back to the history of machine learning (Rosenblatt, 1961).[10]

This returns me to the question of nonhuman intelligences and memories. The pursuit of machine learning since the 1950s has been about revising cognition but also understanding what might denote human history or perception. The very first model of a neural network—the perceptron—was never introduced as a model of "artificial intelligence." The author of the paper, psychologist Frank Rosenblatt, argued it was to fulfill "neurodynamic" principles. The perceptron would teach us about "natural intelligence." The perceptron was "not an invention for pattern recognition. As a brain model, its utility is in enabling us to determine therefore physical conditions for the emergence of various psychological opportunities" (Rosenblatt, 1958, p. 1) (Fig. 8.8).

Arranged in layers that made decisions cumulatively and statistically, the perceptron forwarded a new concept of intelligence as networked. Rosenblatt stated, "It is significant that the individual elements, or cells, of a nerve network have never been demonstrated to possess any specifically psychological functions, such as 'memory,' 'awareness,' or 'intelligence.' Such properties, therefore, presumably reside in the organization and functioning of the network as a whole rather than in its elementary parts" (pp. 9–10). By induction, this intelligence, therefore, might not reside in any one neuron and perhaps not even one body.

While many mutations have occurred along the road to contemporary deep learning and neural nets, insofar as most machine learning methods required training data—the computer equivalent of a parent correcting a child as the latter seeks to identify objects in the world—computers could,

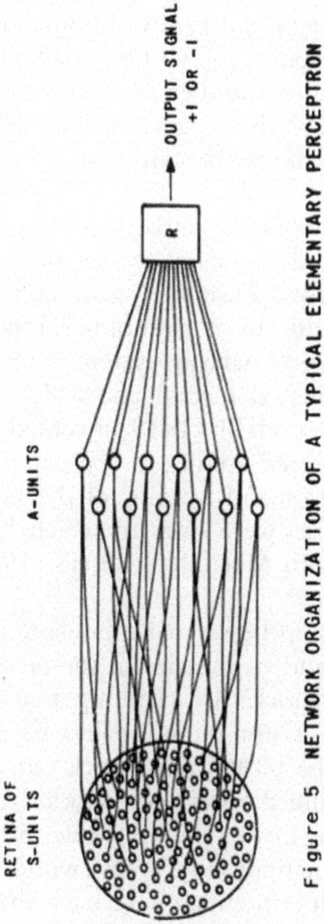

Fig. 8.8 From Rosenblatt (1961)

in principle, be trained on what was in essence population-level experience. Experience here, is moved outside of the individual; it's the data set, environment, or sensor system that becomes the object of design. That is, though each human individual is limited by that set of external stimuli to which he or she is in fact exposed, a computer can draw on huge databases of training data that were the result of judgements and experiences of not just one individual but large populations of human individuals. These infrastructures are ubiquitous today; think of the MINST data set, Google image training sets, the massive number of click farms spread around the world, or the massive geological data sets that monitor and make "decisions" in real time to continue the extraction of ever rarer materials (Arboleda, 2020).

The inspiration for this model of networked cognition lay in many places, but above all in the work of economist Friedrich Hayek and psychologist Donald Hebb. Rosenblatt laudingly mentions Hayek (1952/2012) as the most significant of psychological theorists to envision the subjective and nonhierarchical nervous system in his work *The Sensory Order*. For Hayek, an unregulated market and a decentralized nervous system were the "natural" order. Hebb (1949) invented Hebbian learning in neural networks and pioneered studies in sensory deprivation. These concepts of revising the interior and exterior of the human subject and modelling neurons as networks were ones to which Rosenblatt (1958) was greatly indebted along with McCulloch-Pitts's (1943/1970) model of neurons.

This genealogical relationship between Rosenblatt, Hayek, and Hebb returns us to Chile, history, and its legacies in the present. Naomi Klein built her argument about "shock" by claiming that methods derived from Hebb's research (even if not intentionally) became the template for torture at the hands of the CIA. This "shock" torture mirrored the neoliberal mandate for creating disasters or "shocks" that served as the bedrock for structural readjustment policies. Chile in the 1970s was an experiment in these tactics, inaugurating a new world of planetary-scale tests, in which the "shock" doctrine may have been the first, and experiments at population level managed not through older calculi of territory, eugenics, and Malthusian economics, but through new economic calculative instruments closely attached to our intelligent machines.

I wonder then at this condition we live in and its link to artificial intelligences that have fundamentally positioned experience as a matter of extra-human or personal relations, perhaps beyond Terran experiences.

We have turned our whole planet into a device for sensing the deepest, coldest space; the first wager in perhaps the biggest gamble we are taking as a species. If optimization is the "event horizon" of earthbound ecologies—representing the limit of the historical imaginary of economy by making it difficult to imagine running out of materials or suffering catastrophic events—then the event horizon appears as the very image to replace the finitude of the earth.

In a pessimistically optimistic vein, however, might this also be the final possibility to undo the fantasies of modern imperialism and anthropocentrism? There is hope in those infinitesimally specific signals found in a black hole, from eons ago beyond human or even Terran time. They remind us that there are experiences that can only emerge through the global networks of sensory and measuring instrumentations, and that there are radical possibilities in realizing that learning and experience might not be internal to the subject but shared. Perhaps these are just realizations of what we have known all along. We know that our worlds are comprised of relationships to Others, but there is a possibility that never has this been more evident or made more visible than through our new technologies, even our financial technologies and artificial intelligences. As they automate and traumatize us, they also reveal perhaps what has always been there—the sociotechnical networks that exist beyond and outside of us. Realities impossible to fully visualize. Upon introducing the perceptron, Rosenblatt spoke of "psychological opportunities"; what might these be?

These new assemblages of machines, humans, physical force, and matter also allow a reflexive critique and create new worlds. We do not know what the EHT will unearth, but we do know, especially now as we are in the midst of a global pandemic, that only our big data sets and simulations will guide us. For the first time in history as a species, perhaps, we are regularly offered different futures, charted from different data sets and global surveillance systems. Should we continue aggressive containment strategies against COVID-19? Do we prefer human life over market life? How can the sensor systems and experimental systems, the testing that is now sensing for this disease, be utilized in the future for equity or social justice? Our planet has become a vast dataset, every cell phone and many bodies (although not all, invisibilities and darknesses are also appearing) serving as recording devices that allows us to track this disease and, with it, the violences and inequities of our society. But the question is: how shall we mobilize this potential? The same distributed systems of sensors, analytics, and data collection offer many options. Totalitarian states and democratic governance through data, improved health and consciousness of social inequity, or terrible economic disenfranchisement through futures markets that even now play on the disaster and use data simulations to make bets on negative futures for humanity. We are in a massive and ongoing test scenario, mirrored by the tests we are all taking for diseases. Different forms of governance are being experimented with, different understandings of data and what imaginaries they engender, but the planetary test is not a controlled experiment; its stakes cannot be fully known and may be terminal.

The event horizon telescope is an allegory for this condition. It presents us with the radical encounter with our inability to ever be fully objective and the possibility that there are things to learn and forms of experience that are beyond the demands of capital or economy in our present. In many ways it is one possible culmination of a history of rethinking sensation, perception, and scientific epistemologies. But it is not the only possibility in a world of probabilities. Reactionary politics and extreme extractionism emerge from a perverse use of new media networks—not to recognize our subjective and interconnected relatedness but rather to valorize older forms of knowledge and power: those of myth, cartesian perspectivalism, and "nature" as a resource for "human" endeavors. Those are the politics that separate figures from grounds, maintain the stability of objects, and understand the future as always already foreclosed and known.

When we discuss AI in terms of national competition or the ongoing abstraction and rationalization from an analogue world, are we taking seriously enough the reformulations of time and space facilitated by these very techniques? Or our own investment and entanglement with sociotechnical systems? Or history? Do we ignore the landscape and the ecology of interactions when we frame ethics in terms of decisions made at singular points in time? Our dominant discourses on AI repeat ideas that we can still control the future or that technology is not natural. These are logics of the event that ignore its horizon. My hope is that perhaps in encountering the impossibility of ever imagining the reality of the event horizon, we might finally be able to witness and engage the precarious reality of life on Earth.

Acknowledgements This project was supported by the Australian Research Council grant "Logistical Worlds". Special thanks to Ned Rossiter, Brett Neilson, and Katie Detweiler for making the research possible.

Notes

1. For an extensive discussion of the history of objectivity and the relationship between objectivity, perception, and technology see Daston and Galison (1992) and Crary (1990).
2. The observatory is also the harbinger of new forms of territory, a location that transforms the boundaries and borders between ourselves and outer-space, but also the spaces of the Earth. The installation is run by a consortium headed by the European Southern Observatory, a number of United States universities, and a series of Japanese institutions (European Southern Observatory, n.d.). Just as ALMA envisions a new world beyond our own, it is also part of producing a new geography on our planet, a world of new zonal logics. In 1990, ALMA was bequeathed to the international consortium that runs it, but Chile had already granted concessions to the European Southern Observatory in 1963 across the Atacama for observatories. ALMA is therefore a unique extraterritorial zone, part of the history of a massive astronomical collaboration engineered in the Global South in order to create the European Union through scientific cooperation in the post-World War II years. ALMA in its extraterritorial governance and work to produce new political-economic institutions—primarily the European Union—appears as an allegory for the post-planetary imaginaries which its science fuels.
3. Interviews conducted at ALMA on my visit on March 13, 2019, and at the ESO Data Center in Santiago on March 20, 2017, revealed that many of the staff had been working on satellites and related information and communication problems before applying their research on to the study of the stars. ALMA has pioneered work on exo-planets and finding asteroids and other potentially mineable objects on Earth. Interviews with Yoshiharu Asaki, Associate Professor National Astronomical Observatory of Japan (ALMA), and Chin-Shin Chang, Science Archive Content Manager (Santiago).
4. See also Jennifer Gabrys' (2016) work on the idea of the planet as programmable through sensor infrastructures.
5. Lithium was first discovered 1817 by Swedish chemist Johan August Arfwedson. Arfwedson, though, wasn't able to isolate the metal when he realized petalite contained an unknown element. In 1855, British chemist Augustus Matthiessen and German chemist Robert Bunsen were successful in separating it. It is one of the lightest and softest metals

known to man. In fact, it can be cut with a knife. And because of its low density, lithium can even float in water (Bell, 2020).

6. Alejandro Bucher, Technical Manager SQM, March 23, 2017.
7. See also https://earthobservatory.nasa.gov/images/144826/salt-flats-mountains-and-moisture.
8. For work on debt and financialization as well as the place of ideas of information, computation, and algorithms in the production of these markets see Mirowski (2002), Harvey (2007), and LiPuma and Lee (2004). For an excellent summary of capital and extraction in Chile, including discussion of the way new information technologies and financial strategies are allowing a new "margin" of extraction and extension of mining capacities see Arboleda (2020).
9. For more on the specific use of AI and machine learning in mine reclamation programs see Halpern (2018).
10. Please note that this segment on Rosenblatt was conceived with Robert Mitchell as part of our joint project and future monograph *The Smartness Mandate*.

References

Arboleda, M. (2020). *Planetary mine: Territories of extraction under late capitalis*m. Verso.

Bell, T. (2020, January 24). *An overview of commercial lithium production*. The Balance. https://www.thebalance.com/lithium-production-2340123.

Boyle, R. (2018, November 28). The search for alien life begins in Earth's oldest desert. *The Atlantic*. https://www.theatlantic.com/science/archive/2018/11/searching-life-martian-landscape/576628/.

Carrere, M. (2018, December 16). *Chile renews contract with lithium company criticized for damaging wetland* (S. Sims, Trans.). Mongabay. https://news.mongabay.com/2018/12/chile-renews-contract-with-lithium-company-criticized-for-damaging-wetland/.

Crary, J. (1990). *Techniques of the observer: On vision and modernity in the nineteenth century*. MIT Press.

Daston, L., & Galison, P. (1992). The image of objectivity. *Representations, 40,* 81–128. https://doi.org/10.2307/2928741.

Edwards, J. (2017, April 6). *Goldman Sachs: Space mining for platinum is "more realistic than perceived."* Business Insider. https://www.businessinsider.com/goldman-sachs-space-mining-asteroid-platinum-2017-4.

European Southern Observatory. (n.d.). *ESO & Chile—A scientific and cultural bridge*. Retrieved June 27, 2019 from https://www.eso.org/public/about-eso/eso-and-chile/.

Event Horizon. *Wikipedia*. https://en.wikipedia.org/wiki/Event_horizon.

Gabrys, J. (2016). *Program earth: Environmental sensing technology and the making of a computational planet*. University of Minnesota Press.

Grossman, L., & Conover, E. (2020, April 10). The first picture of a black hole opens a new era of astrophysics. *Science News*.

Gúzman, L. (2018, December 7). The fight for the control of Chile's lithium business. *Diálogo Chino*. https://dialogochino.net/15614-the-fight-for-control-of-chiles-lithium-business/.

Halpern, O. (2014). *Beautiful data: A history of vision and reason since 1945*. Duke University Press.

Halpern, O. (2018, April 10). Golden futures. *LIMN* (10). https://limn.it/articles/golden-futures/.

Harris, P. (2020, January 27). *Chile seawater desalination to grow 156%*. Mining Journal. https://www.mining-journal.com/copper-news/news/1379729/chile-seawater-desalination-to-grow-156.

Hart, D. (2018, June 20). *Cooking up the world's driest desert—Atacama Rover Astrobiology Drilling Studies*. NASA. https://www.nasa.gov/image-feature/ames/cooking-up-the-world-s-driest-desert-atacama-rover-astrobiology-drilling-studies.

Harvey, D. (2007). *Limits to capital*. Verso.

Hayek, F. (2012). *The sensory order: An inquiry into the foundations of theoretical psychology*. University of Chicago Press (Original work published 1952).

Hebb, D. (1949). *The organization of behavior: A neuropsychological theory*. Wiley.

IndustriALL Global Union. (2016, May 10). *Industrial Chile sponsors bill to declare lithium a strategic national resource*. http://www.industriall-union.org/industral-chile-sponsors-bill-to-declare-lithium-a-strategic-national-resource.

Klein, N. (2007). *The shock doctrine: The rise of disaster capitalism*. Picador.

Klein, N. (2010, March 3). Milton Friedman did not save Chile. *The Guardian*. https://www.theguardian.com/commentisfree/cifamerica/2010/mar/03/chile-earthquake.

Kroener, B. I. (2008, November 6). The Saudi Arabia of lithium. *Forbes*. https://www.forbes.com/forbes/2008/1124/034.html#1fdfe4254dee.

LiPuma, E., & Lee, B. (2004). *Financial derivatives and the globalization of risk*. Duke University Press.

McCulloch, W., & Pitts, W. (1970). A logical calculus of ideas immanent in nervous activity. In W. McCulloch (Ed.), *Embodiments of mind* (pp. 20–24). MIT Press (Original work published 1943).

Mining Journal. (2019, March 26). *Codelco to deploy AI solution*. https://www.mining-journal.com/innovation/news/1359598/codelco-to-deploy-ai-solution.

Mirowski, P. (2002) *Machine dreams: Economics becomes a cyborg science*. Cambridge University Press.
Nye, D. (1994). *American technological sublime*. MIT Press.
Overbye, D. (2019, April 10). Darkness visible, finally: Astronomers capture first ever image of a black hole. *The New York Times*.
Overbye, D. (2020, March 28). Infinite visions were hiding in the first black hole image's rings. *The New York Times*.
Oxford English Dictionary. (n.d.). Event horizon. In *Oxford English dictionary*. Retrieved August 11, 2019.
Parro, V., de Diego-Castilla, G., Moreno-Paz, M., Blanco, Y., Cruz-Gil, P., Rodríguez-Manfredi, … Gómez-Elvira, J. (2011). A microbial oasis in the hypersaline Atacama subsurface discovered by a life detector chip: Implications for the search for life on Mars. *Astrobiology*, *11*(10), 969–996. https://doi.org/10.1089/ast.2011.0654.
Pinch, T., Gooding, D., & Schaffer, S. (Eds.). (1989). *The uses of experiment: Studies in the natural sciences*. Cambridge University Press.
Rosenblatt, F. (1958). The perceptron: A probabilistic model for information storage and organization in the brain. *Psychological Review, 65*(6), 386–408.
Rosenblatt, F. (1961). Principles of Neurodynamics. Perceptrons and the Theory of Brain Mechanisms (No. AD0256582). Defense Technical Information Center. https://apps.dtic.mil/sti/citations/AD0256582.
Temming, M. (2019, April 10). How scientists took the first picture of a black hole. *Science News*.
Vertesi, J. (2015). *Seeing like a rover: How robots, teams, and images craft knowledge of Mars*. University of Chicago Press.
Zhang, Y., & Zhao, Y. (2015). Astronomy in the big data era. *Data Science Journal, 14*(11), 1–9. https://doi.org/10.5334/dsj-2015-011.

CHAPTER 9

Critical Perspectives on Governance Mechanisms for AI/ML Systems

Luke Stark, Daniel Greene, and Anna Lauren Hoffmann

As the use of artificial intelligence (AI) systems grounded in various forms of machine learning (ML) and statistical inference has grown, the hype around these technologies has grown faster. AI/ML technologies will, according to their extollers, usher in a "Fourth Industrial Revolution," purportedly providing data-driven insights and data-driven efficiencies reshaping labor, medicine, urban life, and consumption (Schwab, 2017) is highest. Enthusiasm for AI/ML technologies is rampant in global corporations, national governments, and even nongovernmental organizations. Critiques of the adverse societal impacts of these systems have intensified

L. Stark (✉)
University of Western Ontario, London, ON, Canada
e-mail: cstark23@uwo.ca

D. Greene
University of Maryland, College Park, MD, USA
e-mail: dgreene1@umd.edu

A. L. Hoffmann
University of Washington, Seattle, WA, USA
e-mail: alho@uw.edu

© The Author(s) 2021

J. Roberge and M. Castelle (eds.), *The Cultural Life of Machine Learning*, https://doi.org/10.1007/978-3-030-56286-1_9

in response to this upsurge in AI boosterism (Benjamin, 2019; Eubanks, 2018) but have at times struggled to gain traction with policymakers (Crawford et al., 2019).

In this chapter, we provide a critical overview of some of the proposed mechanisms for the ethical governance of contemporary AI systems. These strategies include technical solutions intended to mitigate bias or unfairness in the design of AI systems as well as legal, regulatory, and other social mechanisms intended to guide those systems as they are built and deployed. Academics and industry teams have developed technical tools for the development of fair, trustworthy, and interpretable AI systems; socio-legal governance mechanisms include projects from civil society groups, local, state and supranational governments, and industry actors. These latter solutions include high-level values statements and sets of principles around AI ethics, promulgated by actors in all three of the above categories; AI-specific laws and regulations from governments, alongside voluntary standards proposals from business and civil society groups; and the application of existing human rights frameworks and discourses of "securitization" to the governance of AI/ML technology.

Focusing on these interventions primarily in their North American and European contexts, we describe various proposed mechanisms for AI/ML governance in turn, arguing each category of intervention has in practice supported the broader regimes of corporate and state power under which AI/ML technologies are being developed. The various AI/ML governance mechanisms being proposed by states and corporate actors do not function independently of each other. As Nissenbaum (2011) observes, "law and technology both have the power to organize and impose order on society" (p. 1373). Technical and social governance mechanisms act together as sociotechnical systems, and understanding how these elements interact in the hands of state and corporate actors is critical in ensuring that the governance of AI/ML is not only most effective but also most just. The mutual interdependence of various material, regulatory, and rhetorical governance mechanisms can work together for less than ideal ends: to subvert one form of effective governance by undercutting it through other means, or to confound, confuse, and delay the exercise of oversight through emphasis on a different governance mechanism. The interrelationship between governance mechanisms can thus do as much to hinder as to help the causes of equality and justice. Here, we critique many of the proposed solutions for AI/ML governance as supporting a narrow, unjust, and undemocratic set of norms around these technologies' design and deployment, grounded in the exigencies of both computational media and neoliberal capital (Deleuze, 1990). We conclude by highlighting alternative perspectives—including labor movements such as the Tech Won't Build It campaign and social justice groups such as the Movement for Black Lives—committed to dismantling and transforming both the AI/ML technologies supporting the broader twenty-first-century neoliberal surveillance economy, and that economy itself (Zuboff, 2019).

Governance Through Tools

Some of the most commonly proposed solutions to the shortcomings of contemporary AI systems have been technical fixes, i.e., changes to machine learning processes and practices to diagnose and diminish statistical biases or omissions in these systems' outputs (Narayanan, 2018). As "Big" data analysis and AI/ML have become ubiquitous, the longstanding critiques of social bias expressed via digital systems drawn from science and technology studies (STS) (Friedman & Nissenbaum, 1996) have gained traction in computer science and data science. Philosophers and social theorists of technology such as Nissenbaum (2010), Gandy (2009), Johnson (2007), Pfaffenberger (1992), and Winner (1988) have variously argued technical specifications can and should be only one element of a broader, multidisciplinary assessment of digital technologies and their social impacts. In 2013, Dwork (a computer scientist) and Mulligan (a legal scholar) argued for "greater attention to the values embedded and reflected in classifications, and the roles they play in shaping public and private life," observing digital analytics "promised—or threatened—to bring classification to an increasing range of human activity" (Dwork & Mulligan, 2013, p. 35). With the increasing ubiquity of AI/ML technologies, computer scientists began to follow the lead of Dwork, Friedman, Mulligan, Nissenbaum, and others in working to analyze, and in some cases formalize abstract values such as fairness, accountability, transparency, and interpretability, particularly in the context of machine learning systems. Yet while necessary for addressing the governance of AI systems, these tools address only a small fraction of the governance challenges provoked by these technologies.

Techniques for diminishing technical definitions of bias and unfairness have been developed by corporate (Zhang, Lemoine, & Mitchell, 2018), scholarly (Kearns, Roth, & Wu, 2017), and civil society actors (Duarte,

2017). These efforts have historical parallels in the social sciences, particularly around quantitative educational, vocational (Hutchinson & Mitchell, 2019), and psychometric testing (Lussier, 2018). Fairness, Accountability, and Transparency in Machine Learning (FATML) workshops, held yearly in conjunction with the International Conference on Machine Learning (ICML) from 2014 to 2018, were organized by a group comprised largely of computer scientists. In 2018, the first dedicated FAT* Conference was held in New York City, and in 2019 the second edition of the conference became associated with the Association of Computing (ACM) conference series, a testament to the quick increase of interest in the field from machine learning practitioners and other computer science researchers.

Technical tools for mitigating bias in AI systems have coalesced around strategies for ensuring fairness (Kleinberg, Ludwig, Mullainathan, & Rambachan, 2018)—though what the term "fairness" means, and how that definition subsequently shapes computational bias solutions, has remained an open question (Narayanan, 2018). Technical solutions have been developed to ensure both individual statistical fairness (Hardt, Price, & Srebro, 2016) and statistical fairness across pre-defined groups (Verma & Rubin, 2018), while related work has explored human perceptions of algorithmic bias and fairness in everyday contexts (Lee, 2018; Woodruff, Fox, Rousso-Schindler, & Warshaw, 2018). Scholarship has also begun to connect computational models of fairness with extant formalizations from philosophical theories of political and economic equality (Heidari, Loi, Gummadi, & Krause, 2018).

A second cluster of technical work has centered on ensuring AI algorithms and statistical models are accountable and explainable—or "transparent"—to human users and auditors (Miller, 2019). Much like fairness, the definitions of these terms lack consensus (Caplan, Donovan, Hanson, & Matthews, 2018). Tools intended to enable such accountability and transparency tend to focus on demonstrating either the provenance of training data sets or the decision-making processes through which machine-learning models make use of such data, defining terms like accountability and transparency narrowly as referring to a system's usability or the clarity of its interface design (Ananny & Crawford, 2017). Scholars have noted further that transparency and accountability are, like fairness, fundamentally social concepts (Brown, Chouldechova, Putnam-Hornstein, Tobin, & Vaithianathan, 2019; Veale, Van Kleek, & Binns, 2018).

The focus on narrow technical definitions of terms like accountability, bias, or unfairness on the parts of computer scientists and especially large digital technology firms has led many scholars to note such tools are necessary, but entirely insufficient, to address the full spectrum of sociotechnical problems created by AI systems (Selbst, Boyd, Friedler, Venkatasubramanian, & Vertesi, 2019). These scholars draw on the STS and critical legal studies literatures noted above, alongside scholarship in critical race studies, women's, gender, disability, and queer studies, and other fields interrogating social/institutional structures of power and domination. Scholars such as Noble (2018), Eubanks (2018), Broussard (2018), and Benjamin (2019) have documented and analyzed the failures of digital tools to properly account for race, gender, sexuality, and other facets of human diversity. Focusing specifically on fairness, Hoffmann (2019) observes that discourses around rights, due process, and antidiscrimination often fail to overcome animus and have at times even "hindered ... the transformative and lasting structural change that social justice demands" (p. 901). Costanza-Chock (2018) calls for the application of design justice, or "theory and practice that is concerned with how the design of objects and systems influences the distribution of risks, harms, and benefits among various groups of people," to AI/ML and other digital systems.

These scholars and others have both challenged the emphasis on technical solutions as the primary mechanisms to govern AI/ML systems and the contention that such solutions are value neutral in their execution. No technical solution to the governance of technical systems such as AI/ML is advisable on its own; as Nissenbaum (2011) observes, "however well-designed, well-executed, and well-fortified ... [technical] systems are, incipient weaknesses are inevitable and pose a threat to their programmed action" (p. 1386). Such "weaknesses" are the elements of the system that predispose it toward particular normative outcomes that are incommensurate with social values like fairness, democratic accountability, and justice; as Nissenbaum notes further, "an important role for regulation is to remove the temptation to exploit these [technical] weaknesses" (p. 1386). Yet many of the regulatory efforts around AI/ML to date have the opposite valence. As in other recent cases involving novel technologies, the interests and concerns of these technologies' powerful proponents have sought to capture the discourse around social, legal, and regulatory responses to AI/ML technologies.

Governance Through Principles

In conjunction with work on technical mechanisms for governing AI/ML systems, industry players and nonprofit groups have also produced high-level AI "values statements," articulating guidelines for the development and deployment of these technologies. In recent work (Greene, Hoffmann, & Stark, 2019), we interrogated a sample of these statements released by high-profile actors in the area, such as nonprofit AI research company Open AI, industry group the Partnership for AI, and the tenets of the AI Ethics Board for Public Safety of Axon Corporation (formerly Taser). In the interim, a slew of similar statements from corporations, governments, and civil society groups have been announced. Jobin, Ienca, and Vayena (2019) observe some high-level principles such as transparency are commonly invoked across many of these statements, while others, like sustainability and solidarity, are far less common. The diversity of principles and codes around the world makes synthetic analysis of such statements complex, with discourse in the Anglosphere tending to overlook principle sets in languages other than English or not easily accessible via conventional digital channels.

We concluded in (2019) that the AI values statements we analyzed offered a deterministic, expert-driven vision of AI/ML governance, the challenges and pitfalls of which are best addressed through technical and design—not social or political—solutions. In the interim, little has changed. These statements both reflect and reify what Abend (2014) calls the "moral background" for AI/ML development, or the parameters under which ethics are understood and delimited. Perhaps unsurprisingly given the involvement of tech sector companies in many of these statements, there is little acknowledgement in these documents that AI/ML can be limited or constrained by social exigencies or democratic oversight. The rush to apply AI/ML during the COVID-19 pandemic to digital contact tracing, automatic temperature tracking, and other technical interventions with little constraint is a sobering case in point.

High-profile AI vision statements are distinguished by several shared traits. These include an insistence that the positive and negative impacts of AI are a matter of universal concern amenable to a common ethical language; an emphasis on AI governance as an elite, expert project of technical and legal oversight despite a desire to pay lip service to broad stakeholder input; a paradoxical insistence on the inevitability of AI technologies while placing the ethical onus for their governance on humans;

and a focus on technical solutions and design elements such as transparency, and not on the broader political economy in which these systems are embedded, as the necessary locus of ethical scrutiny and AI governance (Greene et al., 2019). These values statements are couched in the descriptive language of STS and the philosophy of technology, indicating that these critical fields have had at least some rhetorical effect.

Recently released AI vision and value statements have deviated little from the core themes described above. The Organization for Economic Cooperation and Development (OECD)'s Principles on AI, adopted in mid-2019, emphasize the development of "trustworthy AI" in order to fuel "inclusive growth" and argue for the facilitation of AI development, not its regulation or potential curtailment ("OECD Principles on Artificial Intelligence," n.d.). Even the Vatican's recent "Call for an AI Ethics," signed in Rome in February 2020, echoes already extant AI principles, calling for AI to be transparent, inclusive, reliable, secure, and impartial—values described in the call's press release as "fundamental elements of good innovation," but with seemingly little connection to Christian ethical traditions (Pontifical Academy for Life, 2020). The Vatican document was cosigned by both IBM and Microsoft, suggesting the effort was as much a public relations exercise as a serious attempt to grapple with the social impacts of AI and automation more broadly.

While the ethical design parameters suggested by AI vision statements share some of the elements and framing of STS and other critical fields, they differ implicitly in normative ends, with explicit goals around social justice or equitable human flourishing often missing. The "moral background" of these ethical AI/ML statements is thus closer to conventional business ethics (Metcalf, Heller, & Boyd, 2016; Moss & Metcalf, 2020), typified by codes of ethical conduct that foreground protecting and consolidating professional and corporate interests (Stark & Hoffmann, 2019). Indeed, the focus on developing high-level principles around AI ethics could be considered strong evidence for the field's attempt to consolidate itself—with many technical divisions and differences across practitioners, agreements around high-minded yet abstract principles can potentially serve not only as a sop to governance efforts from other actors, but also as mechanisms to signal professional membership and insider status.[1] AI/ML ethics statements buttress business-as-usual approaches within technical fields while helping to strengthen the professional clout of AI/ML practitioners.

Governance Through Regulations and Standards

Most national governments responding explicitly to the growth of AI research and development to date have done so primarily through national AI strategies, documents that frequently echo the broad principles of corporate and civil-society vision statements described above (Dutton, Barron, & Boskovic, 2018). Canada was the first country to announce a nationally funded AI strategy in March of 2017. Some of these strategies are paired with increased financial investment in various aspects of AI research and development. As of the end of 2018, the Canadian Institute for Advanced Research (CIFAR) lists nine national AI strategies with funding commitments, while another twenty countries had produced or were at work on AI guidance documents (Dutton et al., 2018, pp. 5–7). In the European Union, both various national governments and the European Commission have produced AI strategic planning documents, the latter including the European Commission's *Ethical Guidelines for Trustworthy AI* (AI HLEG, 2019) developed in 2019. While some national jurisdictions have begun to move forward on binding regulatory regimes for AI and automated systems, this progress has been slow. In tandem with its *Ethical Guidelines*, the European Commission published a white paper in February 2020 on "a European approach" to artificial intelligence intended as the groundwork for binding EU regulations (European Commission, 2020), though critics have noted the EC's recommendations seek to regulate, but not ban, certain applications of AI such as facial recognition (Baraniuk, 2020).

Regional and municipal governments have been more active and successful at developing regulatory responses to AI. Local regulation of AI-enabled facial recognition technologies (FRTs) has been a particularly active area of policymaking. Full or partial bans and moratoria on the deployment of FRTs by local governments and law enforcement agencies have been passed in jurisdictions in the United States, Europe, and elsewhere (Leong, 2019) as the dangers of these technologies to human equality (Stark, 2019) and civil liberties (Hartzog & Selinger, 2018) have become more widely recognized. These regulatory moves are partial ones; they generally do not cover private sector deployment of FRTs (Wright, 2019), nor the deployment of these technologies in educational institutions (Andrejevic & Selwyn, 2019). Moreover, these regulations often fail to address the wide range of AI-equipped analytic technologies designed to surveil elements of human bodies and behavior alongside the face—such as gait recognition or emotion analytics. Nonetheless, local regulation of AI technologies is a welcome regulatory first step—and has often been catalyzed by the work of social justice groups such as the Movement for Black Lives (more below).

Another potentially promising set of mechanisms for regulating the application of AI systems are algorithmic impact assessments (AIAs) (Reisman, Schultz, Crawford, & Whittaker, 2018; Selbst, 2017): procedural mechanisms through which institutions systematically assess the potential risks and outcomes of automated decision systems before they are deployed. Based on a variety of similar impact assessment processes in environmental regulation, human rights law, and more recently digital privacy scholarship (Bamberger & Mulligan, 2008), AIAs have attracted interest from varying levels of government, including the New York City municipal and the Canadian federal governments (Cardoso, 2019). New York City formed an Automated Decision Systems Task Force in 2017 to assess how such mechanisms were being used in the municipal context and provide recommendations for their regulation. The Task Force's report (New York City, 2019) released in late 2019, advocated for the creation of a city Algorithms Management and Policy Officer but was criticized for its lack of other specific policy suggestions (Lecher, 2019); a Shadow Report from the AI Now Institute (Richardson, 2019) argued for broader and more rigorous application of AIA processes in all levels of government, including broad applicability and periodic external reviews of their effectiveness. The uneven implementation of AIAs suggests the challenge of moving to binding regulation around automated systems—not so much because of technical difficulties as due to political pressures to ensure the powerful continue to benefit from the deployment of these technologies.

High-profile national AI policies and supranational statements of principle are also quickly being supplemented by more granular corporate mechanisms for the governance of AI/ML systems: internationally recognized technical standards and sets of ethical design principles. These mechanisms extend the technocratic, processes-grounded and expert-focused themes often found in AI vision statements. As such, they are a means to cement such solutions to the societal problems posed by AI/ML systems as the main field of debate for practitioners and policymakers. Standards, unlike regulation, implicitly work within the growth plans of industry and serve to coordinate individual enterprises around interoperability and consistency; they support, rather than hinder, the notion of regulation as an enabler of the tool-focused approach preferred by AI/ML companies.

A variety of private and public organizations at the national and international level have begun the process of developing standards around AI (Cihon, 2019). The International Organization for Standardization (ISO), an independent, nongovernmental international organization, has begun to develop standards around AI in conjunction with the International Electrotechnical Commission (IEC) through Subcommittee 42 of the two organizations' Joint Technical Committee (JTC) 1, the latter formed in 1987 to develop global digital technology standards. The ISO/IEC JTC 1/SC 42 process is in its early stages and has produced a number of drafts currently being developed in committee around AI topics including ISO/IEC WD 22989: Artificial intelligence—Concepts and terminology and ISO/IEC WD 23053: Framework for Artificial Intelligence (AI) Systems Using Machine Learning (ML).

The AI standards-making activities of the Institute of Electrical and Electronics Engineers (IEEE), which describes itself as "the world's largest technical professional organization for the advancement of technology" are somewhat more advanced. As part of its *Global Initiative on Ethics of Autonomous and Intelligent Systems*, the organization has published an omnibus set of high-level AI ethics principles, *Ethically Aligned Design* (IEEE, 2019) and is in the process of developing particular standards through a variety of focused working groups on topics such as Transparency of Autonomous Systems (P7001), a Standard for Child and Student Data Governance (P7004), and a Standard for Ethically Driven Nudging for Robotic, Intelligent and Autonomous Systems (P7008).[2] Of particular relevance to contemporary discussions is working group P7013 on Inclusion and Application Standards for Automated Facial Analysis Technology. The group seeks to create "phenotypic and demographic definitions that technologists and auditors can use to assess the diversity of face data used for training and benchmarking algorithmic performance" as well as "a rating system to determine contexts in which automated facial analysis technology should not be used."[3] The IEEE has also begun an Ethics Certification Program for Autonomous and Intelligent Systems (ECPAIS), the goal of which is to "offer a process and define a series of marks by which organizations can seek certifications for the processes around the A/IS products, systems, and services they provide."[4] As the IEEE notes, participation in this metrification of AI governance requires an IEEE Standards Association Corporate Membership.

In the United States, the White House Office of Science and Technology Policy under the Obama administration identified the AI-adjacent field of "big data" as both a strategic priority and an area of legal and ethical concern through a series of reports between 2014 and 2016 (Muñoz, Smith, & Patil, 2016). In early 2019, the Trump administration released an Executive Order on "Maintaining American Leadership in Artificial Intelligence," which laid out some elements common to other national AI strategies (White House, 2019). The US Commerce Department's National Institute of Standards and Technology (NIST) was charged with developing national AI standards in a February 2019 Executive Order; they produced a plan for federal engagement in the topic in August of 2019 (NIST, 2019). The plan's recommendations focus narrowly on developing benchmarks, tools, and metrics for AI systems with little attention to the broader societal impacts of AI and automation.

Governance Through Human Rights

The pitfalls apparent in partial technical solutions, nonbinding national strategies, and voluntary standard setting as AI governance mechanisms have prompted many civil society actors to call for an approach grounded in global human rights discourse. According to Latonero (2018), AI's "design and deployment should avoid harms to fundamental human values," while "international human rights provide a robust and global formulation of those [same] values" (p. 5). Donahoe and Metzger (2019) argue human rights provide "a framework that can claim global buy-in and that addresses the roles and responsibilities of both government and the private sector when it comes to accountability for the impact of AI-based decisions" (p. 118). The authors cite the 2011 UN Guiding Principles on Business and Human Rights (known colloquially as the Ruggie Principles) as a key mechanism to ensure private companies apply human rights law to their own products, services, and operations.

Other scholars have advanced more cautious endorsements of the application of human rights frameworks to AI governance. Daniel Munro (2019) observes that while the "shared ethical language" of extant human rights conventions can "help to overcome the challenge of coordinating multiple, and sometimes incompatible, frameworks," he also warns of three pitfalls to such an approach. The first concerns enforcing human rights covenants against the private businesses and other entities manufacturing and selling AI systems. Munro notes the Ruggie Principles do provide some guidance on the parameters of such an approach but that concrete enforcement mechanisms remain inadequate. Second, high-level human rights frameworks suffer from some of the same problems around the interpretation of abstract principles as other extant AI ethics codes.

Third, and to our mind most critically, Munro shares the concern of philosophers such as Mathias Risse, who observe the "minimal standards" approach to much human rights discourse is insufficient to account for positive values of both distributive and relational justice and equality (Anderson, 1999). This critique—that at best such rights frameworks are conceptually too narrow, trading positive visions of radical social and economic justice for a cramped vision of negative political liberty—is just one of many leveled by progressives at human rights as an ethical framework.[5] Critics often note the centrality of political rights to human rights discourse, in contrast to the relative paucity of effort to protect economic and social rights. Others argue the international legal regimes enabling and enforcing such rights are imperialistic, exporting Western values around the world (Anghie, 2005, 2013), and that human rights are explicitly neoliberal, guaranteeing the survival of populations and individuals only so that they can be further exploited by global capital (Anghie, 2005, 2013; Moyn, 2011, 2013, 2018). Moyn (2018) also observes that human rights principles often fail to guarantee human flourishing and diminish human suffering in practice precisely because they lack reliable mechanisms for dispute by which they can be activated.

Unfortunately, suggested applications of human rights frameworks to AI governance often duplicate many of the limitations we identified in other high-level AI ethics principles described above. These limitations include a focus on design as the locus of ethical activity in work around human-rights-by-design. While salutary, such a design focus does not grapple sufficiently with the systemic logics behind many of AI's deleterious effects (Penney, McKune, Gill, & Deibert, 2018). A focus in human-rights-by-design on the need for technical and business transparency is also paralleled in high-level ethics codes. Yet emphasis on transparency as a procedural virtue is insufficient when considering the real costs to human flourishing produced by many AI-driven technologies. In sum, governance strategies for AI/ML based on traditional human rights frameworks have not yet avoided the insufficiencies of similar high-level statements of principle; major companies such as Salesforce have already grounded their AI policies in human rights principles, a testatment to how closely corporate and human rights ethics discourses can potentially overlap.

Our aim here, however, is not to further denigrate human rights discourse. As Latonero observes, human rights provide a familiar framework legible to a wide array of actors around the world. It is notable that the surge in academic and public conversations around AI has returned human rights to the fore in a historical period in which the human rights apparatus, always more honored in the breach than in the observance, has been under attack from many quarters. If human rights frameworks are applied both carefully and radically to the governance of artificial intelligence, both those systems and human rights discussions themselves stand to be improved and strengthened as a result.

Governance Through Securitization

Security policymakers have long sought to frame the digital world in terms with which they are already familiar, drawing on a broader discourse around "cyberspace" already extant in popular literature and society from the mid-1980s (Eriksson, 2001). Newly developed AI technologies have been slotted neatly into this vision by policymakers and defense pundits: frequent references in the media to a new "AI arms race," particularly between China and the United States, have threatened to recast Cold War patterns of competition as models for contemporary AI governance. Artificial intelligence technologies are certainly of major interest to the defense sector, sparking reasonable anxieties around AI/ML systems as military assets, either to augment conventional warfare, such as through their use in unmanned aerial vehicle (UAV) or drone technologies, or as aides in cyberattacks. Moreover, reports that international technology companies are willing to work closely with, or in some cases directly as proxies for, national governments have also associated national AI policies with espionage.

However, this emphasis on AI through the lens of already existing cybersecurity discourses and as a national security problem risks further entrenching AI policy in the hands of the few. Securitization theory argues that discourses around "security" deploy particular "grammars of securitization" to connect "referent objects, threats, and securitizing actors together" to both depoliticize and control particular sociotechnical arenas (Hansen & Nissenbaum, 2009). AI's securitization shares similar traits with those of cybersecurity more broadly (which itself draws strongly from Cold War discourse around nuclear arms). AI's "grammar of securitization" both reinforces AI's status as an elite technical discourse and distracts from the effects of that same discourse on AI policymaking across the board. Hansen and Nissenbaum (2009) identify three "securitization modalities" which they suggest are particularly powerful in broader cybersecurity discourse: hyper-securitization or "a tendency both to exaggerate threats and to resort to excessive countermeasures"; everyday security practices, i.e., "situations in which private organizations and businesses mobilize individual experiences" to "make hyper-securitization scenarios more plausible by linking elements of the disaster scenario to experiences familiar from everyday life"; and technification, "a particular constitution of epistemic authority and political legitimacy" whereby some subjects are depoliticized into the realm of the "expert" (p. 1164).

The concept of technification aligns closely with our observations in past work (Greene et al., 2019) and above: that most AI vision statements or sets of ethical principles seek to restrict debates around the societal impacts of AI to a coterie of technical experts whose positions are posited, chiefly by themselves, as technocratic and thus apolitical. Securitization rhetoric thus allows both industry and governments free reign to set the parameters for AI governance on their own terms. In its simultaneous insistence on the inevitability of AI technologies and that experts' hold responsibility for ethical AI governance, much AI discourse also performs a flavor of hyper-securitization, hyping the disruption being produced by AI systems while disavowing the role of policy choices in accepting the deployment of problematic technologies. And in line with other surveillance technologies such as CCTV cameras, institutional actors are rapidly securitizing AI as a threat in itself if deployed by the wrong hands, while also advocating its use as a means to identify threats to the national polity (Cassiano, 2019; Chen & Cheung, 2017).

The securitization of AI discourses and technologies also further exacerbates existing patterns of digital inequality and power asymmetries between the global North and South. Rumman Chowdhury and Abeba Birhane argue the extractive data practices of many AI firms constitute "algorithmic colonialism," a digital analogue to the exploitative material extraction of natural resources and human capital to which the Global South has been subjected for centuries (Chowdhury, 2019). Algorithmic colonialism entails both the depredations of neocolonial powers (in particular the United States and China) and those of local elites supported by broader networks of global capital (Couldry & Mejias, 2019); it also includes algorithmic settler colonialism, through which settler colonial states look inward to exploit and dispossess the data heritage of indigenous populations (TallBear, 2013). Finally, it relies on globalized digital infrastructures to outsource and occlude the immense amounts of human labor of which "AI" services often actually consist: workers around the world are paid meagerly to clean and tag data, train models, and facilitate other purportedly automated services, while the more privileged developers of these systems reap the lion's share of the financial reward (Gray & Suri, 2019; Poster, 2019a, 2019b).

Securitization discourse, particularly around technification, thus seeks to push AI/ML systems out of the hands of citizens in both the global North and South and to install them as yet another weapon in the game of neoliberal great power politics. More broadly, securitization supports and underpins the various regulatory, technical, and discursive proposals outlined above designed to narrow the range of people and institutions able to have a say in the governance of AI/ML—to varying degrees, the proposed governance mechanisms for these technologies ensure their fate lies with a particular subset of more or less privileged individuals.

Conclusion: Future Alternatives for AI/ML Governance

None of the various existing or proposed mechanisms for AI/ML governance, ranging from computational tools to global regimes around human rights and securitization, are entirely antithetical to the broader systems of neoliberal governance and capitalist accumulation responsible for the development and deployment of contemporary AI/ML technologies—a fact hardly surprising. What are our proposed alternatives? As a baseline, truly just and equitable governance of AI/ML technologies will have to more or less radically transform the development and deployment of those technologies themselves; in turn, the future development of these transformed AI/ML technologies cannot be grounded in the values of the Deleuzian "society of control" (Deleuze, 1990), wherein societal life is modulated through digital manipulation overseen by state and corporate power. This is a tall order, requiring the work of many hands. Elsewhere, we have variously described some of the strategies required, including foregrounding data justice (Hoffmann, 2019), dissecting digital inequality (Greene, forthcoming), overhauling professional ethics in the

AI/ML space (Stark & Hoffmann, 2019), and engaging with a diverse array of queer ethical traditions (Stark & Hawkins, 2019).

One through-line across this and much related scholarship is the necessity of foregrounding and centering the expertise of communities affected by AI/ML systems in their design and use (Costanza-Chock, 2018; Forlano & Mathew, 2013; Madaio, Stark, Wortman Vaughan, & Wallach, 2020; Sloan, Moss, Awomolo, & Forlano, 2020). Politics is a social system of collective deliberation around decision making and collective distribution around resource matching. Parallel political projects for technological reform and governance thus suggest alternative ways both to govern who makes decisions about technologies such as AI/ML and who benefits from their effects. Workplace labor movements such as the Tech Won't Build It campaign and the abolitionist and antisurveillance work of the Movement for Black Lives (MBL) are thus exemplary of alternative paradigms for AI/ML governance.

The Tech Won't Build It campaign coalesced in 2018 around Google employee labor action against the company's involvement in the United States Department of Defense's Maven contract for targeted autonomous weapons systems. Workers from multiple companies, including Microsoft, Salesforce, Amazon, and Palantir, began to protest similar entanglements by their firms with both military and immigration enforcement efforts by the US government. These protests have grown to include work stoppages, open letters illustrating the gap between espoused corporate values and actual corporate practices, and support for other social justice organizations.

Tech Won't Build It is broadly a movement focused on cultivating workplace democracy through labor action, holding that workers developing AI/ML should have a say in how such technologies are deployed. This focus is distinct from the narrow focus on expertise in AI ethics statements and other governance mechanisms—tech sector workers here claim a seat at the table not because of their qualifications but because of their position in the production process. The labor power of technology workers is both a statement of legitimacy and a threat due to their strategic position, with an explicit focus on reducing profits (or at least redirecting them away from morally indefensible ends).

The Black Lives Matter movement was begun in 2013 by Alicia Garza, Patrisse Cullors, and Opal Tometi after George Zimmerman's acquittal for the murder of Trayvon Martin; it has since become an international movement committed to creating a world where police and prisons—violent institutions that exacerbate social problems—are unnecessary. As an abolitionist project, the Movement for Black Lives' policy platform provides a useful contrast to ethical design manifestoes. Under the section "An End to the Mass Surveillance of Black Communities, and the End to the Use of Technologies that Criminalize and Target Our Communities," the MBL policy platform addresses many of the same technologies addressed by ethics principles and other governance mechanisms. However, in contrast to the narrow, elite-focused stance of most governance mechanisms, MBL frames the solution to AI/ML governance as increased democratic oversight of technological procurement and deployment.

The abolitionist perspective of the MBL differs from other governance mechanisms described above in at least two ways. First, the project of defining harm and redress takes a longer and more contextualized view; while everyone might benefit from MBL's policy prescriptions, prison abolition and police violence are historically specific problems afflicting Black people in colonial societies. Second, rather than beginning with abstract ideal principles, the MBL platform is grounded in its vision of the ideal community—one in which prison abolition is a reality—and works backward to identify general principles and then the specific policy stances and campaigns they imply. Unlike many of the governance mechanisms we describe, this is also a mass mobilization document that embraces conflict and agonism as mechanisms for democratic change.

Not only do these movements encourage a broader governance conversation focused explicitly on social justice and AI/ML—urgently needed as these technologies become ubiquitous—they also point toward ways in which technical and social governance can interoperate for the benefit of all. What are our various collective visions of the ideal community, and how can the governance of AI/ML systems play a part? And how can members of diverse communities, often with asymmetric access to wealth and power, work together to ensure justice, equality, and fairness exist not just in principle but also in practice? We hope these questions can open a more radically inclusive and democratic conversation around AI governance—one that surpasses technical fixes and narrow expert guidelines to embrace the heterogeneity of needs and desires centered on human intelligence, ability, and solidarity.

Notes

1. We are grateful to Bart Simon for crystallizing this observation.
2. See https://standards.ieee.org/content/ieee-standards/en/industry-connections/ec/autonomous-systems.html.
3. https://standards.ieee.org/project/7013.html.
4. https://standards.ieee.org/industry-connections/ecpais.html.
5. Conservative critiques invariably assail the notion of human rights as a mechanism through which tenets of natural law are subverted, leading to various forms of social malaise and decay.

References

Abend, G. (2014). *The moral background: An inquiry into the history of business ethics*. Princeton University Press.

AI HLEG. (2019). *Ethics guidelines for trustworthy AI*. European Commission. https://ec.europa.eu/digital-single-market/en/news/ethics-guidelines-trustworthy-ai.

Ananny, M., & Crawford, K. (2017). Seeing without knowing: Limitations of the transparency ideal and its application to algorithmic accountability. *New Media & Society, 20*(3), 973–989. https://doi.org/10.1177/1461444816676645.

Anderson, E. S. (1999). What is the point of equality? *Ethics*, *109*(2), 287–337. http://www.philosophy.rutgers.edu/joomlatools-files/docman-files/4ElizabethAnderson.pdf.

Anghie, A. (2005). *Imperialism, sovereignty and the making of international law*. Cambridge University Press.

Anghie, A. (2013). Whose Utopia? Human rights, development, and the Third World. *Qui Parle, 22*(1), 63–69. https://doi.org/10.5250/quiparle.22.1.0063.

Andrejevic, M., & Selwyn, N. (2019). Facial recognition technology in schools: Critical questions and concerns. *Learning, Media and Technology* (2), 1–14. http://doi.org/10.1080/17439884.2020.1686014.

Bamberger, K. A., & Mulligan, D. K. (2008). Privacy decisionmaking in administrative agencies. *Chicago Law Review, 75*(1), 75–107.

Baraniuk, C. (2020, February 19). EU to tackle AI "Wild West"—But still to say how. *BBC News*. https://www.bbc.com/news/technology-51559010.

Benjamin, R. (2019). *Race after technology: Abolitionist tools for the New Jim Code*. Wiley.

Broussard, M. (2018). *Artificial unintelligence: How computers misunderstand the world*. MIT Press.

Brown, A., Chouldechova, A., Putnam-Hornstein, E., Tobin, A., & Vaithianathan, R. (2019). *Toward algorithmic accountability in public services* (pp. 1–12). Presented at the 2019 CHI Conference, New York, NY, USA: ACM Press. http://doi.org/10.1145/3290605.3300271.

Caplan, R., Donovan, J., Hanson, L., & Matthews, J. (2018). *Algorithmic accountability: A primer*. Data & Society Research Institute.

Cardoso, T. (2019, May 28). Federal government unveiling risk assessment tool for artificial intelligence. *The Globe & Mail*. https://www.theglobeandmail.com/politics/article-federal-government-unveiling-risk-assessment-tool-for-artificial/.

Cassiano, M. S. (2019). China's Hukou platform: Windows into the family. *Surveillance & Society, 17*(1/2), 232–239.

Chen, Y., & Cheung, A. S. Y. (2017). The transparent self under big data profiling: Privacy and Chinese legislation on the social credit system. *The Columbia Science & Technology Law Review, 12*(2), 356–378. https://doi.org/10.2139/ssrn.2992537.

Chowdhury, R. (2019). *AI ethics and algorithmic colonialism*. https://www.mcgill.ca/igsf/channels/event/rumman-chowdhury-ai-ethics-and-algorithmic-colonialism-300414.

Cihon, P. (2019). *Standards for AI governance: International standards to enable global coordination in AI research & development*. Future of Humanity Institute, University of Oxford.

Costanza-Chock, S. (2018). *Design justice: Towards an intersectional feminist framework for design theory and practice*. Presented at the Design Research Society. http://doi.org/10.21606/dma.2017.679.

Couldry, N., & Mejias, U. A. (2019). Data colonialism: Rethinking big data's relation to the contemporary subject. *Television & New Media, 20*(4), 336–349. https://doi.org/10.1177/1527476418796632.

Crawford, K., Dobbe, R., Dryer, T., Fried, G., Green, B., Kaziunas, E., ... Raji, D. (2019). *AI now 2019 report*. AI Now Institute.

Deleuze, G. (1990). Postscript on control societies. In *Negotiations, 1972–1990* (pp. 177–182) (M. Joughin, Trans.). Columbia University Press.

Donahoe, E., & Metzger, M. M. (2019). Artificial intelligence and human rights. *Journal of Democracy, 30*(2), 115–126. https://doi.org/10.1353/jod.2019.0029.

Duarte, N. (2017, August 8). *Digital decisions tool*. Center for Democracy & Technology. https://cdt.org/insights/digital-decisions-tool/.

Dutton, T., Barron, B., & Boskovic, G. (2018). *Building an AI world*. Canadian Institute for Advanced Research.

Dwork, C., & Mulligan, D. K. (2013). It's not privacy, and it's not fair. *Stanford Law Review Online, 66*, 35–40.

Eriksson, J. (2001). Cyberplagues, IT, and security: Threat politics in the information age. *Journal of Contingencies and Crisis Management, 9*(4), 211–222.

Eubanks, V. (2018). *Automating inequality: How high-tech tools profile, police, and punish the poor*. St. Martin's Press.

European Commission. (2020). *Artificial intelligence—A European approach to excellence and trust* (No. COM[2020] 65 final). European Commission. https://ec.europa.eu/info/sites/info/files/commission-white-paper-artificial-intelligence-feb2020_en.pdf.

Forlano, L., & Mathew, A. (2013). *The designing policy toolkit*. Urban Communication Foundation.

Friedman, B., & Nissenbaum, H. (1996). Bias in computer systems. *ACM Transactions on Information Systems, 14*(3), 330–347.

Gandy, O. H. (2009). Engaging rational discrimination: Exploring reasons for placing regulatory constraints on decision support systems. *Ethics and Information Technology, 12*(1), 29–42. https://doi.org/10.1007/s10676-009-9198-6.

Gray, M. L., & Suri, S. (2019). *Ghost work*. Houghton Mifflin Harcourt.

Greene, D., Hoffmann, A. L., & Stark, L. (2019). Better, nicer, clearer, fairer. In T. X. Bui & R. H. Sprague (Eds.), (pp. 2122–2131). Presented at the Proceedings of the 52nd Hawaii International Conference on System Sciences (HICSS). https://hdl.handle.net/10125/59651.

Hansen, L., & Nissenbaum, H. (2009). Digital disaster, cyber security, and the Copenhagen School. *International Studies Quarterly, 53,* 1155–1175.

Hardt, M., Price, E., & Srebro, N. (2016). *Equality of opportunity in supervised learning*. arXiv:1610.02413 [cs.LG], pp. 1–9.

Hartzog, W., & Selinger, E. (2018, August 2). Facial recognition is the perfect tool for oppression. *Medium*. https://medium.com/s/story/facial-recognition-is-the-perfect-tool-for-oppression-bc2a08f0fe66.

Heidari, H., Loi, M., Gummadi, K. P., & Krause, A. (2018, September 10). *A moral framework for understanding of fair ML through economic models of equality of opportunity*. arXiv:1809.03400 [cs.LG]. https://arxiv.org/abs/1809.03400.

Hoffmann, A. L. (2019). Where fairness fails: Data, algorithms, and the limits of antidiscrimination discourse. *Information, Communication & Society, 22*(7), 900–915. https://doi.org/10.1080/1369118X.2019.1573912.

Hutchinson, B., & Mitchell, M. (2019). *50 years of test (un)fairness* (pp. 49–58). Presented at the Conference on Fairness, Accountability, and Transparency 2019, New York, NY, USA: ACM Press. http://doi.org/10.1145/3287560.3287600.

IEEE/The IEEE Global Initiative on Ethics of Autonomous and Intelligent Systems. (2019). *Ethically aligned design, first edition*. https://ethicsinaction.ieee.org/.

Jobin, A., Ienca, M., & Vayena, E. (2019). The global landscape of AI ethics guidelines. *Nature Machine Intelligence*, 1–11. http://doi.org/10.1038/s42256-019-0088-2.

Johnson, D. G. (2007). Ethics and technology "in the making": An essay on the challenge of nanoethics. *Nanoethics, 1*(1), 21–30. https://doi.org/10.1007/s11569-007-0006-7.

Kearns, M., Roth, A., & Wu, Z. S. (2017). *Meritocratic fairness for cross-population selection* (pp. 1–9). Presented at the Proceedings of the International Conference on Machine Learning, Sydney, Australia.

Kleinberg, J., Ludwig, J., Mullainathan, S., & Rambachan, A. (2018). Algorithmic fairness. *AEA Papers and Proceedings, 108*, 22–27. https://doi.org/10.1257/pandp.20181018.

Latonero, M. (2018). *Governing artificial intelligence*. Data & Society Research Institute. https://datasociety.net/output/governing-artificial-intelligence/.

Lecher, C. (2019, November 20). NYC's algorithm task force was "a waste," member says. *The Verge*. https://www.theverge.com/2019/11/20/20974379/nyc-algorithm-task-force-report-de-blasio.

Lee, M. K. (2018). Understanding perception of algorithmic decisions: Fairness, trust, and emotion in response to algorithmic management. *Big Data & Society*, *5*(1). http://doi.org/10.1177/2053951718756684.

Leong, B. (2019). Facial recognition and the future of privacy: I always feel like . . . somebody's watching me. *Bulletin of the Atomic Scientists, 75*(3), 109–115. http://doi.org/10.1080/00963402.2019.1604886.

Lussier, K. (2018). Temperamental workers: Psychology, business, and the Humm-Wadsworth Temperament Scale in interwar America. *History of Psychology*, 1–22. http://doi.org/10.1037/hop0000081.

Madaio, M. A., Stark, L., Wortman Vaughan, J., & Wallach, H. (2020). *Co-designing checklists to understand organizational challenges and opportunities around fairness in AI* (pp. 1–20). Presented at the CHI 2020: Proceedings of the SIGCHI Conference on Human Factors in Computing Systems, Honolulu, HI. http://doi.org/10.1145/3313831.3376445.

Metcalf, J., Heller, E. F., & Boyd, D. (2016). *Perspectives on big data, ethics, and society*. The Council for Big Data, Ethics, and Society.

Miller, T. (2019). But why? Understanding explainable artificial intelligence. *XRDS: Crossroads, the ACM Magazine for Students, 25*(3), 20–25. http://doi.org/10.1145/3313107.

Moss, E., & Metcalf, J. (2020). *Ethics owners: A new model of organizational responsibility in data-driven technology companies*. New York: Data & Society Research Institute. https://datasociety.net/pubs/Ethics-Owners.pdf.

Moyn, S. (2011). *The last Utopia*. Belknap Press.
Moyn, S. (2013). The continuing perplexities of human rights. *Qui Parle, 22*(1), 95–115. https://doi.org/10.5250/quiparle.22.1.0095.
Moyn, S. (2018). *Not enough: Human rights in an unequal world*. Belknap Press.
Munro, D. (2019, July 12). *Artificial intelligence needs an ethics framework*. Centre for International Governance Innovation. https://www.cigionline.org/articles/artificial-intelligence-needs-ethics-framework.
Muñoz, C., Smith, M., & Patil, D. J. (2016). *Big data: A report on algorithmic systems, opportunity, and civil rights*. Executive Office of the President.
Narayanan, A. (2018). *Translation tutorial: 21 fairness definitions and their politics*. Presented at the FAT* 2018, New York.
National Institute of Standards and Technology (NIST). (2019). *U.S. leadership in AI: A plan for federal engagement in developing technical standards and related tools*. https://www.nist.gov/system/files/documents/2019/08/10/ai_standards_fedengagement_plan_9aug2019.pdf.
New York City. (2019, November). *Automated decision systems task force report*. https://www1.nyc.gov/assets/adstaskforce/downloads/pdf/ADS-Report-11192019.pdf.
Nissenbaum, H. (2010). *Privacy in context: Technology, policy, and the integrity of social life*. Stanford Law Books.
Nissenbaum, H. (2011). From preemption to circumvention. *Berkeley Technology Law Journal, 26*(3), 1367–1386.
Noble, S. U. (2018). *Algorithms of oppression: How search engines reinforce racism*. New York University Press.
OECD Principles on Artificial Intelligence. (n.d.). https://www.oecd.org/going-digital/ai/principles/.
Penney, J., McKune, S., Gill, L., & Deibert, R. J. (2018, December 20). Advancing human-rights-by-design in the dual-use technology industry. *Journal of International Affairs*. https://jia.sipa.columbia.edu/advancing-human-rights-design-dual-use-technology-industry.
Pfaffenberger, B. (1992). Technological dramas. *Science, Technology and Human Values, 17*(3), 282–312.
Pontifical Academy for Life. (2020). *Rome call 2020*. https://romecall.org/romecall2020/.
Poster, W. R. (2019a). Racialized surveillance in the digital service economy. In R. Benjamin (Ed.), *Captivating technology: Race, technoscience, and the carceral imagination* (pp. 133–169). Duke University Press.
Poster, W. R. (2019b). Sound bites, sentiments, and accents: Digitizing communicative labor in the era of global outsourcing. In D. Ribes & J. Vertesi (Eds.), *DigitalSTS: A field guide for science technology studies* (pp. 240–262). Princeton University Press.

Reisman, D., Schultz, J., Crawford, K., & Whittaker, M. (2018). *Algorithmic impact assessments*. AI Now Institute.

Richardson, R. (Ed.) (2019). *Confronting black boxes: A shadow report of the New York City automated decision system task force*. AI Now Institute. https://ainowinstitute.org/ads-shadowreport-2019.html.

Schwab, K. (2017). *The fourth industrial revolution*. Portfolio Penguin.

Selbst, A. D. (2017). Disparate impact in big data policing. *Georgia Law Review, 52,* 109–195.

Selbst, A. D., Boyd, D., Friedler, S. A., Venkatasubramanian, S., & Vertesi, J. (2019). *Fairness and abstraction in sociotechnical systems* (pp. 59–68). Presented at the Proceedings of the Conference on Fairness, Accountability, and Transparency, New York, NY, USA: Association for Computing Machinery. http://doi.org/10.1145/3287560.3287598.

Sloan, M., Moss, E., Awomolo, O., & Forlano, L. (2020). *Participation is not a design fix for machine learning* (pp. 1–7). Presented at the Proceedings of the International Conference on Machine Learning, Vienna, Austria.

Stark, L. (2019). Facial recognition is the plutonium of AI. *XRDS: Crossroads, the ACM Magazine for Students*, *25*(3), 50–55. http://doi.org/10.1145/3313129.

Stark, L., & Hawkins, B. (2019, 9 December). *Queering AI ethics: Pedagogy and practice*. Thirty-third Conference on Neural Information Processing Systems (NeurIPS), Queer in AI Workshop, Vancouver, BC.

Stark, L., & Hoffmann, A. L. (2019). Data is the new what? Popular metaphors & professional ethics in emerging data culture. *Journal of Cultural Analytics*, 1–22. http://doi.org/10.22148/16.036.

TallBear, K. (2013). Genomic articulations of indigeneity. *Social Studies of Science, 43*(4), 509–533. https://doi.org/10.1177/0306312713483893.

Veale, M., Van Kleek, M., & Binns, R. (2018). *Fairness and accountability design needs for algorithmic support in high-stakes public sector decision-making* (pp. 1–14). Presented at the Extended Abstracts of the 2018 CHI Conference, New York, New York, USA: ACM Press. http://doi.org/10.1145/3173574.3174014.

Verma, S., & Rubin, J. (2018). *Fairness definitions explained* (pp. 1–7). Presented at the 2018 ACM/IEEE International Workshop on Software Fairness, New York, New York, USA: ACM Press. http://doi.org/10.1145/3194770.3194776.

White House. (2019, 11 February). *Executive Order on maintaining American leadership in artificial intelligence*. https://www.whitehouse.gov/presidential-actions/executive-order-maintaining-american-leadership-artificial-intelligence/.

Winner, L. (1988). Do artifacts have politics? In *The whale and the reactor* (pp. 19–39). University of Chicago Press.

Woodruff, A., Fox, S. E., Rousso-Schindler, S., & Warshaw, J. (2018). *A qualitative exploration of perceptions of algorithmic fairness* (pp. 1–14). Presented at the Extended Abstracts of the 2018 CHI Conference, New York, New York, USA: ACM Press. http://doi.org/10.1145/3173574.3174230.

Wright, E. (2019). The future of facial recognition is not fully known: Developing privacy and security regulatory mechanisms for facial recognition in the retail sector. *Fordham Intellectual Property, Media & Entertainment Law Journal, 29*(2). https://ir.lawnet.fordham.edu/iplj/vol29/iss2/6.

Zhang, B. H., Lemoine, B., & Mitchell, M. (2018). Mitigating unwanted biases with adversarial learning. arXiv:1801.07593 [cs.LG]. https://arxiv.org/abs/1801.07593.

Zuboff, S. (2019). *The age of surveillance capitalism*. PublicAffairs and Hachette.

Index

© The Editor(s) (if applicable) and The Author(s), under exclusive license to Springer Nature Switzerland AG 2021

J. Roberge and M. Castelle (eds.), *The Cultural Life of Machine Learning*, https://doi.org/10.1007/978-3-030-56286-1

The manufacturer's authorised representative in the EU is Springer Nature Customer Service Centre GmbH, Europaplatz 3, 69115 Heidelberg, Germany. If you have any concerns regarding our products, please contact ProductSafety@springernature.com

Printed and bound by CPI Group (UK) Ltd, Croydon, CR0 4YY

22/09/2026

02220948-0006